American Animated Cartoons
of the Vietnam Era

American Animated Cartoons of the Vietnam Era

A Study of Social Commentary in Films and Television Programs, 1961–1973

CHRISTOPHER P. LEHMAN

McFarland & Company, Inc., Publishers
Jefferson, North Carolina, and London

LIBRARY OF CONGRESS CATALOGUING-IN-PUBLICATION DATA

Lehman, Christopher P., 19XX–
    American animated cartoons of the Vietnam era : a study
of social commentary in films and television programs, 1961–
1973 / Christopher P. Lehman.
        p.   cm.
    Includes bibliographical references and index.

    ISBN-13: 978-0-7864-2818-2
    ISBN-10: 0-7864-2818-X
    (softcover : 50# alkaline paper) ∞
    xxxxxx
    xxxxxxxx
    xxxxxxx   2006
    xxxxx'x — dc21   XXXXXX

British Library cataloguing data are available

Cover information xxxxxxxxxxxxxxxxxxxxxxx.

Manufactured in the United States of America

*McFarland & Company, Inc., Publishers
  Box 611, Jefferson, North Carolina 28640
  www.mcfarlandpub.com*

ACKNOWLEDGMENTS

Over the past ten years, I had the fortune of communicating with several animation veterans. I am extremely grateful to Howard Beckerman, Doug Crane, Vicki Lee Gailzaid, the late Faith Hubley, Ken Spears, Noel Paul Stookey, and Morrie Turner for the time they took to write or talk to me about their work.

I thank Mary Welsh and Barbara Davis of the New Rochelle Public Library for their hard work in helping me track down information about the Terrytoons animation studio. Their resources greatly contributed to my research.

I am extremely grateful for the love and support of my family. My mother, father, and brother have encouraged me as long as I can remember. My daughter, Imani, is a tremendous source of inspiration. My wife, Yolanda, has stood by me through all of the time it took to write the manuscript and motivated me when I felt most exhausted. This book exists because of Imani and Yolanda.

TABLE OF CONTENTS

PREFACE

American Animated Cartoons of the Vietnam Era discusses the evolution of U.S. animation during the period 1961–1973 — from militaristic and violent to slightly more liberal and pacifist — and the role of the Vietnam War in this development. Various kinds of animated films — theatrical short films or "shorts," theatrical features, and television series — receive coverage. The studios examined are the commercial theatrical operations linked to Hollywood distributors and the studios producing for television. Independent studios are discussed where they of exceeded commercial expectations with popular, successful films.

Generally, each chapter focuses on films released or broadcast during a particular year of the Vietnam War. The first, second, and eighth chapter cover two-year periods because of the similarities among the films from each year of those periods. Some cartoons released during a particular year were produced more than a year earlier. However, they are discussed according to the year of release as a means of comparison with other contemporary works released at the same time to audiences.

The book draws upon interviews with people involved in the production of some of the films. It also looks at the effect of the Vietnam War on the promotion of the films in trade periodicals. Film critics responding via newspaper columns to the cartoon innovations also served as invaluable references.

Very few books give much examination to cartoons of this period — even fewer to the theatrical shorts. The cartoons are frequently dismissed as cheap and unoriginal. However, such analyses avoid exploration of

1

social trends and issues covered in the cartoons. *American Animated Cartoons of the Vietnam Era* seeks to place the films in the context of the social upheaval of the Vietnam period and show how the cartoons reflect their times.

INTRODUCTION: ANIMATING TURBULENT TIMES

In 1961 the American animation industry experienced rejuvenation after a few years in the doldrums. Throughout the 1950s some of the most successful cartoon studios had stopped producing theatrical short films, including Walt Disney Productions (the home of "Mickey Mouse" cartoons), Metro-Goldwyn-Mayer's cartoon department ("Tom and Jerry"), and United Productions of America ("Mister Magoo"). Their distributors felt content to reissue earlier cartoons to exhibitors and make nearly the same amount of money. However, according to *Newsweek* magazine, movie audiences missed seeing new cartoons before feature presentations. The distributors relented and, by 1961, had contracted with animation studios to produce new cartoons. In the meantime, William Hanna and Joseph Barbera launched a successful television cartoon studio after MGM fired them in 1957. The cartoon industry showed potential for success.

At the same time, the United States was about to embark on a major military commitment to South Vietnam. The United States had a foreign policy of containment, resolving to prevent communism from spreading beyond its borders. Concerning Indochina, America endorsed the "domino theory"— the idea that if communist North Vietnam were to conquer its southern neighbor, then communism would spread throughout Southeast Asia, into Cambodia, Laos, and Thailand. In 1961, however, with John F. Kennedy just entering the presidency, the U.S. military presence in South Vietnam was but a few hundred advisers.

Over the next twelve years, as U.S. involvement in the Vietnam War rose and then fell to its pre–Kennedy level, the American animation industry experienced its own turmoil. The 1960s and early 1970s were extremely lean years for cartoon studios. Theatrical operations experienced the devastating effects of television wooing potential movie patrons to stay home. At first, the theatrical studios had an advantage because television cartoon studios were few and far between. But by the late 1960s, the television operations outnumbered and out-produced their theatrical competition. The number of cartoon releases in theaters, rose and shrank in a manner that somewhat paralleled the U.S. military presence in South Vietnam.

More importantly, theatrical and television cartoon studios responded to U.S. participation in the Vietnam War through animation between 1961 and 1973. The artists produced several commentaries on the federal government, the armed forces, the draft, peace negotiations, the counterculture, and pacifism. They never directly referred to Vietnam, unlike the dozens of World War II–era cartoons poking fun at Adolf Hitler and Emperor Hirohito. Animators of the Vietnam era generally avoided overtly topical content, reasoning that films with timeless stories (usually chases) were more attractive for television networks to rerun for years to come. Nevertheless, the cartoonists made subtle references to popular opinion about war.

The references were most subtle in the early 1960s. As several movies and television programs featured nostalgic depictions of earlier wars, animators comically but patriotically remembered the Revolutionary War, the Civil War, and both World Wars. Hollywood was not ready to illustrate contemporary race relations in live-action or animated films; for both kinds of films, independent studios took up that challenge.

In the 1960s, most animators were mired in production techniques of World War II. Gags and story formulas had hardly changed since than. The theatrical studios still used many of the same stars of the 1940s for cartoons of the early 1960s. Television animators also relied heavily on tried-and-true theatrical animation devices such as humanized animals, slapstick violence, and recognizable celebrity voices or approximations. Moreover, since the end of World War II, studios had not critically approached the subject of military conflict. They did not start doing so concerning Vietnam before 1965.

For animation, the most dramatic event of the period was the loss of originality in animation as a result of successful licensing. King Features Syndicate started the trend in television cartoons in 1965 by caricaturing the Beatles and constructing simple stories in which to inject recordings by the rock music group. The next year, Filmation Associates brought the comic-book figure Superman to television animation and boosted CBS-TV's Saturday morning ratings. Having opened the Pandora's box of borrowing established properties, the studios found that networks increasingly wanted them to simply find the right property instead of trusting animators to think of original characters. In contrast, theatrical studios had no such licensing boon to keep them afloat and consequently started to die in the late 1960s. Meanwhile, as U.S. participation dramatically increased between 1965 and 1968, U.S. animation changed in other ways. Initially, in 1965 and 1966, studios were politically divided among themselves. Some cartoons promoted militarism and social conformity. For example, television studios found their niche with "superhero" cartoons and all-white, middle-class casts. On the other hand, theatrical cartoons questioned war itself and slightly backpedaled on violent content. When MGM produced "Tom and Jerry" cartoons in the mid–'60s, the cat and mouse hardly laid a hand on one another — a sharp contrast from the episodes of the '40s.

Cartoon violence served as a barometer to national sentiment on Vietnam. When most Americans supported the war in the 1960s, scenes of bombings and gunfire were very prevalent in animated films. Suddenly, in 1968 the violence of the Vietnam War era caught up with animators. In the year of the Tet Offensive and the killings of Rev. Dr. Martin Luther King, Jr., and Senator Robert Kennedy, U.S. audiences began to sour towards violent films. Parents grew more critical of films offered to juvenile audiences. As a result, television networks discouraged studios from producing any further "superhero" cartoons and heavily censored cartoons for violent content by the 1970s. Although, ironically, a new movie ratings system in 1968 gave animators more leeway concerning content, theatrical studios censored themselves by producing G-rated cartoons, suitable for later television broadcast. As a result, physical slapstick humor vanished.

Racism present in cartoons also reflected anxieties roused by the Vietnam War. In 1961, Asian images generally looked the same as during World War II — nearsighted, buck-toothed, diminutive figures with diagonal lines representing slanted eyes. Although Japan was the enemy to the United States in that war, animators indiscriminately applied the features to the Chinese and other Asian ethnic groups. The studios also committed "Asian minstrelsy" by having white actors provide thickly accented voices for the Asian characters. The longer the Vietnam War lasted, the more the Asian caricature worsened. Only after the United States left the war in 1973 did the imagery improve.

Depictions of the counterculture in animation evolved significantly over the course of the war. However, in contrast to the worsening and later improvement of Asian figures, the counterculture images improved but then devolved into broad caricature. The sunglasses-wearing beatniks of the 1960s turned into lazy, hairy hippies in the 1970s. In between, a few cartoonists tried to capture the visual appeal of the counterculture, especially via dream sequences full of swirling psychedelic colors. By and large, the animators of this period were mostly twenty-year employees of various studios, having careers older than the hippies they caricatured. In this context, the derisive image of the beat culture as lazy rock musicians is unsurprising; most longtime animators simply could not relate to it.

Nevertheless, psychedelic animation, inspired by modern film techniques like rapid editing of multiple scenes and deliberately blurred focus, became standard in the industry as the films attracted audiences and earned fortunes for studios. King Features Syndicate had the most success in this kind of cartooning by using Beatles caricatures in the feature-length cartoon *Yellow Submarine* in 1968. Television studios immediately co-opted the graphics for weekend cartoons about rock musicians — the most popular of which was Filmation's adaptation of teenage comic-book star Archie. Even the usually conservative Walt Disney Productions got into the act and embraced "head" cartooning to great accolades.

Even fewer animators could relate to the drama surrounding the issue of racial integration throughout the Vietnam years. Students conducted sit-ins to desegregate businesses and public facilities throughout the early 1960s, while live-action as well as animated films had mostly segregated casts. The Civil Rights Movement won major legislative victories — the Civil Rights Act (outlawing racial segregation) and the Voting Rights Act (outlawing voter discrimination) — in the mid 1960s. Then, Americans saw integration on a constant basis for years, for television viewers watched African Americans fighting alongside whites in Vietnam throughout the war's duration. However, American animation did not illustrate black and white characters outside of servant-master relations until the end of the 1960s. After all, Hollywood cartoonists had no experience in anyting but buffoonish caricatures of Stepin Fetchit and jazz musicians.

In the early 1970s, as President Richard Nixon called on a "Silent Majority" to support his management of the Vietnam War, theatrical cartoonists briefly returned to patriotic, militaristic imagery. Films still questioned war in general. However, radicals received more skewering than in recent years. Draft-card burners appeared as craven cowards, and musical hippies were stooges for talking animals.

At the same time, television cartoons began promoting messages of cooperation and unity. Black characters starred in television cartoons and did not play buffoons or savages. Rather, they sang, played sports, solved mysteries, and learned moral lessons. By 1972 even hippies received more sympathetic treatment, having civil conversations with other characters in the series *Wait Till Your Father Gets Home*.

With U.S. involvement in the war winding down the following year, both theatrical and television studios had settled into "peacetime" animation. The racial stereotypes of the past were largely gone. Violence disappeared, too; characters no longer shot or punched one another. Instead, cartoons minimal on character movement and full of dialogue filled movie and television screens. For example, superheroes returned — but only to lecture villains about morality instead of hitting them. A new age of animation had surely arrived.

1

THE CARTOONS OF
1961–1962

In 1961 and 1962, the Cold War dominated news reports in the United States. President John F. Kennedy waged an aggressive campaign against communism in the first two years of his term. He sent U.S. troops to Cuba for the ill-fated Bay of Pigs invasion in 1961, but he held his ground against Cuba through a missile crisis the next year. He also significantly increased the number of U.S. military advisors to South Vietnam. Within days of Kennedy's authorization of the advisors to fire weapons in self-defense, the first of nearly sixty thousand servicemen killed in action in South Vietnam over twelve years died.

In the meantime Hollywood did not dramatize these current military conflicts but rather romanticized earlier ones. World War II was the war of choice for the movie industry. Television programs recreated battles of that war on a weekly basis, and the networks discovered that viewers were not too weary from news about Vietnam or Cuba to watch sugarcoated depictions of World War II. Among the popular television shows were the drama *Combat* (1962–67) and the situation comedy *McHale's Navy* (1962–66).

U.S. animators also drew from earlier wars for the first cartoons of the Vietnam War. As in *McHale's Navy*, the war imagery in the animated films was comedic. Cartoon animals donned military uniforms and fought in caricatured versions of historic battles. As the fiftieth anniversary of the start of World War I approached, several animated figures appeared as pilots in dogfights against representations of the Red Baron. The animated war imagery of 1961 and 1962 was rarely more complex than a series of dogfight or gunfire gags strung together. Discussions of the homefront attitudes of wars were not part of the nostalgia; the post–World War I "lost generation" of Ernest Hemingway and F. Scott Fitzgerald hardly figured into these films.

Although the studios kept imagery of contemporary Southeast Asia out of the cartoons, the politics of the Vietnam War shaped many gags. Animated characters in most films of this period practice the Cold War tactic of limited war — using weaponry short of nuclear bombs to defeat an enemy. For example, the Warner Brothers cartoon *Beep Prepared* (1961) starts with Wile E. Coyote aiming an arrow at the Road Runner but ends with him using a machine gun. Other films show two characters engaging in brinksmanship — matching each other, weapon for weapon, in military buildup.

In contrast to the mostly symbolic depictions of modern militarism, animators directly made statements about several aspects of present-day homefront culture during the early Vietnam War. The first cartoons to exploit the counterculture of the 1960s minimize the radical aspects of beatniks and make them more juvenile in order for them to appeal to children. The *Popeye* television cartoon "Coffee House" treats the beat culture as a fad. In one episode Olive and Brutus dress in berets and glasses and chant, "Cool, cool." In addition, although "rock and roll" music had survived branding as "nigger music" and payola scandals to remain popular with teenagers regardless of race, the songs had lost their rawness and became rather sedate by this time. The cartoon studio Format Films capitalized on the relative safeness of the music style. Borrowing from the fictional "chipmunk" characters of a humorous rock novelty recording by Ross Bagdasarian, Format's television series *The Alvin Show* muted whatever was left of the genre's threatening nature by giving it a pre-pubescent sound and look. The series ties rock music to vaudeville. The program has short skits by various stars and comedic interpretations of songs.

Format was by no means alone in watering down popular culture for juvenile audiences. Based in New Rochelle, New York, the Terrytoons studio had survived for three decades by primarily catering to the tastes of children. From the start, producer Paul Terry populated his cartoons with small anthropomorphic animal figures for parodies of fairy tales or cartoons filled with chase scenes. When Terry sold the studio to CBS-TV and retired in 1955, successor Bill Weiss continued in Terry's tradition. 20th Century–Fox — Terrytoons' distributor since 1938 — was pleased with the consistent popularity of the cartoons and kept releasing them to theaters despite the studio's transitions.

Terrytoons drew from World War II when bringing its most popular star from that conflict to the early Vietnam War. Its character Mighty Mouse had initially appeared in theaters in 1942 as a parody of the popular DC Comics hero Superman, whom Max Fleischer had first successfully adapted to animation in shorts for Paramount Pictures one year earlier. Superman's image of a powerful fighter for "truth and justice" had appeal to audiences right after the Pearl Harbor attack, and Terrytoons capitalized on that appeal for Mighty Mouse albeit in a more slapstick fashion. Both the mouse and the man had similar costumes and super powers—flying fast and possessing super strength. Terrytoons even borrowed Superman's "Man of Tomorrow" nickname for the title of Mighty Mouse's debut *The Mouse of Tomorrow*. The rodent survived the war and starred in new cartoons until the mid–1950s, at which point CBS-TV began airing the figure's old episodes on television under the package *The Mighty Mouse Playhouse*. He then became the top animated hero on television and remained on the network for eleven years. Terrytoons briefly capitalized on his renewed popularity by producing more "Mighty Mouse" episodes from 1959 to 1961, at which point the United States began its long military commitment to South Vietnam.

Terrytoons used other war-related imagery to keep the business afloat in the early 1960s. Hector Heathcoate — a patriotic but hapless soldier of the Revolutionary War era — was one of the first successful new characters from the studio since the sale to CBS-TV. In 1956 the network had hired Gene Deitch as the supervising director of Terrytoons. Deitch tried out new but unappealing characters. Weiss fired him in 1958, cut production budgets, and replaced the "replacement characters" with still newer ones like Heathcoate. The only surviving figure from Deitch's short stay — and, perhaps not coincidentally, the last Terrytoons character to star in an Academy Award–nominated cartoon — was a whiny elephant named Sidney.

Terrytoons gave Hector's clumsiness a patriotic quality. His mishaps inadvertently allow the United States to win decisive battles — a stark contrast to cartoons starring military figures during World War II. Back then, animators used their work either to tell cautionary tales of incompetence or rally the homefront viewers via patriotic and victorious soldier images. The cartoons were part of the war effort, and the federal government discouraged uncomplimentary caricatures of the troops. Studios produced films in which careless officers like Warner Brothers' Private Snafu and Walt Disney's Donald Duck (in a few cartoons as a reluctant draftee in 1942 and 1943) wreaked havoc at their bases and, as punishment, peeled potatoes. On the other hand, more coordinated and careful figures like Paramount

Pictures' Popeye and Superman helped the U.S. Armed Forces win animated battles. Two decades later, the studios did not make cartoons to either rally behind or instruct soldiers; rather, they sought to entertain children watching television at home or viewing cartoon matinees in theaters. As a result, animators took their films much less seriously than earlier, as exemplified by Hector Heathcoate causing his fellow troops to trip over themselves but still saving the day by inadvertently blowing up an enemy camp with explosives.

In addition to Hector's comic colonial adventures, the studio romanticized another concluded war but from the standpoint of a former enemy instead of the United States. Between 1959 and 1963, several cartoons from Terrytoons starred a Japanese mouse named Hashimoto, whose best friend was G. I. Joe, a reporter from the United States. The series was a novelty in U.S. entertainment, for studios largely avoided illustrating Japan outside of the setting of World War II despite improving relations between the two countries in the sixteen years since the end of the war. Terrytoons took the bold step of showing the American mouse and the Japanese mouse shaking hands and calling each other "friend." More importantly, the series gave human qualities to citizens of a former enemy of the United States.

Terrytoons was no more likely than other animation studios in developing a Japanese protagonist so soon after World War II. In line with the practices of the film industry during that conflict, Terrytoons produced films featuring derogatory caricatures of the Japanese. In 1942 20th Century–Fox distributed two such films from the studio — *The Outpost* and *Somewhere Over the Pacific* — within months of each other; in both cartoons U.S. servicemen pursue bucktoothed Japanese figures shown as squealing pigs. Two decades later much of the Terrytoons staff remained the same. For example, the studio still employed the director of the two aforementioned anti–Japan cartoons, whose name was Mannie Davis.[1]

Much of the credit for the sympathetic Japanese imagery of the series belongs to Bob Kuwahara, a Japanese American director and the creator of Hashimoto. He was one of the first minorities in the animation industry, working in cartoons for Disney in the 1930s. Internment in a Japanese American Relocation Camp in the 1940s brought his career to a halt. Upon becoming a director at Terrytoons in the late 1950s, one of his first orders of business was a series of cartoons containing positive images of Japan. Although Kuwahara directed most of the entries of the series, other staffers also handled "Hashimoto" films; Mannie Davis himself supervised a couple of cartoons. In most of the films, Hashimoto boasts about his country's richness of beauty and culture — sentiments rarely expressed about Japan in U.S. movies of the early 1960s.

To effectively present the pleasant images of Japan, the "Hashimoto" cartoons circumvent direct discussion of the war that brought Hashimoto and G. I. Joe together. The episodes either show one person visiting the other's country for a tour or consist of Hashimoto telling the journalist a story from Japanese folklore. None of the cartoons are propagandistic "flashbacks" to World War II, in which Japan and the United States fought each other. Instead, the episodes are on par with Hollywood's simultaneous attempts at depicting Asians sensitively in such films as *The Bridge on the River Kwai* (1957) and *Flower Drum Song* (1961).

Terrytoons found its greatest success of the Vietnam War by tapping into the growing popularity of rural imagery. The studio produced over one hundred *Deputy Dawg* episodes for television syndication. Focusing on a dim-witted canine police officer in charge of keeping animals out of a henhouse, the series spread to major cities in 1961. The program was part of a wave of popular television situation comedies set in small towns such as *The Real McCoys* (1957–63) and *The Andy Griffith Show* (1960–68). Due to multiple requests, Terrytoons allowed 20th Century–Fox to release *Deputy Dawg* episodes to theaters in 1962.

Although the characterization of the unintelligent rube did not flatter the South, southern exhibitors especially enjoyed the character Deputy Dawg. In a sense, he embodied the predicament of the pro-segregation southern state during the early Vietnam War. Many politicians and police officers of the region complained that the federal government should not impose racial integration on them. At the same time, some African American civil rights demonstrators broke the law by conducting sit-ins, illegally placing themselves in "white" sections of facilities to protest the moral wrong of segregation. Mississippi, in particular, constructed a state sovereignty commission in 1956, using taxpayer dollars to prevent federal interference and spy on civil rights activists and their supporters. *Deputy Dawg* never specifically mentions blacks or segregation, but the star is a "middleman" figure, just as the segregationist states presented themselves. The clumsy and incompetent Deputy Dawg constantly suffers the haranguing of his sheriff, while animal figures Muskie Muskrat and Vincent Van Gopher steal henhouse eggs right under the dog's nose.

A new television studio provided some of the Vietnam War period's most gruesome pro-war imagery. Leonardo-Total Television Productions illustrated World War I negatively for the United States in the episode "Failspin Tooter" from the series *King Leonardo and His Short Subjects*. In the film a wizard grants Tooter Turtle his wish to become a U.S. fighter pilot during World War I. He becomes a pilot only after a German caricature shoots down every U.S. combat plane. The episode shows the planes full of holes and the pilots falling out of them. The wizard morosely narrates, "Every day the Americans was [sic] losing more and more men, until only one pilot was left." The film even implies that Germany won the air war, because the German figure shoots down Tooter before the wizard magically brings him back to the 1960s.

At the start of the Vietnam War, as in the early years of World War II, Warner Brothers Cartoons was one of the most promising theatrical animation departments. In the 1940s the studio made irreverent films starring cocky and brash characters like Bugs Bunny and Daffy Duck. The figures were the first successful challenges to the popularity of Disney's more reserved stars Mickey Mouse and Donald Duck. In the early '60s, the studio was Disney's only competitor still received Academy Award nominations for its cartoons. Warner Brothers Cartoons also triumphantly entered television with *The Bugs Bunny Show*—a program that aired for four decades in various formats on network television.

The sixties, however, also provided significant challenges for the studio to overcome. In contrast to the new direction the animators pioneered in cartoon humor during World War II, the start of U.S. involvement in the Vietnam War did not spark any creativity or innovation in the artists. Even new staff members surrendered to the stagnant formulas the facility had developed. John Dunn, the most Oscar-nominated cartoon writer of the Vietnam War era, did not shine while working at Warner Brothers. He was consigned to writing for long-developed cartoon characters. In addition, he had to fashion scripts for the different styles of each director.

Despite these setbacks, the most popular cartoon character of World War II, Bugs Bunny, remained as popular during the start of the Vietnam War as during the previous conflict. In between the two wars, Warner Brothers Cartoons made him very understated, letting adversaries cause their own failures. His change in personality paralleled the studio's shift in focus from flamboyant and sometimes hyperactive figures like Daffy Duck and the early Bugs Bunny to strong and violent gags resulting from the flaws of the characters. More importantly, the evolution allowed him to have an uninterrupted reign as the top theatrical short subject series among exhibitors from 1944 to 1960.

Cartoon director Isadore "Friz" Freleng glorified war for Warner Brothers during the 1960s. He had previously poked fun at military enemies of World War II, developing incompetent Japanese soldiers for *Bugs*

Bunny Nips the Nips (1944) and caricaturing Adolf Hitler and Hermann Göring in *Herr Meets Hare* (1945). Now, as the Vietnam War began, Freleng presented militarism as productive in the "Looney Tunes" film *The Jet Cage* (1962). However, the imagery also reflected the creative stagnation of the studio after thirty years of existence, for the military references merely serve as a means of rehashing old jokes and animation to flesh out a story. In the cartoon Tweety Bird imitates an Air Force pilot when his owner gives him a cage that can fly. The film provides a final opportunity for the use of such World War II-era lines as "Pilot to bombardier! Pilot to bombardier!" The scene with this line concludes with Tweety dropping Sylvester Cat, hidden behind the bird, through a bomb chute at the floor of the cage.

The references to World War II, although borrowed from earlier cartoons, still made *The Jet Cage* relevant to contemporary popular culture. At the time of the film's release, Hollywood was producing television series and movies about that conflict. The war-inspired content of *The Jet Cage* became an asset for the film in terms of marketability. For example, a movie theater in New Orleans booked the cartoon with the live-action feature *Term of Trial*, which concerns World War II.

Tweety's Civil War satire *Rebel without Claws* (1961) also contributes to the war nostalgia of the early Vietnam War years. At the time, the United States was observing the centennial of the "War Between the States." Civil rights movement activists frequently used the event to dramatize their century of struggle towards social and political equality. One particular rallying cry was "Free by '63", in observance of the hundredth birthday of the Emancipation Proclamation. Meanwhile, other centennial observances had to do with the superficial — the production of Union or Confederate soldier hats, the flying of "rebel" flags. *Rebel without Claws* was among the superficial. The film establishes its setting merely by putting Union and Confederate hats on Sylvester Cat and Tweety Bird, respectively, and music director Milt Franklyn integrated tunes of the period into his score. Otherwise, the gags involving guns and explosives could have taken place in any "Tweety" film.

Freleng significantly streamlined the Civil War by reducing it to a "chase cartoon." However, this simplistic revisionism results from the studio's sensitivity towards contemporary sectional tensions over the issue of civil rights. In *Rebel without Claws* (1961), Confederate officer Tweety tries to avoid the clutches of Union soldier Sylvester while delivering a message. Several traditional elements of Civil War films were missing in the cartoon. As the United States publicized itself as democratic and fair during the Cold War, the studio avoided casting slave characters in the film. In fact, no black figures appear in the cartoon. Furthermore, with states in the South upset at federal intervention of high-profile desegregation crises, *Rebel without Claws* did not mention the Confederacy or secession. It was a far cry from *Confederate Honey* (1940) — a Civil War satire from two decades earlier, in which Freleng used slave figures and satirized the movie *Gone with the Wind* (1939).

Freleng also demonstrated in *D-Fightin' Ones* (1961) that he could not intelligently discuss race via animation. He had a perfect opportunity to use animal figures to satirize race relations while drawing from the race-themed feature film *The Defiant Ones* (1958). Instead of a black man and a white man handcuffed together, the director cleverly pairs a white dog with the black cat Sylvester. Freleng could have made the stereotypical cat-mouse hatred a context for exploring black-white tensions. However, any discussion by the cat and dog of their animosity towards one another does not extend beyond a terse "I hate you." As the civil rights movement conducted sit-ins and freedom rides to force the issue of segregation into the U.S. media, Freleng retreated from the issue by using old slapstick gags.

With *The Pied Piper of Guadalupe* (1961), Freleng relies upon verbal and visual racial humor instead of the animal-as-minority representation in *D'Fightin' Ones*. *The Pied Piper of Guadalupe* is one of many cartoons in which Sylvester Cat chases Speedy Gonzales — a mouse caricature of a Mexican peon possessing super speed. Vocal artist Mel Blanc delivered Speedy's lines with a stereotypical prolonging of vowel sounds, which Blanc had used for earlier comical Mexican characters. However, this cartoon has something different — the *gringo* Sylvester engaging in racial humor at Speedy's expense. At the end of the film, the mouse retrieves the cat's flute and asks, "Don't you want heem [him]?" Sylvester, injured and bitter, sneers in dialect, "No, I don't want heem!" Thus, even as Speedy physically bested the cat, Sylvester fell back to racism to demean the Mexican mouse.

The Academy Award nomination of *The Pied Piper of Guadalupe* ensured the prolonging of the "Speedy Gonzales" series and its derogatory Mexican imagery. For years Warner Brothers had released only one or two episodes per year. However, over the next two years, the distributor released six "Speedy" films. Speedy was the last recurring character of the studio to receive the Oscar nomination — an honor that usually increased the attractiveness of a cartoon and its star to exhibitors. As a result of his popularity, the distributor became increasingly reliant on him to sell cartoons.

Freleng's colleague Chuck Jones addressed the concerns of the Civil

Rights Movement when illustrating social conformity. In his "Looney Tunes" episode *Martian Through Georgia* (1962), a Martian, feeling out of place on his home planet, travels to Earth to assimilate there. Despite his best efforts in studying humanity, he looks too different for people to welcome him as a fellow Earthling. The story was too eerily similar to the plight of African Americans in segregated areas. Although they had rights as U.S. citizens, city and state governments kept them from voting and told them which bathroom to use, from which water fountain to drink, and where to sit on a bus or in a movie theater.

Jones also associates space with race by dubbing the "Negro problem" a "monster problem" instead. A subplot of *Martian Through Georgia* concerns the Martian's resolve to capture a monster lurking nearby. He hears people reporting about the creature frightening Earthlings. He is completely unaware that he himself is the "monster." When he finally makes the connection, he immediately feels dejected and returns to Mars, where he had once been happy with his own kind. Thus, the film does not encourage social integration but rather people of different groups living in their own separate areas in order to keep the peace. The message is totally out of step with the support of a growing number of U.S. citizens with the civil rights movement's push for racial integration.

Jones' cartoons also stifle the agency of female characters. He wrote and directed *Nelly's Folly*, about a giraffe leaving her jungle to professionally sing but returning there when her career fizzles. Jones also wrote the feature film *Gay Purr-ee* (1962) with wife Dorothy for the animation studio United Productions of America. In the movie a French cat leaves her rural environment for Paris but is kidnapped there. The films are similar to those made just before World War II, when women were portrayed as helpless. The film did not perform well in theaters, suffering not only from slow-paced direction but also from unfavorable timing; movie musicals like *Gay Purr-ee* were in decline in the 1960s. With an unfavorable pun, one critic called the plot for *Gay Purr-ee* "a very old sardine."[2]

Warner Brothers Cartoons withdrew from the present in more ways than merely political ones. Its television program *The Bugs Bunny Show* resembles vaudeville via the stage setting, multiple segments, and the striped jackets of the characters. To be sure, the nostalgia evoked in this series is on par with some contemporary shows on the air. For example, the format of *The Bugs Bunny Show* is not unlike contemporary variety shows like *The Ed Sullivan Show* (1948–71). However, Sullivan used the format to exploit both old and new acts — from ventriloquists to rock musicians. In *The Bugs Bunny Show*, the stars appeared in new animation on a stage setting merely as a tool for showcasing old Warner Brothers shorts.

Walter Lantz — an independent animation producer since the 1920s — also failed to offer much novelty in his films of the early Vietnam War. Like Warner Brothers Cartoons, he had the same major star in 1961 as in 1941. His most popular character Woody Woodpecker had caught audiences off guard in his first films with his staccato laugh, cockiness, and revelry in his mental unbalance. Twenty years later he possessed a calmer demeanor, which hardly caused a stir with viewers. The bird was no longer revolutionary.

Lantz also shared with Warner Brothers Cartoons a willingness to use characters to express Cold War views. He entered the Vietnam War era by illustrating the colonialism of the U.S. military role through a new character. Before the war, Lantz's major stars were Woody Woodpecker and Chilly Willy the Penguin. Then, in 1961, the producer created international policeman Inspector Willoughby. As a heroic human figure, he is a radical departure from Lantz's tendency to choose relatively unused animals and birds as funny cartoon characters. More important, he travels to different countries to capture foreign criminals. Therefore, he symbolizes the United States in their attempt to stop the overseas spread of Communism.

Lantz fashioned the "Inspector Willoughby" cartoons as comedies instead of adventures in foreign intrigue. The episodes consist of gags involving bombs and guns, just like in cartoons from every other studio. As comedies, the films do not build much suspense, nor are the villains menacing. The Inspector himself uses the self-defense of martial arts instead of violent firepower to subdue his adversaries. Lantz even treats these scenes in comedic fashion by contrasting the tall height and muscular build of the criminals with the diminutive stature and skinny physique of the officer. In so doing, the producer draws from World War II-era animation, which featured small protagonists representing the United States — the underdog of the war who was attacked by surprise by Japan.

In 1962 the studio created the longest running theatrical cartoon series of the Vietnam War by isolating the characters from contemporary trends. In fact, "The Beary Family" — consisting of father Charlie Beary, mother Bessie Beary, and children Junior and (until 1963) Suzy — borrows from entertainment predating World War II. Lasting until 1972, the series contained few entries in which the Bearys venture outside their house, and the studio never changed the wardrobe of the figures. The excessive domesticity and the absence of fads over a period of ten years make the series very similar to the television situation comedy *My Three Sons* (1960–72), but "The Beary Family" is more slapstick than its television counterpart. Also, the Beary characters are not as developed as those of the television series. Nevertheless, the survival of the two series throughout most of the war reveals that characters with conservative values and attire found loyal audiences and had more staying power than the trendy films.

Charlie Beary was part of a wave of bumbling father figures emerging as the United States experienced a low point in the Cold War. As Charlie struggled in his leadership of the Bearys, the United States faced a difficult recovery from the USSR's lead in the race to a manned lunar landing, the abortive Bay of Pigs invasion, and the negative global publicity surrounding violent mobs attacking peaceful civil rights demonstrators. The other Bearys respect Charlie's role in the family as the father, but they have a low opinion of him. They often expect him to fail at his tasks. He is an animated counterpart to humorous television fathers on *Bachelor Father* (1957–62) and *The Dick Van Dyke Show* (1961–66).

In contrast to Lantz's success with new series, Paramount Pictures' Cartoon Studio was in a dire situation. By 1960 the eighteen-year-old studio had sold the rights to all its characters and started the decade without major stars. Publicists for the facility put a positive spin on its troubles by saying that it was always looking for new stars. To be sure, the studio's search for a hit character ensured that the cartoons offered a variety of stars. On the other hand, exhibitors looking for proven hit characters found Paramount's offerings too risky in which to invest.

To alleviate the dilemma, Paramount simply reinvented popular characters of the studio's past. For example, the animators pacified the war-related gremlin figure by turning him into a character similar to Casper the Friendly Ghost — a helpful and young apparition who enjoyed playing with children and animals. The tactic had previously worked well for the studio, because it had created the long-running character Little Audrey (1948–58) after losing the license to animate the comic-strip character Little Lulu in 1948. However, Goodie did not have the appeal of Casper or Audrey and died a quick death in theaters.

Paramount's most culturally relevant cartoons of the early Vietnam War had no recurring stars at all. The studio produced some inventive suburban satires that commented on frequent criticisms of suburbanites. Affluent suburban figures were still the order of the day in modern movies and television. The poor were ignored in these films, for their appearances would have given Communist viewers a negative image of the United States. *The Robot Ringer* (1962) addresses the problem of conformity. In the film a white-collar business mistakes an android for a person. The machine physically resembles its coworkers in body and clothing. The cartoon uses humor to reinforce criticism of U.S. business and society from books like David Reisman's *The Lonely Crowd* and William Whyte's *The Organization Man*. The robot embodies the soulless office worker.

The Robot Ringer is notable for its urban scenery. Paramount began setting cartoons in cities after years of fantasy or countryside backgrounds. The new metropolitan cartoons, however, lack the grittiness of the studio's films produced by Max Fleischer from the 1920s to 1942. The newer cartoons present clear skies, clean streets, and contemporary skyscrapers, in contrast to Fleischer's run-down tenements. Then again, he made sexually suggestive cartoons for adult audiences during the Great Depression, as opposed to the juvenile-targeted films Paramount made as the Vietnam War dawned.

Like other cartoon studios, Paramount used outer space as a setting for political statements. The moon serves as a place of exile as well as a symbol of U.S. colonization in *It's for the Birdies*. After an annoyed gopher in a hole sends a bothersome golfer to the moon, the golfer grabs golf flags out of thin air and plants them on lunar soil by several craters. Thus, although banished to the desolate satellite, he transforms it in order to maintain his earthly lifestyle on it. *Funderful Suburbia*, meanwhile, makes outer space a symbol of the trend of "white flight." In this cartoon a white family leaves the planet Earth, seeking escape from assorted social problems. Both cartoons are similar to current movies about space. In both animated and live-action films, only white characters possess control of the exploitation of the moon, and planetary bodies serve as Earth's extended jails, resorts or suburbs.[3]

In contrast to Paramount's theatrical failures, the studio produced very successful television cartoons starring popular characters. Episodes of "Popeye and Sailor" and "Beetle Bailey" appeared in television syndication for several years. The only problem was that Paramount did not own the stars; King Features Syndicate did. As a result, King made more money from the television stations paying to air the films than Paramount did as one of several outfits contracted by King to make cartoons. In addition, Paramount was not the only studio contracted with King; others included Larry Harmon Productions (the makers of *Bozo the Clown* television cartoons) and Halas and Batchelor (a British studio, best known for its animated adaptation of George Orwell's *Animal Farm*).

Nevertheless, Paramount was the facility that could best transition the character from theatrical shorts to television. As in the final films to theaters in the 1950s, the studio entered the Vietnam War by keeping Popeye on the homefront. During World War II, the studio had depicted Popeye as a Navy serviceman, replacing his dark uniform with "Navy whites." In addition, he often appeared on battleships defending the United States from various enemies. After World War II ended, the studio retained this appearance but made him a civilian until the theatrical series folded in 1957. The wardrobe proved practical for animators by that time, for studio budgets shrank and the simplistic design of the uniform meant less time and money into the animation of intricate details. For the television cartoons, Paramount kept Popeye in "Navy whites" but neither referred to the sailor's past military service nor implied any new overseas campaigns. Most importantly, the character designs had hardly changed in the transition from theaters to television, because the staff at Paramount remained largely intact.

Paramount was also consistent in how it used the "Popeye" cartoons for survival. As during World War II, the popularity of the series helped keep the studio afloat during its turbulent times of the early 1960s. The studio had previously used the "Popeye the Sailor" films to provide stability in the 1940s. When Paramount Pictures replaced cartoon producer Max Fleischer in 1942, the new animation producer kept the "Popeye" cartoons in production, thus providing consistency in product. Nearly twenty years later, King Features Syndicate paid the studio to resume making "Popeye" films — an arrangement Paramount needed because of the lack of success it had with new stars.

The "Popeye" cartoons of the 1960s are punctuated by formulaic violence, like the World War II episodes. In most episodes the sailor and his civilian adversary Brutus quarrel. Brutus hits Popeye, who then eats spinach and strikes Brutus much harder. In addition, Popeye remains a small underdog — another vestige of animation from the earlier war. Thus, his blows to the larger Brutus are meant to elicit sympathy and reinforce the longstanding moral of the cartoons: "Might makes right."

However, some aspects of the series did not survive from one war to the other. The depiction of Olive Oyl during the early Vietnam War has considerably less agency than in earlier periods. She is a very dependent woman in the King Features Syndicate *Popeye* series. As in the final "Popeye" theatrical films from Paramount Cartoon Studio, the King television episodes consist of her needing Popeye to rescue her from danger. The final episodes imprison her in a formula in which she wavers between dating either Bluto or Popeye. In contrast, in the films made during World War II, she exercises significant independence from Popeye and Bluto. Some episodes of the '40s do not even focus on a Popeye-Olive-Bluto love triangle but rather other aspects of Olive's personality. She takes care of herself and needs no rescuing.

Some exceptions do exist for Olive. A few King episodes illustrate her as a precursor for future animated heroines of the Vietnam War. When a female adversary knocks Popeye down, Olive eats his spinach and punches out his opponent for him. She occasionally tries to fight male characters, but her blows do not even register with them. Still, she receives superhuman powers long before physically strong female characters like Wonder Woman start appearing regularly in both animated and live-action films. Therefore, King was somewhat progressive in female imagery with those exemplary "Popeye" episodes.

The next year Paramount and King Features revived another dormant genre in animation — the film set on a military base. A cartoon character had not regularly appeared in military uniform for homefront audiences since the end of World War II, when Walt Disney stopped depicting Donald Duck as a reluctant army private. The syndicated television series *King Features Trilogy* accurately adapted Mort Walker's comic strip "Beetle Bailey" to animation. Beetle is similar to Donald in that both characters are clumsy and inadvertently wreak havoc on their respective bases. They also intensely frustrate their sergeants.

In contrast to the formulaic "Beetle Bailey" films, television cartoon producer Jay Ward created a unique military character in the 1960s. "Dudley Do-Right"— a component of *The Bullwinkle Show*— satirizes both silent-era melodrama and the Mounted Police. The title-character is an officer who, although rescuing a damsel from a mustachioed villain, displays more affection for his horse than for the lady. "Dudley Do-Right" was but one of Ward's many irreverent twists on established film genres, which helped define television animation in the early Vietnam War.

Ward also made films that gave some depth to caricatures of American enemies. During the Cold War, movies and television programs depicted communists as one-dimensional figures bent on destroying the United States. In contrast, Ward's series *The Bullwinkle Show* humanized Communists by presenting them as witty. Ward was practical in doing so, for buffoonish images of Soviets would have downplayed the seriousness of Cold War tensions and of significant events like President Kennedy's public request for the nation to have Americans land on the moon.

The Bullwinkle Show slightly masked the ethnic identities of antagonists Boris Badenov and Natasha Fatale. The series identifies Boris and Natasha as spies from Pottsylvania, not the Soviet Union. Still, vocal artist

Paul Frees voiced Boris like Balkan actor Akim Tamiroff and the "Mad Russian" character of comedian Eddie Cantor's radio show. The name "Badenov" pokes fun at *Boris Godenov*. According to producer Peter Piech, Japan's Soviet attaché protested the series, and the Japanese network that had aired the show stopped doing so.[4]

To be sure, *The Bullwinkle Show* presents Communists in a ghoulish manner. Boris and Natasha have very pale "skin." The color is white, as opposed to the pink or salmon hues of most animated caricatures of Europeans Americans. The only human figures with white bodies in cartoons tend to be characters becoming frightened, vampires, and ghosts. Thus, the color of Boris and Natasha is as much of a visual sign of a foreboding presence as are their jet-black clothes — a typical method of imaging evil in the movies.[5]

Rembrandt Films — a studio in the Communist country of Czechoslovakia — similarly transcended Cold War hostilities by producing popular cartoons for U.S. audiences. Producer William Snyder arranged to have Metro-Goldwyn-Mayer (MGM) distribute "Tom and Jerry" cartoons made in Czechoslovakia by former Terrytoons supervising director Gene Deitch. Between 1939 and 1957, William Hanna and Joseph Barbera had directed the series, which focused on a cat (Tom) chasing a mouse (Jerry). Exhibitors enjoyed the cartoons, and some episodes won Academy Awards for Best Cartoon Short Subject. MGM fired the directors and reissued old episodes for three years but then gave in to audience demand for new "Tom and Jerry" cartoons. By contracting with an independent overseas studio, the distributor minimized costs in financing the series.

Deitch gave the violence in "Tom and Jerry" more of an emotional context than Hanna and Barbera had. The original directors kept the "chase cartoon" formula fresh for nearly twenty years by offering new images of exaggerated physical abuse. In contrast, Deitch prolonged characters' facial expressions of pain and explored the feelings of the cat and mouse during their chases. As a result, Rembrandt's episodes resemble Disney cartoons more than the original "Tom and Jerry" films, for the Disney studio often indulged in "personality animation" for its characters at the expense of story timing. Moreover, the expressions of the feelings in the Rembrandt cartoons are not funny. For example, *Mouse into Space* (1962) shows Tom's emotional dependency on Jerry. When the mouse leaves home for space training after the cat shoots him, a sorrowful Tom frantically tries to convince him to stay. At one point, the cat places a bomb in his own mouth and dares Jerry to light the fuse with a match.[6]

Mouse Into Space is also noteworthy in its dual association of outer space with escapism and patriotism. As in Paramount's *Funderful Suburbia*, this cartoon depicts space as an escape from problems on Earth. Jerry becomes an astronaut because he is tired of being assaulted by Tom. However, upon Jerry's return, Tom admires the medals from Jerry's trip and respectfully shakes the mouse's hand. The positive treatment of space travel in the cartoon reflects support for President Kennedy's promotion of U.S. space exploration and also shows how well Deitch and company divorced themselves from the politics of their country to glorify the United States.

In only one capacity does *Mouse into Space* vaguely hint at sensitivity towards Communism. For a few seconds, the film features a canine cosmonaut sharing the skies with Jerry. The brief scene is one of the few acknowledgments in animation of the United States engaging with the Soviet Union in a "space race." However, most of the cartoons produced in the United States during the 1960s propagandistically depict cosmonauts in unflattering manners. In contrast, the imported *Mouse into Space* from Eastern Europe does not; the dog lacks any broad visual caricature at the expense of Communists. The animal merely looks annoyed when Tom accidentally opens his rocket capsule while in orbit.

The Snyder-Deitch "Tom and Jerry" shorts helped take the series to new heights of success. To be sure, none of the episodes received Academy Award nominations, unlike the shorts produced between 1939 and 1957. In addition, MGM continued to release old films along with the new ones. Nevertheless, in 1961, exhibitors voted "Tom and Jerry" the top money-making short subject series of the year. The cat and mouse displaced "Bugs Bunny" cartoons, which had held the top spot for sixteen years. "Tom and Jerry" repeated the victory in 1962. The theater owners' embrace of the violent twosome over the sly and understated bunny signaled shifting tastes as U.S. participation in the Vietnam War began.

The studio gained even more experience in animating to American tastes by agreeing to produce dozens of "Popeye" cartoons for King Features Syndicate. Snyder and Deitch followed the violent story formula that Paramount Cartoon Studio had previously established. Rembrandt frequently drew from contemporary American topics, thus adding some unique variation to the repetitiveness of Popeye punching Brutus to save Olive. However, even the modern references soon became formulaic themselves, for King wanted Rembrandt to produce a significant number of "Popeye" cartoons in a short amount of time; space travel alone is the focus of the episodes *Astro-Nut, From Way Out, Partial Post,* and *There's No Space Like Home.* Nevertheless, the films aired for years in syndication, which meant that the studio on the other side of the "iron curtain" ironically contributed to U.S. militaristic imagery via one of the country's best-known serviceman characters.

Risky humor at the expense of the U.S. military won Snyder and Deitch their greatest success in the United States. In their cartoon *Munro*, the federal government mistakenly drafts a child into the Armed Forces. Paramount Pictures distributed the film, which won the Academy Award in 1961. The distributor continued to release films by Snyder and Deitch over the next seven years. Ironically, Paramount Pictures never won the Oscar for any films produced by its own animation studio.

William Hanna and Joseph Barbera — the directing pair who received multiple Oscars for "Tom and Jerry" films in the 1940s and '50s — won over audiences if not critics in the early years of the Vietnam War. Now owners of their own studio, they modeled *The Flintstones*, a prime-time cartoon series debuting in 1960 on ABC-TV, after the situation comedy *The Honeymooners* via plots, characterizations, and character designs. However, the cartoon is a parody of prehistoric times. *The Flintstones* drew humor not only from the get-rich-quick schemes of its two main male figures but also from anachronistic references to the suburban sprawl of the first twenty years after World War II. Animals and birds serve as "modern" appliances. Stone Age "automobiles" are large wooden structures powered by people running inside of them. The stone houses in neighborhoods looked alike.

Hanna and Barbera promoted the purpose of animation as maximizing the bottom line. They milked story formulas and characterizations for original series *ad nauseam* and drew from others' creations when tapped out of their own. In addition, the producers did not even complain of the high costs of animation, unlike Walter Lantz. On the contrary, they set out to redefine animation by limiting it. Whereas theatrical studios tried to maintain full, fluid animation in the face of rising expenses, Hanna and Barbera made characters move only when absolutely necessary. They declared, "All that motion is passé."[7]

Hanna-Barbera altered its "anachronistic suburbia" format of *The Flintstones* for the new television series *The Jetsons* (1962–63). Its imagery of the future consists of white people colonizing outer space. In a sense it is a half-hour series adaptation of Paramount's cartoon *Funderful Suburbia*. The main difference is the nature of the colonization. Paramount shows outer space as a place for white people to colonize in order to escape Earth's problems. In *The Jetsons* the colonization is already established. Why humans have taken over outer space is irrelevant. Thus, *The Jetsons* does not have to directly satirize social problems; instead, the series can leave the social commentary unsaid and focus on rehashing standard television sitcom fare.[8]

The studio also made cartoons starring animal characters but in a completely different social context than "Tom and Jerry." Whereas the antagonism between the cat and the mouse had symbolized the battles between the Allied and Axis Powers in the 1940s, many of Hanna-Barbera's new animal figures related to human ones in ways that mirrored race relations of the early 1960s. In these cartoons the casts would consist solely of caricatures of white people and talking anthropomorphic animals, thus presenting the non-human figures as an "other" or an alternate to the white image. The studio set itself apart from its competition with these cartoons; other animation facilities cast animals either as mute pets to humans or as human-like, independent creatures with their own homes and freedom to move about as they pleased. Moreover, just as African Americans continued to suffer legally imposed racial segregation, Hanna-Barbera's animal characters had their own designated social "place" and suffered consequences for venturing outside it.

Yogi Bear, a character who received his own show in 1961 after having appeared in a component of *The Huckleberry Hound Show* for the previous two years, symbolizes blacks staying within their "place." The bear is restricted to Jellystone Park and is overseen by a white park ranger. However, Yogi makes the most of his social confinement by resorting to theft; he steals picnic baskets. Despite his survivalist criminality, he is fashioned as a sympathetic protagonist via his maintenance of the park's social hierarchy. Unlike the African American civil rights demonstrators, portrayed by news reporters and southern politicians as radicals for wanting to move beyond their "place" and integrate, Yogi does not directly confront the ranger in order to achieve more autonomy in the park.

By 1961 Hanna-Barbera was willing to acknowledge growing discontent among the disenfranchised concerning their social segregation without compromising support for the status quo. The television series *Top Cat* concerns a group of cats constantly longing to escape their poor alley environment. The program borrows from the live-action television comedy *The Phil Silvers Show* in that the leader of the cats devises various abortive "get rich quick" schemes. In addition, the cats run afoul of a human police officer, whose successful policing of the cats' activities keeps the animals in the alley. The show is politically consistent with *Yogi Bear*, for just as the bear is rewarded for not disrupting social order, the cats are thwarted at every opportunity they take in moving beyond their "place."

In 1962, the "survivalist comic animal" formula started to wear thin. Hanna-Barbera borrowed from its own shows in creating yet another animal figure dealing with social boundaries placed by human characters. Like Yogi's confinement to a park and care from a ranger, alligator Wally Gator lives in a zoo and is supervised by a zookeeper. Similarly to Top Cat's wishes to leave the alley, Wally desires to escape the zoo. The alligator does but is always returned or voluntarily returns to the zoo by the end of each episode. Thus, the studio adds to its theme of "proper place" by illustrating how an "other" figure to the white characters struggles and ultimately fails to fit in to society. The status quo remains preserved.

Even the studio's theatrical work promoted this theme. Since 1959, Columbia Pictures had distributed Hanna-Barbera's "Loopy De Loop" shorts to movie houses. The series concerns a French wolf trying to improve the image of his species; he wants to be a good wolf instead of a big, bad one. However, the people for whom he attempts to perform good deeds reward his generosity by attacking him. Thus, Loopy is persecuted because of his looks and the bad reputation of his species. As these films appeared on wide screens across the nation, blacks similarly challenged poor yet socially ingrained racial stereotypes like the humble servant, oversexed brute and childlike simpleton when trying to integrate into U.S. society. Like Loopy, African Americans of the early 1960s faced an uphill battle in getting rid of its "image problem."

Interestingly, the "Loopy De Loop" series lasted throughout the most progressive period of the civil rights movement. Between 1959 and 1965, activists won several hard-fought victories such as desegregation of businesses and institutions in local areas, the March on Washington, the Civil Rights Act of 1964, and the following year's Voting Rights Act. When the movement's participants demonstrated, they used nonviolent tactics and spoke about love when doing so; they referred to the goal of integration as a means to a "beloved community." Meanwhile, Hanna-Barbera's choice of French as Loopy's ethnicity is significant. To be sure, other studios had used the French language to illustrate characters' loving feelings, but Loopy is different. Although the figure's personality draws heavily from the amorous but malodorous skunk Pepe Le Pew, a character from Warner Brothers Cartoons between 1945 and 1962, the love displayed by the wolf is more *agape* than *eros*.

Meanwhile, Walt Disney discovered how to use physical humor and animal characters to reinforce social conformity. While driving to the lake for a boat ride in *Aquamania* (1961), Goofy causes a pile-up accident in which all the others cars also have boats hitched to the rear bumpers. In addition, all of the contestants in a boat race look like Goofy. However, except for the pile-up gag, Disney does not poke fun at conformity. Rather, the studio accepts it as a fundamental aspect of U.S. society. In the opening scenes, Goofy appears in a business suit, and Disney does not make any jokes about the dog's appearance as a suburbanite.

The production of *Aquamania* reveals the durability of the conformity that started at the conclusion of World War II. Disney had initially cast Goofy as a suburban "everyman" in the late 1940s. The studio removed his facial stubble and protruding teeth, thus giving him a more refined look. He began wearing business suits instead of casual clothes. He began to look more human, hiding his ears in his hat, and when Disney gave him a wife and son in 1951, the wife had a human form — the face was never seen — and the son lacked ears. *Aquamania* reuses animation from *Get Rich Quick* (1951), in which Goofy appears without ears and in a suit, and Goofy's son looks exactly the same as in the episodes of the 1950s. *Aquamania* won an Academy Award nomination, which validated Disney's prolonging of the status quo of the previous decade.

Goofy was not the only Disney character to suffer stagnation in the early 1960s. The studio's story formulas for theatrical shorts in general had hardly changed since the 1950s. The "Donald Duck" episode *The Litterbug* (1961) combines themes and formats from several of the studio's old cartoons. The pro-ecology theme of *The Litterbug* has roots in the cartoon *In the Bag* (1956), in which a park ranger tricks bears into picking up litter. In addition, the cartoon is the latest of films in which the studio uses Donald Duck as an educational tool. Earlier examples of his role as a model of how not to behave include *How to Have an Accident in the Home* (1956). Even earlier, during World War II, the studio had cast Goofy in similar cartoons, but Goofy's appearances were in parodies of "how-to" films — not seriously educational shorts.

Disney also tried to beat United Productions of America (UPA) at its own game. UPA had won over critics with its narrated, heavily stylized cartoons that minimized slapstick humor in the 1950s. Several of the studio's films won Academy Awards that decade, but Disney only received one — the UPA-like cartoon *Toot, Whistle, Plunk and Boom* (1953), which featured narration and graphic stylization. Eight years later *The Saga of Windwagon Smith* presented the narrated story of a man seeking to cross the United States in a contraption combining a ship and a covered wagon. However, the formula may have run dry by then, for the cartoon — one of only four from Disney in 1961 — did not even receive a nomination.

Disney fared better the next year by returning to its own recent successful techniques. To be sure, *A Symposium on Popular Songs* (1962) borrows from UPA's "narration/stylization" trend in its story of the long music career of the duck Ludwig Von Drake. On the other hand, Disney repeats the formula of *Toot, Whistle, Plunk and Boom* by illustrating music history through humor; the duck plays the songs he popularized from the start of the 1900s to the 1960s. Also, three years after the studio's Academy Award nomination for *Noah's Ark* (1959) — a stop-motion cartoon, making moving "characters" out of foreign objects — *A Symposium on Popular Songs* spotlights this technology for some segments. For the studio's efforts, the cartoon won an Academy Award nomination.

One of the more remarkable aspects of *A Symposium on Popular Songs* is its recognition of African American music as part of U.S. musical history of the twentieth century. Drake does not mention the ethnic group by name. However, some of the songs have stylistic roots in music developed by blacks. One of his earliest "famous" songs is a ragtime piece, which comes from a genre pioneered by composer Scott Joplin. Near the end of the film, Drake showcases a couple of rock-and-roll numbers, whose genre was only recently damned as "nigger music" because of its roots in African American "rhythm and blues." Drake himself plays guitar and sings a rock song in the conclusion — a unique move, considering that no theatrical star had previously done so. Moreover, the studio itself had come a long way towards embracing black music; during World War II, Disney had equated zoot-suited musicians, whose swing-style "boogie woogie" jazz served as a precursor to rock, with the Axis powers.

Disney's homage to black music is part of the studio's slow but steady improvement in African American representation over the past few years. To be sure, Disney had a long history of depicting blacks as buffoons and shuffling servants. As late as 1954, its cartoon *Social Lion* presented sleepy-eyed, grass-skirted indigenous Africans as servants to white hunters. But then in 1958, the studio's *Paul Bunyan* briefly paid tribute to U.S. folk heroes, one of which was the steel-driving black man John Henry. Disney gave the figure a muscular physique but hid his face between his arms. For whatever reason, the studio chose not to try to make a definitive break from the standard bug-eyed and big-lipped caricatures, but at least a strong heroic black character was a start. *A Symposium on Popular Songs* continues in that "inch-by-inch" progressive vein in its promotion of black music without discussing the racial group itself.

Unfortunately, Disney's ethnic sensitivity did not extend to Asian Americans. One of the stop-motion scenes features a crudely constructed, slant-eyed Asian puppet. He appears in a song patterned after the Andrews

Sisters in terms of its swing rhythm and harmonizing patterns. The tune identifies him as the "Oriental Fortune Cookie Man." He is a rather nondescript character, constantly smiling while baking the dessert. However, Disney's apolitical image of him at the start of the Vietnam War is a decisive break from the studio's much cruder and more pejorative figures of World War II.

Meanwhile, UPA sold its soul to adapt Chester Gould comic-strip detective Dick Tracy to animation. Worse, however, was how the studio constructed the series, which had little to do with UPA's reputation for quality work. Earlier cartoons illustrate many issues facing U.S. citizens during the 1950s — insecurity during the Cold War, social conformity, and the booming economy. However, the studio fell victim to business realities and focused on Mister Magoo. Then, the studio received a new executive producer and abandoned theatrical production. Then, an influx of longtime animation veterans to replace the young artists abandoning the complacent studio further prevented the studio from adapting its films to modern times. Consequently, after having enlightened adult audiences with sophisticated artistic and political productions, the studio now pandered to children with slapstick. Once a studio championing racial tolerance in films like *Brotherhood of Man* (1947), UPA now used ethnic stereotypes for characters assisting Dick Tracy. Although heroes, these figures were broad caricatures providing comic relief to the crime stories.

Fortunately, the legacy of UPA survived despite itself. An independent studio provided the most direct commentary on war and racial integration. Former UPA director John Hubley and his wife Faith made *The Hole*, in which two construction workers discuss nuclear war while at work. The film itself was a radical exercise in racial tolerance. One of the main characters was black, and the other was white. In addition, one character did not serve another, but instead both performed the same labor. The vocalist for the black character was black jazz musician Dizzy Gillespie. With *The Hole* the Hubleys did what UPA had originally planned to do — use cartoons to directly address social issues.

The Hubleys proved that African American cartoon figures could be witty characters. Such characters in earlier films are clownish and servile. Hollywood drew humor from how they thought blacks should speak instead of giving them funny dialogue. In contrast, the Hubleys trusted Gillespie enough as a performer to treat his character with dignity. Faith Hubley had nothing but praise for him as "a brilliant man, a true friend and a gigantic sense of humor, a wise man, a poet. We all know about his music." She considered his vocal acting skills "on par with his exemplary musicianship." No "Amos 'n' Andy"-like malapropisms and incorrectly conjugated verbs come from the actor's mouth in *The Hole.*[9]

The Hubleys' treatment of Gillespie is also important in that they are not seeking to exploit his music. Most cartoons starring black musicians before 1962 feature very little acting but a significant amount of jazz or swing. In the 1930s, during the early years of sound-synchronized animation, Max Fleischer arranged for the entertainers to perform songs for his cartoons and caricatured them as various figures. One decade later, Walter Lantz and Warner Brothers Cartoons occasionally hired African American swing musicians, but these studios only wanted their music — not their likenesses. The Hubleys extend beyond these earlier efforts in jazz animation by presenting a highly developed character played by Gillespie and by placing his music in the background instead of the forefront.

The federal government's hunt for Communists in the 1950s indirectly caused the making of *The Hole.* John Hubley left UPA during the House Un-American Activities Committee hearings. Blacklisted from Hollywood studios, he and Faith opened their own facility. Free from the power of Hollywood distributors, the co-producers made films dear to them; African American jazz, for example, serves as the music genre of choice for nearly all of their cartoons. Faith Hubley remarked, "John and I are both dedicated jazz fans — before and after our partnership. To not embrace jazz is like denying one's major influence."[10]

Ironically, the positive ethnic imagery in *The Hole* was to the advantage of the United States during the Cold War. The film provides an optimistic depiction of race relations in the United States at a crucial point in the nation's history. As the civil rights movement began, Communist countries saw marches, boycotts and sit-in demonstrations in the American South and questioned whether the United States truly granted freedom and democracy to its citizens. Therefore, the scenes of black and white social equals in *The Hole* presented a change from the usual images of racial tension in the news.

While the Hubleys made progressive racial films, other artists regressed. Freeman Gosden and Charles Correll — the white creators and voices of the African American radio characters Amos and Andy — brought their famous characterizations to animation for the television series *Calvin and the Colonel.* The program was very similar to the radio show *Amos 'n' Andy.* Both series feature characters leaving the rural South for the urban North. The characters get involved in shady "get rich quick" schemes to establish themselves in their respective cities. The only major difference between the two programs (besides animation) is that the characters in *Calvin and the Colonel* are animal figures, not blacks.

The civil rights movement indirectly played a major role in the development of the series. The animalizing of *Amos 'n' Andy* for *Calvin and the Colonel* results from the racial politics of the earlier series. One decade earlier the National Association for the Advancement of Colored People (NAACP) had vigorously campaigned to have CBS-TV cancel its televised adaptation of *Amos 'n' Andy*, which the network did after two years of having aired the series. The negative publicity soured the networks toward stereotypical depictions of African Americans. By revamping the figures as "southern" animals, Gosden and Correll avoided complaints of racism.

Most of the content in *Calvin and the Colonel* is more relevant to the Civil War than to the Vietnam War. The humor is derived from nineteenth-century blackface minstrelsy routines. Gosden and Correll, former minstrels themselves, had integrated some of their ethnic jokes into *Amos 'n' Andy* scripts and reused them for episodes of *Calvin and the Colonel*. Ironically, almost thirty years earlier, they had allowed another studio to animate *Amos 'n' Andy* as six-minute shorts, but the excessive reliance on verbal humor bogged down the films. *Calvin and the Colonel* suffered the same flaw and did not last beyond its first season.

However, *Calvin and the Colonel* helped define Vietnam War-era animation by pioneering the practice of adapting a popular live-action film or person into cartoon form. Sensitive networks kept Gosden and Correll from literally animating *Amos 'n' Andy* in the 1960s, as opposed to the 1930s. Still, the cartoon briefly served as a medium to which the entertainers could perform their old routines one last time. Throughout the course of the war, studios improved upon *Calvin and the Colonel* by finding fresher commodities to animate and in more innovative ways.

Space, race, and conformity characterized the early cartoons of the Vietnam War. Most theatrical animators refused to break from the formulas with which they had worked since the 1940s. Thus, World War II–type humor dominated as the new war began. Meanwhile, television animators drew from milquetoast sitcoms instead of producing innovative shows. The studios making cartoons for either medium failed to capitalize effectively on the resurrected popularity of their art. In the mid–1960s, they paid dearly for their error.

2

THE CARTOONS OF
1963–1964

In the spring of 1963, the popularity of the Hubleys' film *The Hole* (1962) dovetailed with the events of the civil rights struggle in Alabama. On April 7, teenage police officers in Birmingham, Alabama arrested young civil rights demonstrators. Police Commissioner Eugene "Bull" Connor ordered one officer to allow two police dogs to attack a teenager, and footage of the incident made news headlines around the world. On the following day, *The Hole*— a dialogue between a black figure and a white one about politics — won the Academy Award for Best Cartoon Short Subject of 1962. The Academy's decision showed the animation industry that cartoons with political content had value, and it validated the work of the Hubleys — especially John, who had left UPA years earlier because his equality-themed work made him and the studio vulnerable to accusations of Communist sympathies.

The Hubleys capitalized on their win by making another racially political cartoon. In addition, they used racial imagery to satirize war. In their cartoon *The Hat*, two soldiers on either side of an international border prepare to shoot each other after one accidentally drops his helmet across the border to the enemy's land. The Hubleys once again called upon Dizzy Gillespie to voice the black serviceman, and comedian Dudley Moore voiced the white officer. It was the first brilliant satire of war since Gene Deitch's *Munro* (1960) and, unfortunately, one of the last direct animated commentaries on both race relations and war.

Despite *The Hole*'s Academy Award, no studio followed in the footsteps of the Hubleys and made political cartoons. Rather, the animation industry entered a period of transition and made as few changes as possible to the content of their films. For example, as television continued to take people away from theaters and the market for family films shrank, Hollywood scrambled to bring audiences back to see live-action and animated films. Some distributors replaced key cartoon studio personnel like producers and directors. Others made contracts with new studios to produce cartoons starring popular characters. The East Coast theatrical studios — Terrytoons and Paramount — tried to please their distributors by creating several new characters, so that at least one of them could become a hit with audiences. On the other hand, the West Coast animators milked dry long-running series in order for exhibitors to continue renting cartoons on the basis of a character's proven popularity with audiences. The animators of both coasts had in common their preserving of slapstick comedy in cartoons instead of making issue-oriented dramas work like *The Hole*.

As long as distributors offered cartoons to theaters, exhibitors were still willing to promote the films. To be sure, fewer theaters paid for newspaper advertisements of animated shorts paired with features. Those that still did, however, tended to connect the films by distributor or theme or both. When features focused on war, some exhibitors found cartoons that did, too. For example, in a New Orleans theater during March 1963, the aforementioned Warner Brothers cartoon *The Jet Cage* played with the movie *Term of Trial*— a Warner Brothers movie which, like its accompanying cartoon, contains references to World War II. One year later a local theater showed the Warner Brothers cartoon *Hawaiian Aye Aye* (1964), about Sylvester Cat pursuing Tweety in the Pacific Ocean, with a feature set in that same body of water during World War II: *Ensign Pulver* (1964).

Still, the press noticed the animation crisis. Journalists reported that distributors released fewer shorts in 1963 and 1964 than in 1961. Reporters frequently referred to the theatrical animation industry as either dead or in limbo. The editor of *Film Quarterly* stated that "the commercial role of shorts has collapsed." Harriet Polt more frankly titled a *Film Comment* article "The Death of the Animated Cartoon." However, the reporters mostly concentrated on the few releases from Disney and MGM or the imminent closing of Warner Brothers. In so doing, they often overlooked that the East Coast studios had never closed and were more stable than their West Coast competitors.[1]

One East Coast facility — Terrytoons — was busy redefining its product. The studio ceased production of all its current theatrical series in 1963 to make a clean slate for next year's releases. The era of the animated clumsy U.S. soldier in theatrical shorts ended when Terrytoons dropped the "Hector Heathcoate" series. Hector was one of the last vestiges of the "military goof" characterization of World War II cartooning. Disney had long stopped putting Donald Duck in military fatigues, and no other theatrical studio had cast their major stars as soldiers regularly before Terrytoons created Heathcoate.

However, the hapless soldier did not completely disappear. That same year CBS-TV started broadcasting *The Hector Heathcoate Show* (1963–65), which featured episodes made for television instead of old theatrical shorts. The Revolutionary War character was now part of a television genre of "military goof" figures. Quinton McHale of *McHale's Navy* (1962–66) and Gomer Pyle of *Gomer Pyle, USMC* (1964–69) were Hector's live-action television counterparts during the run of *The Hector Heathcoate Show*.

Meanwhile, the final "Hashimoto" film from Terrytoons marked several milestones in the imaging of Asians by the U.S. animation industry. No more theatrical cartoons from any studio starred an Asian figure as the main character. Animation for theaters and television did not present an Asian family for nine years. However, live-action television was just as negligent, if not more so, in terms of having an Asian family as leads — not guest roles — of a series. "Hashimoto" was also the last cartoon series for over a decade to star only Asian figures. In the interim, both animation and live-action studios caricatured Asians as servants and martial arts experts. In late 1964, the death of Bob Kuwahara — the creator of "Hashimoto" and its sole director for its final two years — effectively sealed the fate of Asian imagery in cartoons, for only he had been willing to depict the group with sensitivity.

With new characters Terrytoons continued to produce cartoons paralleling developments in the Vietnam War. The studio's films for theaters in 1964 still promote multiculturalism but by addressing cultural insensitivity instead of presenting diverse ethnic groups. The new "Astronut" series consists of episodes in which an alien from outer space introduces his culture to his friend on Earth — a man named Oscar Mild. Astronut, largely ignorant of the effects of bringing his artifacts to Earth, unintentionally causes havoc with each gift he brings. As Americans worried about entering the Vietnam War and President Lyndon Johnson promised the nation that the United States would not escalate involvement, the "Astronut" films warned audiences not to enter into a foreign land without knowing about the area.

Like "Hector Heathcoate," "Astronut" also had a contemporary in television with the live-action situation comedy *My Favorite Martian*

(1963–66). This program concerns a man named Tim, who befriends a wayward Martian and names him "Uncle Martin." The major difference between the two series is that Uncle Martin looks human and only has to hide his antennae. Thus, much of the humor comes from people mistaking him for a fellow earthling. In contrast, Astronut produces comedy by struggling to fit into U.S. society despite his green color.

The "Astronut" films made a telling but symbolic commentary on race relations during one of the most violent periods of the civil rights movement. The friendship between the white Oscar and the green Astronut illustrates the peaceable coexistence of figures of different cultures and colors. However, the chaotic situations resulting from people's frightened reactions to Astronut's green body present a struggle towards social integration. The scenes of apprehension are on par with those from the cartoon *Martian Through Georgia* and from contemporary "B movies" about outer space invaders, most of which were destructive antagonists either killed by humans or sent back to their home planets. Unlike Astronut's contemporaries, he has a friendly demeanor, and his adventures show integration as good instead of a danger to be thwarted. As his first episodes played in theaters that summer, three young male civil rights activists — two white and one black — lost their lives in Mississippi. They were part of a group of young adults traveling from across the country to that state to train the local blacks about their voting rights. Local whites considered them invaders and saw their arrival as a threat to the state's segregationist society.

In contrast to the imagery representing racial equality, Terrytoons also produced colonialist imagery. In the theatrical series "Luno the Flying Horse," a white boy on a flying horse finds adventure in Third World countries. To be sure, the series is similar in format to the live-action program *Lassie* (1954–71), in which a boy and his dog experience dramatic adventures. However, *Lassie* takes place in the rural United States, unlike the element of foreign intrigue in "Luno." Moreover, the people Luno conquer are often brown-skinned indigenous figures, as opposed to the white criminals Lassie helps apprehend.

"Luno" and "Astronut" collectively mark a shift in the Terrytoons studio towards white characters. For example, while most of the humor in "Astronut" comes from the alien's ability to metamorphose, the series also features amusing human characterizations. Vocal artist Dayton Allen provided humorously nervous stuttering for Astronut's timid Earthling friend Oscar and shouted impatient rants for Oscar's boss, the ironically named Mr. Nicely. The studio's transition to white figures was also numerical. Unlike the year 1963, in which the episodes starring Hector Heathcoate were a small fraction of Terrytoons' mostly animal-populated releases (the "Sidney" and "Hashimoto" series), "Luno" and "Astronut" cartoons dominated the 1964 releases.

Paramount Cartoon Studio joined Terrytoons not only in developing several new figures but also in producing films with themes related to white supremacy. Like Luno from Terrytoons, Paramounts' cartoon *Laddy and His Lamp* promotes colonialism. In the film a little white boy (Laddy) controls a genie caricatured as a West Asian figure. This domination is similar to that of Luno over the indigenous antagonists he defeats overseas. However, Laddy and the genie have a friendly relationship, and the genie is ready to serve the boy immediately upon being freed from the lamp. They have no tension between each other.

Despite a major change in personnel at Paramount a short while later, colonialist imagery still shaped cartoons. Laddy was one of the last creations of producer/director Seymour Kneitel, who died in July 1964. His replacement Howard Post presented internal colonialism in his first film *Homer on the Range* (1964). In the film a white cowboy has an Indian sidekick. Thus, a white figure is still able to dominate a minority character and explore new land. The difference is that the land is not a foreign country but rather the American West.

Paramount contributed to the whitening of U.S. culture in 1964 by casting white human caricatures for nearly all of the studio's releases. In the "Modern Madcap" entry *Robot Rival*, such figures exclusively colonize different planetary bodies. In contrast to most cartoons about outer space, this film features no aliens at all. Another episode from the series, *Near Sighted and Far Out* identifies the "star" as a little boy named Squeegee, although he plays the "straight man" role to an anthropomorphic, talking anteater.

More importantly, Paramount's first new theatrical series in two years starred two white figures. "Swifty and Shorty" episodes consist of the attempts of a tall confidence artist (Swifty) in swindling a naïve, diminutive man (Shorty). The series has several precedents and counterparts in television, most notably the aforementioned *McHale's Navy* and the earlier series *The Phil Silvers Show*. Although Kneitel directed some "Swifty and Shorty" cartoons before his passing, Howard Post made additional entries. Thus, he was able to keep Paramount's product consistent for exhibitors.

Post also continued Paramount's "Noveltoons" and "Modern Madcaps" series. However, both series became indistinguishable. The latter took on the elements of the former by introducing new "stars" and featuring settings beyond the present-day United States. Despite having two series as outlets for potentially popular characters, none of the new figures connected with audiences. The studio's old approach to selling characters was not working anymore.

Meanwhile, in California Walter Lantz stuck to characters and formulas that did work. The Old West, the North Pole, and the suburbs were the principal settings of Lantz's films from 1963 until the studio's demise nine years later. The producer made savvy choices in his backgrounds for cartoons. To be sure, Chilly Willy had no live-action counterpart in contemporary films as a polar protagonist. The strength of that series lay in the comedy drawn from the penguin's antagonizing of Smedley Dog. However, Westerns and suburban situation comedies ruled the television airwaves in the mid-1960s. Lantz continued to produce his own sitcom-like "Beary Family" entries, and he resurrected a dormant character — Sugarfoot Horse — from the defunct hillbilly series "Maw and Paw" to serve as Woody Woodpecker's sidekick in several Western parodies through 1972.

Sugarfoot became the first of many co-stars for Woody in his later episodes. The frequency of the team-ups suggested that the bird could not carry a film anymore. It was a sad fate for a character who had wowed audiences in his debut (*Knock Knock* in 1940) and had stolen the spotlight from the film's milquetoast "star" Andy Panda. While director Paul J. Smith used the horse, Sid Marcus created a small but ferocious dog named Duffy to keep Woody company. The dog draws laughs from his ability to open his mouth wider than the size of his body, and his bark is the combined sounds of an elephant's shriek and a lion's roar.

Some Lantz cartoons went beyond the formulas and were somewhat timely. For example, in this era of black students breaking segregationist laws via sit-ins for the cause of equality under the law, civil disobedience made its way into Lantz's work. Borrowing from the legend of Robin Hood, *Robin Hoody Woody* (1963) features the woodpecker in the role of the famous figure. Ironically, as a character successful in stealing something from another character, Woody takes on the persona of Lantz's own frequent fish-thief Chilly Willy.

Meanwhile, Metro-Goldwyn-Mayer was competing with its own history. As of July 1963, the distributor had not yet signed anyone to produce more "Tom and Jerry" cartoons. To be sure, the series maintained its popularity under the care of William Snyder and Gene Deitch in Czechoslovakia. Audiences generally did not see aesthetic differences between their films and those of Hanna-Barbera. MGM released six new "Tom and

Jerry" cartoons in 1963 and boasted to the press about the popularity of the series with audiences. In addition, Deitch did not seem too concerned about the possibility of not being rehired.[2]

For the year's releases, Deitch conformed "Tom and Jerry" more to the Hanna-Barbera style. He increased the violent content and decreased the quirky emotional scenes. As a result, a studio in a Communist country helped contribute to the militaristic culture that shaped the U.S. homefront during the Vietnam War. One film for the 1962–63 season, *The Tom and Jerry Cartoon Kit*, features several gags reminiscent of the slapstick humor in the earlier episodes by Hanna-Barbera. In the cartoon Tom and Jerry spit watermelon seeds at each other, and Tom falls through a floor.

Snyder and Deitch "Americanized" their cartoons of the year by borrowing from U.S. popular culture and from the original "Tom and Jerry" series. In so doing they made their foreign films more relevant to U.S. audiences. Just as Hanna and Barbera occasionally set Tom and Jerry in the Old West, so did the Czech studio in *Tall in the Trap*. The cartoon contains references to some television Westerns like *Have Gun Will Travel* and *Gunsmoke*. The studio's final offering, *Carmen Get It*, is set in New York's Metropolitan Opera House and rehashes Hanna-Barbera's *Tom and Jerry in the Hollywood Bowl* (1950), in which Jerry sabotages a concert conducted by Tom.

"Tom and Jerry" was not the only set of relevant cartoons in theaters at the time. In 1964 the periodical *Film Quarterly* described the Warner Brothers cartoons as "cool," in that many of them illustrate old gags in fresh, sometimes abstract, ways. Director Chuck Jones was arguably the most abstract. Some of his films from 1963–64 use titles to accentuate gags, as when the word "Pow" accompanies an explosion in *War and Pieces* (1964). In *Now Hear This* (1963), Jones uses the phrase "Gigantic Explosion" instead of images of flashing light and smoke clouds.[3]

Occasionally Jones' "cool" titles represent his boredom with the studio itself. *Now Hear This* is the first cartoon to do away entirely with the opening and closing graphics of concentric circles encasing the "WB" shield logo. Rather, he makes the letters "W" and "B" out of geometric shapes and replaces the familiar "That's all, folks" closing with the more bland "A Warner Bros. Cartoon." Other directors used the new sequences to start and end their cartoons that did not star established characters. Meanwhile, the circle graphic — a staple of the studio's films since 1936 — remained for the films starring recurring characters.[4]

Like the films from Terrytoons and Paramount that year, Jones' cartoons are part of a growing trend in U.S. culture of popularizing white characters. Two cartoons from 1963 are set in Great Britain and star white human figures. He visits familiar ground for his "Merrie Melodies" episode *I Was a Teenage Thumb*—a reworking of his own *Tom Thumb in Trouble*. In the aforementioned *Now Hear This*, he transforms Great Britain into a sparse, stylized, and exotic land of unusual sounds. In addition, unlike the former cartoon, nobody speaks in the latter.

Warner Brothers Pictures underwent a significant transition in its distribution of animated cartoons, signaling its difficulty in evolving its humor from World War II-era gags to relevance concerning the Vietnam War. Warner Brothers Cartoons closed its doors in 1963, but the distributor immediately contracted with an independent facility to make films starring the famous characters. The studio, formed by Warner Cartoons executive David H. DePatie and director Friz Freleng, retained many of the Warner animators and maintained some continuity in humor although working with half the money of Warner Cartoons' last budget. More importantly, Warner Brothers was able to continue providing cartoons to exhibitors, simply switching from its own final films to the first DePatie-Freleng entries in the fall of 1964.

Bugs Bunny, however, became an early casualty of shifting audience tastes during the war. Although his episodes regained the title of top money-making short subject series in 1963, he lost again to Tom and Jerry the following year. As if borrowing from the violent characterizations of the cat and mouse, Bugs acts more violently than usual in his cartoons from this period. Instead of using his wits to defeat antagonists, he relies increasingly on guns. However, his new demeanor did not reverse the studio's fortunes, and when DePatie-Freleng started producing new cartoons for Warner Brothers, the studio bypassed the bunny for other characters.

Freleng himself had trouble reconciling Bugs to contemporary culture shortly before the studio closed. The director made the bunny a nostalgic figure in the last two "Bugs Bunny" cartoons he made. Neither film is set in the present day. In addition, Freleng reused stories and dialogue from several cartoons. His version of Bugs Bunny was less "cool" than "square."

Devil's Feud Cake (1963) is the least original of Freleng's final pair of "Bugs Bunny" cartoons. The majority of the cartoon consists of clips from earlier episodes of the series. Old scenes of Yosemite Sam hurting himself are linked by new animation in which Satan demands that the cowboy retrieve the bunny. The director borrowed the plot from one of his own films: *Satan's Waiting* (1955), in which the devil sends Sylvester Cat to catch

Tweety. As in the previous year's *The Jet Cage*, this "new" cartoon even throws in the old World War II line, "Pilot to bombardier!"

The Unmentionables (1963) reuses old material with more originality than *Devil's Feud Cake*. *The Unmentionables* concerns Bugs' attempts to bring gangsters Rocky and Mugsy to justice, as in *Bugs 'n' Thugs* (1954). However, the director fashioned the standard gunfire gags as a parody of the live-action television series *The Untouchables*—a crime drama set in the 1920s. Also, the film boasts stylized character designs based on popular graphics of the era, Bugs Bunny and the aforementioned gangsters notwithstanding. Such attention to accuracy in settings was rare from studios by the 1960s, and stories set in the "Roaring Twenties" were just as uncommon until DePatie-Freleng began producing the theatrical "Dogfather" series—spoofing the hit feature film *The Godfather* (1972)—in 1974.

The disappearance of Bugs Bunny after 1964 is ironic, considering his rise to stardom during World War II. When "Bugs Bunny" cartoons first became the top attraction in short films in 1944, his tactics of mind games and minimally violent acts of self-defense against his predators drew audiences. His status as a physical underdog who always wins struck a chord with wartime viewers after the Pearl Harbor attack had caught the United States off guard. Twenty years later, Bugs Bunny's new aggressive streak correlated with the United States fighting the North Vietnamese as a military superpower instead of an underdog. And just as support for the Vietnam War was not as widespread as that for World War II, the appeal of the revamped Bugs paled in comparison to the character's popularity two decades earlier.[5]

Bugs Bunny's sole war-themed film of the Vietnam Era, *Dumb Patrol* (1964), serves as a blueprint for cartoons about "good vs. evil" over the next few years. The bunny here is much different in characterization than during World War II in that he lacks vulnerability. In the films from the earlier conflict, he does not fight his adversaries until attacked first. He frequently announces, "Of course, you know this means war," to prepare audiences for his retaliation. However, in *Dumb Patrol*, he is a pilot during World War I, pursuing Yosemite Sam (as German pilot Sam Von Scham), although Sam has not personally harmed the bunny. Thus, no self-defense takes place. Bugs fights Sam merely because of the German's role as "the enemy." In the superhero cartoons produced by studios through the mid–1960s, the heroes similarly fight villains who have established their "bad guy" status through their crimes against others; they do not hurt the heroes first.

Bugs Bunny also represented American strength via colonialist imagery. The cartoon *Mad as a Mars Hare* (1963) looks at U.S. cultural dominance from the opposite point of view of "Astronut." In contrast to the alien conforming to Earth, Bugs Bunny imposes his Earth ways upon Mars. He plants an "Earth" flag into the soil and, when accidentally given super powers by a Martian, proceeds to literally crush the figure. He colonizes Mars, just as human figures inhabit outer space in Paramount's *Robot Rival*, although the bunny used might to do so.

On the other hand, by the time the "Bugs Bunny" series ended, the directors had experimented with the star's characterization. In some episodes he defeats his adversaries but still experiences trouble either by his own doing or by forces beyond his control. Before 1963 Warner Brothers rarely made Bugs Bunny a loser. This unsuccessful Bugs during the Vietnam War contrasts with the bunny of World War II, who always won despite fighting larger opponents and exemplified the U.S. military effort of that conflict. Perhaps the latter-day Bugs also symbolizes the early Vietnam War by serving as a warning that the mighty can fall. In Freleng's *The Unmentionables*, Bugs captures the gangsters but is imprisoned with them because he forgot the handcuff keys. Director Robert McKimson's *Dr. Devil and Mr. Hare* (1964) ends with the bunny creating a Frankenstein monster who first pummels the Tasmanian Devil and then Bugs himself. The sight of Bugs with a lumped head and his arm in a sling is hardly the image of strength he had projected two decades earlier.

Still, the tweaking of Bugs' heroism was part of a cultural trend in the United States. For years the nation had confronted threats to its post–World War II power. The country was humbled by its own failures and the early successes of the Soviet Union in space exploration in the late 1950s. Racial segregation became a sore spot for the United States; the Soviets referred to it to illustrate the nation's domestic flaws. Correspondingly, a growing number of writers and artists developed protagonist characters as imperfect heroes. Marvel Comics especially pioneered the flawed superhuman in comic book series "Spider-Man" and "The Incredible Hulk" in the early 1960s. The beatings taken by Bugs Bunny in his final years constitute part of this new wave of heroism.

Bugs Bunny's frequent co-star Daffy Duck also undergoes an undesirable transformation. Chuck Jones had changed Daffy from a hyperactive and carefree figure to a greedy, egotistical, and fearful character in the 1950s. The director captured the new personality best in *Duck Amuck* (1953), in which an off-screen cartoonist psychologically breaks the duck down by tampering with the cartoon. By the 1960s, however, other directors took away Daffy's complexity. Instead, the bird is a humorless, unsympathetic villain in *The Iceman Ducketh* (1964). No longer hiding behind booby-traps and pretending to like Bugs Bunny, the duck becomes a bold hunter shooting to kill the bunny. At least the hunter Elmer Fudd had vulnerability by acting gullible and politely. Yosemite Sam, while more cantankerous when firing his pistols, evokes sympathy because he is overcompensating for his short height. In contrast to Elmer wanting to be liked and Yosemite Sam demanding respect, Daffy has no qualities of vulnerability. Also, in earlier films, he plays the role of underdog to Bugs' stardom, but in *The Iceman Ducketh* no relationship between the two exists.

Meanwhile, Freleng's "Speedy Gonzales" cartoon *Chili Weather* (1963) has the rare cartoon theme of civil disobedience. To be sure, it is partially a back-to-roots cartoon, for the film's story of Mexican mouse Speedy Gonzales racing in and out of a cheese factory to feed starving countrymen comes from the 1955 cartoon *Speedy Gonzales*. However, like Woody Woodpecker in *Robin Hoody Woody*, Speedy's altruistic stealing dovetails with the protests of the sit-in activists.

Most of the "Speedy Gonzales" episodes of this period lack this altruism. Like Bugs Bunny, Speedy's heroism is given some tweaking by Warner Brothers Cartoons as the studio ceased operations. The majority of the 1963–64 episodes deviate from the formula of the mouse rescuing or feeding his fellow Mexicans. Most of the films merely feature Speedy running away from Sylvester. One of the least inspired of these final entries is the plotless *Mexican Cat Dance* (1963), in which the mouse acts as a matador to Sylvester in a pseudo-bullfight. The conclusion of *A Message to Gracias* (1964) blurs "good" and "evil" when Speedy commands a defeated Sylvester to pursue a mouse who put Speedy's life in danger for no reason.

The closing of Warner Brothers Cartoons brought an end to the character Foghorn Leghorn after twenty-seven years. In most of his films, this rooster either teases a barnyard dog guarding chickens, or he avoids getting caught by a chicken hawk. In his interactions with other characters, Foghorn is bombastic and blustery, and he refuses to consider the feelings of others. However, he often shows a lack of intelligence. He is similar to other southern fictional figures of the 1940s and is voiced similarly to comedian Kenny Delmar's Dixie character Senator Claghorn. However, in 1963, the image of a bullying southerner was often in the context of violence against civil rights demonstrators, as in Birmingham when Bull Connor unleashed dogs and fire hoses on juvenile marchers. Foghorn's demise that same year was, thus, very timely.[6]

Foghorn's apprehension towards the goateed beatnik rooster in *Banty*

Raids has some parallels to the white South's negative response to the early counterculture. For example, segregationists in Mississippi objected to the convergence of young adult activists to their state not only because of the purpose — ending segregation — but also the appearances of the demonstrators. The grooming of the activists especially had political connotations. Ku Klux Klan branches in Mississippi referred to Michael Schwerner, one of the civil rights workers murdered there in 1964, as "Goatee." To be sure, Foghorn does not attack the beatnik rooster's politics or facial hair but rather complains about the rock music that comes from his guest's shack. Still, the beatnik bird is a sort of "outside agitator" because he sneaks into the barnyard to chase hens. In addition, he stands out because of his stereotypical counterculture look.[7]

This beatnik figure never fully integrates into the cast of *Banty Raids*. He appears as a sort of sideshow freak, for the hens ogle him and Foghorn tries to conform him according to the culture of the barnyard. Also, in contrast to Foghorn's strong characterization, Warner Brothers did not give the beatnik rooster a strong personality. He talks only about himself and his music. Moreover, he spends as much time in the cartoon talking as playing music or listening to it.

The beatnik rooster symbolizes a lack of knowledge on the part of the animators concerning the counterculture of the early 1960s. Warner Brothers does not present many counterculture attributes for the character beyond sunglasses and a goatee. He does not make any references to Jack Kerouac or Alan Watts; in fact, he discusses no poetry or philosophy. He merely speaks in modern slang and plays rock music. *Banty Raids* associates the beat culture (inaccurately) with the rockabilly music genre. Beatniks tended to favor jazz, especially bebop. However, the beatnik rooster in the cartoon sings a brief number in the style of Elvis Presley while strumming a guitar and dancing.

The beatnik rooster is especially disappointing, considering the great care that had once gone into the development of counterculture figures. During World War II, director Robert Clampett commissioned his animators to visit African American nightclubs for a cartoon starring zoot-suited characters; he was satirizing a group of people who drew the ire of U.S. citizens for wearing long suit jackets and baggy pants as the nation rationed fabric for the war effort. The figures the animators designed had accurate clothes and dance steps but were still crude racial stereotypes (protruding lips and dice for teeth, to list some examples). Twenty years later, during the Vietnam War, the studio did not find the counterculture interesting enough to research.

Also notable about *Banty Raids* is the role of rock music. During World War II, the characters of Warner Brothers Cartoons embraced the counterculture of African American jazz artists. Bugs Bunny occasionally spoke in the slang of the day, and Daffy Duck wore a zoot suit. To be sure, rock was not musically far removed from the "swing" music of the 1940s; melodies are similar, but rock focuses more on the guitar and drums than the horn-oriented swing. However, in 1963, rock musicians like the beatnik rooster are antagonists in the studio's cartoons. In addition, none of the Warner Brothers stars make references to contemporary musical tastes or youth-oriented fads. Foghorn Leghorn, in fact, describes rock music as "the most terrifying sounds."

Surprisingly, the rock group the Beatles did not inspire any immediate backlash from theatrical cartoon animators, unlike Elvis Presley. The group did not link rock music to raw sexual energy, in contrast to Presley's pelvic gyrations while performing onstage. The Beatles, thus, appeared more reserved. As "safer" icons, they were more easily marketable than Presley had been. However, the animation industry neglected to take advantage of the group's appeal. Except for Paramount, the studios already had popular (animal) cartoon stars and proven story formulas; the Beatles just did not fit in stories about cat-and-mouse chases and talking bunnies and woodpeckers.[8]

However, the issue of intentional nonconformity, which the Beatles exploited via their long hair length, is the focus of a new cartoon character. Color is central to the identity of the Pink Panther — the first star of a new studio headed by former Warner Brothers Cartoons producer David H. DePatie and director Friz Freleng. Stories about color were rare in cartoons. The closest story to the formula of the panther's painting objects pink is Daffy Duck's drawing of mustaches on portraits in the Warner Brothers animated film *Daffy Doodles* (1946). However, DePatie-Freleng developed several "Pink Panther" stories in which the cat frustrates a white figure by repainting something of his with the color pink. Animation critic Richard Schickel commented on how color itself became a character in the "Pink Panther" series. He acknowledges a moving, white blob as a being by calling it "he" but considers the figure abstract — nowhere near the realism of Disney's characters. Moreover, the use of monochrome backgrounds and characters was a central part of the series' charm for Schickel.[9]

The Pink Phink (1964) — the debut of the "Pink Panther" series — introduces the theme of color-validation to U.S. animation. Both the theme and the character have relevance with the civil rights movement of 1964. That summer the students of SNCC and some black Mississippians had traveled to Washington, DC to ask the federal government to honor the voting rights of African Americans in Mississippi. Both the state and the nation were refusing to enforce the Constitution's Fourteenth and Fifteenth Amendments because of the brown skin color of the disenfranchised. Meanwhile, sit-ins and marches continued across the country. In addition, Black Muslim speaker Malcolm X's commands for his black audiences to look upon their pigmentation and African roots with pride inspired African Americans to develop new means of cultural self-expression. Similarly, although the Pink Panther has no political agenda, he also seeks to establish the presence of his color through unconventional means. In *The Pink Phink* the panther sabotages a house painter's job by changing the color of every wall and floor of a house from blue to pink. Whenever the painter redoes a room in blue to cover the pink, the cat redoubles his efforts to keep his color there.[10]

Although DePatie-Freleng retained many employees from Warner Brothers Cartoons, the new studio offered different political themes than its predecessor. For example, in contrast to the patriotic militarism of *Rebel without Claws* (1961), *The Jet Cage* (1962), and *Dumb Patrol* (1964); the first "Pink Panther" cartoons promote radicalism and non-conformity. One reason is that the panther itself was a radical character, not fitting into the old studio's violent slapstick story formulas. Unlike the cartoons of Sylvester pursuing Speedy Gonzales or Tweety, the panther was not a character who chased an animal for food, nor did anyone else try to eat him. In addition, *The Pink Phink* differs from the standard World War II-era plot of a figure defending himself from an imposing enemy. The panther is the one causing the disturbance by imposing his color onto the painter but is also the protagonist of the film because of his calm demeanor contrasting with the aggressive tantrums of the painter at having his work ruined.

While DePatie-Freleng developed an original character, Walt Disney worked on a mythological one. The studio's feature-length cartoon *The Sword in the Stone* (1963) is a story about Camelot, made during the "Camelot presidency" of John F. Kennedy. The movie is a musical about King Arthur as a boy fulfilling his destiny to fight and lead with the help of a magical sword named Excalibur. Released one month after Kennedy's assassination, the film is one final and bittersweet example of how intensely his presidency influenced U.S. popular culture.

The Sword in the Stone is both a unique and typical Disney cartoon. It differs from previous studio features, because the protagonist is a young boy, unlike Snow White, Cinderella, Alice in Wonderland, and Sleeping

Beauty. However, the boy Arthur has a mentor in the wizard Merlin, just as Cinderella has a fairy godmother. Each previous Disney movie, except for *Victory Through Air Power*, is also a musical. Also, *The Sword in the Stone* is an addition to the genre of boy-heroes, which the East Coast competitor Terrytoons had already started via Luno.

Paramount also cashed in on the genre by resurrecting one of its former stars. The studio produced *The New Casper Cartoon Show* (1963–69) for television, in which Casper the Friendly Ghost travels all over a forest to help people. Similar to the other series starring boys, Casper also has supernatural powers. These new episodes, however, have an advantage over other cartoons via Casper's built-in celebrity; his theatrical episodes of the 1950s had rerun on television in recent years, and he starred in several successful comic-book series from Harvey Comics.

The New Casper Cartoon Show was the studio's most successful television endeavor. The animators eschewed the old format for the friendly ghost's films — cheering up or playing with little animals or children. Casper instead became a righter of wrongs committed by cousin Spooky or the Ghostly Trio — the collective name for Casper's housemates. More importantly, they carry the spirit of the Kennedy presidency of the early 1960s. The new films carry the theme that with (supernatural) power comes responsibility, very similar to President Kennedy's rhetoric of "Ask not what your country can do for you."

The United States was not the only country embracing the boy-protagonist characterization. That same year *Astro Boy*—a Japanese cartoon first shown in the United States in 1963 — introduced a new kind of television cartoon protagonist to U.S. audiences: the militaristic boy. As a weapon-wielding juvenile figure in melodramatic adventures, Astro Boy is a more serious manifestation of what the title-character of *Munro* jokingly was. In only three years since Deitch's film and two years after U.S. servicemen entered South Vietnam, audiences embraced the concept of the boy-soldier.

Meanwhile, a new domestic television cartoon program presenting colonialism via the boy-hero genre in a similar manner to the "Luno" series lasted nearly as long as the Vietnam War itself. Hanna-Barbera's *The Adventures of Jonny Quest* concerns the travels of white figures across the globe and the dangers they face. The series, which began in the fall of 1964 and aired sporadically for the next eight years, depicts countries inhabited by people of color as simultaneously exotic and threatening. The blond-haired and blue-eyed boy Jonny, his father, his tutor, and an Indian boy (the only nonwhite of the cast) come across more monstrous creatures than they do indigenous residents. The dehumanization of the inhabitants of these foreign countries reflects the idea of white superiority.

This new juvenile character of the Vietnam War has roots in an earlier work about a fictional boy of World War II. Co-producer and co-director Joseph Barbera cites the long-running comic strip *Terry and the Pirates* as his inspiration for *The Adventures of Jonny Quest*. Illustrator Milton Caniff had created the strip in the 1930s, in which a white boy named Terry goes on foreign adventures with a white adult figure. The stories for the television show are similar to those from the comic strip, which still appeared in newspapers when the program aired. In fact, Caniff's work outlived Hanna-Barbera's show by one year.[11]

Even the development of the characters in *The Adventures of Jonny Quest* had a quality of colonialism. For creating Jonny's East Indian traveling companion Hadji, Hanna-Barbera did not look to India but rather to Hollywood. Series designer Doug Widey identified the movie actor Sabu, originally from India, as the model for Hadji. As a result, the character reflects Indian culture much less than the U.S. movie industry's depiction of Indians.[12]

Not all television cartoons featured dramatic imagery of white superiority. Leonardo-Total Television Productions made comedy out of colonialism on a weekly basis for the television cartoon *Tennessee Tuxedo and His Tales* (1963–66). One of the components of the series — "The World of Commander McBragg" — features a retired British naval officer recalling overseas adventures to an unimpressed listener. His tales usually end with his conquest of indigenous people of color by some unorthodox means. He occasionally uses the "natives" as servants; they help carry his weapons and other supplies, too.

McBragg is unusual in that he is an unsympathetic protagonist, despite patriotic tone of the cartoons. Other colonialist characters like Luno, Laddy, and Jonny Quest do not have caustic personalities. On the other hand, McBragg resembles Foghorn Leghorn, because both figures incessantly talk without allowing the characters with whom they converse to speak. However, Warner Brothers counterbalanced Foghorn's aggressive personality with compassion, as in his willingness to raise an abandoned orphan in *Banty Raids*. McBragg merely fights characters in their countries and tells his conversing partners a terse "Quiet!"

Leonardo-Total Television also illustrated violence in order to satirize it in the Saturday morning cartoon series *Underdog*. The title-character is a very loose parody of the venerable comic-book icon Superman from DC Comics. Underdog only resembles "the Man of Steel" in that both figures change their clothes in telephone booths, have the ability to fly, and rescue female journalists from danger. Otherwise, unlike the muscular Superman, Underdog is a skinny dog, whether dressed as the hero or in the secret guise of "Shoeshine Boy." His appearance, however, understates his strength. When he punches his adversaries, they usually fall to the ground. Thus, his characterization more closely resembles the puny but powerful dog Droopy (1943–58) from Metro-Goldwyn-Mayer cartoons than Superman.

The *Underdog* episode "Guerilla Warfare" continues in the studio's tradition of glamorizing war. A villain named Riff Raff shows his gang a training film on how to conduct guerilla warfare, which consists of opposing soldiers shooting each other and dropping bombs on one another's camps. Riff Raff orders his men to use the military tactics — hit and run, camouflage, sabotage, and sneak attack — to dispose of Underdog. It was one of very few cartoons, televised or theatrical, to illustrate war tactics with any great specificity. And the enemy's embrace of guerilla tactics corresponds with the fighting style of the North Vietnamese and Vietcong throughout the Vietnam War's duration.

As television broadcasters gravitated towards animated militaristic adventures and slapstick comedies, cartoon satire became endangered. Already plagued by scheduling changes and low prime-time ratings, *The Bullwinkle Show* aired on NBC-TV for its third and final season (1963–64). The series, however, received a new life as reruns on weekend mornings and remained on network television there from the fall of 1964 to the fall of 1973. Its duration of the entire length of the Vietnam War is a testament to not only the humor of the show but also to the relevance of characters like Boris and Natasha to the Cold War.

Hanna-Barbera's *The Flintstones* persevered in prime-time television but lost its satirical edge after 1963. That spring the series introduced a new character in baby Pebbles Flintstone. The infant girl spawned high ratings for the series and several products marketed towards children. However, the program's stories also started to pander to children. *The Flintstones* ceased to resemble *The Honeymooners* from that point onward. Instead of jokes poking fun at modern conveniences in suburban communities, science fiction became more dominant in the stories about *The Flintstones*. Prehistoric cars and talking animals-as-appliances were not the only elements of fantasy. Rather, stories soon involved time-travel, dream sequences, and characters shifting shape and height.

At the same time, the studio shifted gears in its figurative uses of animal figures to illustrate social segregation. *The Yogi Bear Show* ended its run in 1963. The next year the bear starred in his own theatrical movie, *Hey, There It's Yogi Bear*. In bringing the star to the big screen, Hanna-Barbera gave his pilfering of baskets a negative context. In 1964, Hollywood's films abided by a decades-old production code, which included a rule that any illegal activity had to result in a negative consequence for the guilty character. Thus, despite Yogi's imposed isolation at Jellystone Park, he could no longer get away with stealing others' food. Indeed, a major plot development in the feature involves the capture of Yogi's girl-friend Cindy, who receives the blame for looting the baskets that Yogi had actually stolen. To free her, he has to confess his guilt to the ranger and then team up with him to save her.

Hey There It's Yogi Bear was the last Yogi-related product made by the studio for nearly a decade. The movie did respectable business at theaters. However, Hanna-Barbera did not make a sequel. Meanwhile, children had different ideas about the types of cartoon characters they wanted to see on television. In a new era of gimmickry such as outer space settings (e.g. *The Jetsons*) and figures having superhuman powers (e.g. *Underdog*), Yogi belonged to a bygone period.

That same year Hanna-Barbera made one last-ditch effort to milk the *Yogi Bear* formula. The studio offered *The Magilla Gorilla Show*, concerning a primate confined to a pet store. As in *Yogi Bear*, a white man (the storekeeper) takes care of the title-character. Unlike Yogi, Magilla does not resort to any deceptive means to leave the shop. Rather, various white customers purchase him and take him to live with them. However, the gorilla never fits in with his new owners and, at the end of each episode, is back in the pet store. Thus, the series reinforces the idea of non-whites having "their place" by showing how attempts at social integration fail. The theme dovetails with the reluctance on the part of many U.S. citizens to embrace the integrationist goals of the civil rights movement. A common complaint from state and federal government officials was that the demonstrators wanted too much too soon. They reasoned that the country still needed time to honor the rights guaranteed to blacks by the Fourteenth and Fifteenth Amendments, although each document neared a century in age.

In 1963 and 1964, animators made cartoons that truly reflected the times. Ironically, the story formulas and gags they had used since World War II were what audiences of the mid–1960s wanted most. The characters grew cockier, more aloof, and more complicated, reflecting the nation's confidence in handling its many foreign and domestic problems. As the United States continued its military role in Southeast Asia, cartoon characters practiced militarism and colonialism. While segregation remained in place in the South, animators depicted minority groups in unflattering manners. The cartoonists were not alone in their imagery, for Hollywood's movies and television programs offered few alternatives. Major changes in the Vietnam War and the civil rights movement over the next few years tested U.S. animation's long-held traditions.

3

THE CARTOONS
OF 1965

The U.S. animation industry experienced another chance at revitalizing itself in both media in 1965. Theatrical studios developed new characters and novel situations for old stars in the hopes of rekindling interest among film exhibitors for cartoon shorts. In January the New York *Times* optimistically announced, "Animated cartoons, which have almost faded away from movie theater screens, seem ready for a comeback." Meanwhile, television studios experimented with hipper settings and character designs while retaining popular formulas. Television networks seized upon the shows and earned fortunes from them.[1]

The hip quality of the cartoons of 1965 extended beyond how characters looked or acted. The films had relevance to their times, because a significant number of cartoons either directly or symbolically dealt with issues of the Vietnam War. To be sure, the characters did not mention the Civil Rights Act, the War or Poverty, or the arrival of the Marines to South Vietnam. But they did not have to do so. Many stories and settings focused on characters looking different from one another, concerned the poor, or illustrated military conflict. Such imagery is not new to the cartoon, but its increase in 1965 corresponds to how the Johnson administration prioritized them that year.

Some studios stubbornly stuck to old formulas. Walter Lantz's "Chilly Willy" cartoon *Half-Baked Alaska* simultaneous embraces and eschews aspects of traditional gag-oriented animation. The film is one of the few from Lantz to have the format of several quick gags separated by the screen fading to black. The "blackout gag" format first took shape as World War

II dawned in Columbia Pictures' cartoon *The Fox and the Grapes* (1941). Other studios, especially Warner Brothers, used it more than Lantz had. The blackouts were a significant creative change in his films. Corresponding to the increased spotlight on poverty under Johnson's presidency, each gag in *Half-Baked Alaska* concerns an impoverished and starving Chilly's attempts at getting work in order to afford to eat a meal.

Half-Baked Alaska is also notable for the new direction it signaled for the "Chilly Willy" series. Chilly speaks for the first time in the cartoon. While his dialogue with Smedley Dog has humorous touches of the puppet Senor Wences on *The Ed Sullivan Show* (1948–71), the penguin's voicing destroyed the original concept of the character. Back in 1954 Fred "Tex" Avery had developed him as a small mute figure causing mischief to larger but easily perplexed foes. Now, under the direction of Sid Marcus, the penguin is funny not only for what he does but for what he says. As animation budgets shrank for the rest of the '60s, Chilly's voice increasingly became the focal point of his characterization.

Meanwhile, Walt Disney produced films that were conservative in tone. He used conformity to educate children in its two theatrical cartoons of the year. A pair of "Goofy" cartoons—*Freewayphobia* and *Goofy's Freeway Trouble*—instruct viewers on how to drive safely on freeways. As with most "Goofy" episodes produced since the 1940s, all of the characters look like the dog and wear business suits. In an era when DePatie-Freleng's "Pink Panther" cartoons created humor from different-looking figures and the Civil Rights Act forced the federal government to enforce the freedoms of diverse Americans, the sameness of the anthropomorphic dogs is regressive.

For the cartoons Disney substituted visual gimmickry for humor as the educational tool. Neither *Freewayphobia* nor *Goofy's Freeway Trouble* contains many jokes. Moreover, they do not have that much animation. Instead, the film presents diagrams and stop-motion animation of live-action miniatures of cars to demonstrate freeway safety. Interspersed throughout the films are live-action scenes of actual busy freeways, and at the end an animated Goofy is superimposed over the footage.

The "Goofy" episodes of 1965 show that for Disney, the slapstick humor of World War II-era cartoons was dead. The dog had once epitomized that humor for the studio. When Mickey Mouse, Pluto, and Donald Duck appeared in sedate films that drew humor from their reactions to situations during the 1940s and '50s, Goofy tripped over himself and crashed into walls for laughs. *Aquamania* was the last Disney cartoon featuring slapstick as the chief type of humor. Instead, education and camera tricks comprised Disney's approaches to Vietnam War-era animation.

In contrast to Disney's quiet year in theatrical animation, DePatie-Freleng became very famous very quickly. The studio's cartoon *The Pink Phink* (1964) won the Academy Award for Best Cartoon Short Subject in April 1965 — one month after one of the most graphically violent demonstrations of the civil rights movement. In March the Southern Christian Leadership Conference had led a series of marches in Alabama with the goal of crossing the Edmund Pettus Bridge, which connected the cities of Selma and Montgomery. The group's first attempt to cross the bridge had the most brutal response from state troopers using billy clubs and tear gas as well as charging at the marchers on horseback. Barely a week had passed since the last of the marches, which had resulted in a successful crossing, when the annual Academy Award ceremony took place. It was fitting for a cartoon about the validation of a figure's color-based identity to receive the prize for its category.

DePatie-Freleng and its new star received press coverage usually reserved for live-action stars. Instead of merely reviewing a cartoon, periodicals discussed the studio itself. Friz Freleng of DePatie-Freleng told *Time* magazine that topicality made its theatricals stand out among the competition. In the studio's cartoons for United Artists, he is especially accurate. In addition to the color-based conflict that corresponds to the civil rights struggle, "Pink Panther" episodes of the year tackle espionage and the outbreak of war.[2]

Some of the series' entries for 1965 draw from the success in the United States of various representations of European culture. That year the Beatles continued to have successful songs, and other British rock groups sold millions of records. In theaters the fictional secret agent James Bond appeared in the popular movie *Thunderball*, and a sequel to *The Pink Panther—A Shot in the Dark* was released. On television *The Man from UNCLE* capitalized on the spy craze. DePatie-Freleng took notice and forced European culture into the "Pink Panther" series. The cat speaks in a British accent in *Sink Pink* and *Pink Ice*. The episode *Shocking Pink*, meanwhile, has a British-accented narrator.[3]

DePatie-Freleng's major contribution to Cold War-themed animation was *Pinkfinger* — a tale of espionage whose title capitalizes on the popularity of the "James Bond" movie *Goldfinger* (1964). *Pinkfinger* is mostly notable in that it is one of the first animated spoofs of the fictional secret agent, whose movies were wildly popular at the time. Otherwise, the cartoon is standard fare. The evil spies speak in a European accent similar to that of Boris Badenov from *The Bullwinkle Show*. In addition to dynamite explosions and falls into holes, the panther performs one of the oldest slapstick jokes — slipping on a banana peel.

For a discussion on how war begins, the studio made the more original *Pink Panzer*. In this cartoon a devil figure brings morality to animated war — a dynamic not seen since MGM's cartoon *Peace on Earth* (1939). The demon, unseen at first, convinces the panther and his human neighbor that the other seeks to do harm to each character. The friendliness the neighbors exhibit gradually degenerates into open hostility and climaxing with warfare. The topic was timely; United Artists released the film only months after the Marines landed in South Vietnam.

Pink Panzer and *Peace on Earth* have completely different outlooks on war, but the imagery of war corresponds to the wars taking place during the production of each film. In *Peace on Earth*, animals lament that human beings have caused devastation through war. The creatures vow not to follow in the people's footsteps. Thus, MGM's cartoon did not favorably anticipate U.S. involvement in war in Europe. On the other hand, *Pink Panzer* ends with the conflict between the panther and the human figure merely starting. DePatie-Freleng's film, therefore, accepts the state of war as fact while similarly acknowledging its evil origins.

The studio's "Pink Panther" cartoons for the year are more violent than those of the previous year. *Dial "P" for Pink* introduces the Pink Panther to the standard cartoon props of guns and dynamite. When the panther made his debut in 1964, studio writer John Dunn cast him in films whose gags had to do with graphics and color. However, new writer Bob Kurtz wrote *Dial "P" for Pink* and several other films whose humor was heavily reliant on explosives. Eventually Dunn followed suit and wrote similar stories for the panther, even after Kurtz left the studio. In the process, the panther evolved from a unique, graphics-oriented star to just another slapstick cartoon character. Still, the violent approach had been missing in cartoons for a while but now returned as U.S. participation in the Vietnam War escalated.

Despite the change in format for the series, at least the Academy of Motion Picture Arts and Sciences appreciated Dunn's early efforts. Most of the Academy Awards for Best Cartoon Short Subject went to nonviolent, graphic-filled independent and foreign films during the Vietnam War. Such films were a radical contrast to the patriotic war allegories during World War II, in which anthropomorphic animals used the munitions of war to fight each other. However, before DePatie-Freleng, no theatrical animation studio of the 1960s had prioritized graphics over militaristic slapstick. When *The Pink Phink* (1964) won the Oscar, it was the first Hollywood studio cartoon in six years to do so.

Under DePatie-Freleng, the "Merrie Melodies-Looney Tunes" films suffer a similar fate to the UPA product of the late 1950s-stagnation. Just as UPA became increasingly dependent on "Mister Magoo" episodes, none of the Warner Brothers cartoons star any brand new leading characters. During World War II, Warner Brothers Cartoons had used the conflict as a means to experiment with new stylization techniques and characterizations. Now, in the Vietnam War, DePatie-Freleng offered nothing new but instead rested on the laurels of Warner Brothers.

DePatie-Freleng tried to hold on to several traditions of Warner Brothers Cartoons: the "WB" shield in the opening sequence, the concept of the repertory company of characters, and "blackout gags." Only Daffy Duck significantly changed. The zany duck of World War II turned into the angry duck of Vietnam. The studio had not been the first to revamp the bird; at Warner Brothers Cartoons, director Chuck Jones initiated the duck's transformation from a hyperactive troublemaker to a more sedate yet self-absorbed figure. However, DePatie-Freleng amplified Daffy's worst qualities without giving them a humorous spin, as Jones had done.

On the other hand, Daffy Duck is less malicious this year than in 1964. His negative characterization in many of the DePatie-Freleng cartoons stems from his position of power over Mexican characters. He often is cast as a landowner refusing to rent space to others. He pursues Speedy as a matter of protecting property. Therefore, the nature of the chases is different than in *The Iceman Ducketh* (1964), in which a more bloodthirsty Daffy hunts Bugs Bunny simply for money and sport.

The Warner Brothers cartoons by DePatie-Freleng perpetuate the absence of parody that characterizes the final films from the original studio. None of the "Merrie Melodies-Looney Tunes" episodes by the new studio contain celebrity caricatures. Such imagery had once been a hallmark of Warner Brothers animation. Some cartoons of the 1930s and '40s star *only* Hollywood caricatures. The most direct reference to popular culture takes place at the end of *Go-Go Amigo*, when Speedy dances the "Twist."

Unlike the original war satire *Pink Panzer* for United Artists, DePatie-Freleng treaded familiar water when illustrating war for Warner Brothers. In *Assault and Peppered* Daffy and Speedy battle each other from forts. The film reuses gags from the Warner Brothers cartoon *Bunker Hill Bunny* (1950). However, in keeping with the new filmmaking of the Vietnam War, *Assault and Peppered* does not end with a decisive military victory.

Instead, Daffy wins by default after a bored Speedy returns home for supper. Its conclusion is dramatically different than that of *Bunker Hill Bunny*, in which the aggressive villain Yosemite Sam wilts from Bugs Bunny's effective cannonball shots and surrenders to him.

DePatie-Freleng connected poverty with war as civil rights activists started to do the same. Several urban riots took place in the summer of 1965, as in the pervious two summers. Although the civil rights movement had not directly addressed poverty, some people had learned from following the movement's tactics that newsworthy demonstrations often yielded results. However, the urban demonstrators used other means besides nonviolent ones to protest poverty, police brutality, and other problems. Similarly, Speedy Gonzales turns to firepower when championing the economic plight of his countrymen. In *Assault and Peppered*, powerful land baron Daffy Duck whips Mexican mice for trespassing and starving on his property. Speedy then fights for his fellow rodents by engaging in a cannon duel with Daffy.

Assault and Peppered also connects poverty with colonialism. Daffy owns Mexican land and oppresses Mexican mice but is not Mexican himself. This film is one of many in which Daffy-as-colonialist is defeated. As such, it is a rare cartoon for 1965. At the time most studios had cast colonial figures as protagonists and the indigenous characters as enemies, sidekicks, or extras. Now that European characters were in vogue in Hollywood, sympathetic treatment of minorities was even less of a priority for studios besides DePatie-Freleng.

The "Daffy-Speedy" cartoon *Chili Corn Corny* places poverty and colonialism within the context of civil disobedience. Speedy helps a Mexican crow steal corn from a field owned by Daffy in Mexico. As in *Assault and Peppered*, the duck attacks the mouse as a means of defending property. However, the film discourages certain kinds of civil disobedience. The film concludes with the crow successfully taking over Daffy's land and eating his corn. On the other hand, Speedy runs for his life as the duck fires a gun at him for having assisted the crow. Thus, DePatie-Freleng astutely note that while civil disobedience may produce victories for the oppressed, the activists risk their lives for change and receive little appreciation at the time. Indeed, a few activists gave their lives for voter equality in 1965, most notably Rev. James Reeb, Jimmie Lee Jackson, and Viola Liuzzo during Dr. King's marches in Alabama to dramatize the issue.

When DePatie-Freleng's cartoons for Warner Brothers pair Daffy with other characters, the colonialist bent of the Daffy-Speedy films is absent. The duck appears with other figures in films set in the United

States, and his co-stars are not caricatures of minorities. For example, both Daffy and Porky Pig are police officers chasing a crook in *Corn on the Cop*. And in a reversal of Speedy trespassing on land owned by Daffy, the duck unsuccessfully tries to take over land owned by British gophers in *Tease for Two*.

DePatie-Freleng's "Road Runner" cartoons, although more formulaic than the episodes from Chuck Jones, retain the theme of ineffective militarism from the earlier entries. The new directors devise very few original gags appear in their episodes. Friz Freleng reuses animation from some of Jones' entries for *The Wild Chase*, and Robert McKimson borrows a joke from *Show Biz Bugs* for *Rushing Roulette*. Nevertheless, the new films are consistent with the old ones in that the coyote still fails to catch the bird no matter what technology and weaponry he acquires.

Meanwhile, on the east coast, Paramount Cartoon Studio's cartoons for the year are caught between old and new styles of animation. Films directed by Jack Mendelsohn resemble those of the UPA studio from the 1950s. The cartoons by Howard Post, however, are traditional slapstick adventures with conventionally designed figures and backgrounds. The result is an uneven batch of cartoons for 1965 in terms of quality.

Concerning topicality, however, Paramount made some of its most socially and culturally relevant films in years. For example, the studio played with images of ethnicity and class in its caricature of the poor in *The Outside Dope*. A vagrant speaks in a British accent while lying to a police officer about traveling the world on twenty cents per day. The voice, implying elegance and formality, contrasts with the figure's appearance in tattered clothes and a five o'clock shadow. The gag is a creative twist on the stereotypical image of the poor and corresponds to the increasing number of impoverished people, both black and white, in the United States during the 1960s.

Still, *The Outside Dope* is an exception to Paramount's imagery of Europeans. Most of the studio's cartoons promoted European culture in a favorable light. Howard Post continued to frequently use white characters, just as Seymour Kneitel had done before dying in 1964. Post directed new "Swifty and Shorty" cartoons. In addition, two miscellaneous cartoons — *The Itch* and *Poor Little Witch Girl*— feature characters with British accents. The latter film introduced a new recurring but unsuccessful star named Honey Halfwitch.

The emergence of this new character showed that the start of the Vietnam War did not offer promising images of women in cartoons. She was immature and dependent. As such, she was typical of Paramount's animated female characters; the studio's previous female characters were the juvenile figures Little Lulu (1943–48) and Little Audrey (1948–58). All three characters inadvertently cause trouble while playing by themselves or with others, and they share the physical appearance of short height, white skin, and long brown hair. Halfwitch is different in that she is a sorceress-in-training and speaks in a British accent.

Despite Honey's similarities with older cartoon stars, she is still a timely character. Her debut comprised part of an influx of supernatural women in popular culture that year. A new hit television series of the 1964-65 season was *Bewitched*, which concerned the romance between a man and a witch. Then, in the fall of 1965, *I Dream of Jeannie* paired a female magical servant with an astronaut, and *My Mother the Car* featured an elderly lady reincarnated as an automobile. Honey differs from these characters in that she has no limitations to her powers. In contrast, the witch and the genie generally use their powers either to please the men in their lives or to establish order in their homes.

Honey Halfwitch is also relevant in that it is part of a wave of juvenile female protagonists in popular culture. In the fall of 1965, *The Patty Duke Show* started its final season, and both *Gidget* and *Tammy* first aired. The shows did not survive past 1966, as networks decided to attract young female viewers not with teenage girl protagonists with whom they could identify but rather with male pin-ups like the stars of *The Monkees*. Honey is closer in characterization to the adolescent female characters than to the aforementioned witch and genie. However, the fictional teenagers are often infatuated with boys and concern themselves with trendy music and clothes. Honey does not try to woo anyone or follow fads, although her British accent corresponds to the great influx of European influence in U.S. culture during 1965.[4]

Animators made few alternative female characters to Honey Halfwitch at the time. Moreover, those that existed were hardly progressive or culturally relevant. Total Television — Leonardo's *Underdog*, a popular new cartoon series for the 1964-65 season, uses the timeworn, damsel-in-distress formula from silent movies. To be sure, the program parodies the contemporary comic-book hero Superman. However, the show repeatedly places female character Sweet Polly Purebred in danger at the hands of assorted villains. Each of her appearances consists largely of her crying for help or mournfully singing, "Oh, where, oh, where has my Underdog gone?"

However, another clumsy character with superhuman powers is the closest that U.S. animation comes to creating a female superhero. Hanna-

Barbera's Winsome Witch, who appears in her own episodes on *The Atom Ant–Secret Squirrel Show*, uses a magic wand to perform good deeds for others. Thus, she differs from the more self-absorbed Honey Halfwitch. Winsome is also more community-minded than the homebound witch and genie of live-action television.

East Coast animation also drew from television for settings for cartoons. Prominent escapist locales in television series during the Vietnam War were poverty-stricken rural areas. CBS-TV especially popularized rural escapism. It alone broadcast four major situation comedies about poor rural folk. *The Andy Griffith Show* (1960–68), set in the fictional southern town of Mayberry, features strong characterizations and does not exploit the poverty of southerners. *The Beverly Hillbillies* (1962–71) places such characters into a mansion and draws humor from their newness to wealth and urban society, while *Petticoat Junction* (1963–70) and *Green Acres* (1965–71) are set in farming towns populated by shady, dim-witted locals. Terrytoons, which had successfully developed rural humor for its "Deputy Dawg" character, tried to make lightning strike twice in 1965 via "Possible Possum." The studio's creation of the series is hardly surprising, because the same network that aired the live-action rural shows also owned Terrytoons. Now the network had an animated counterpart to its televised shows about hillbillies and small-town citizens.

The owner of Terrytoons was not the only exploiter of the poor in the media at the time. The federal government played a major role in popularizing the poor areas satirized by Hollywood. One year earlier, President Johnson had declared war on poverty. He toured a poverty-stricken Appalachian area. Movie and television producers, however, glossed over those conditions and made the Appalachian valley a fun and carefree place to live, populated by clean and friendly citizens.[5]

The Terrytoons series also shares with current television shows the way in which it depicts the South. As an isolated and underdeveloped area, the setting of "Possible Possum" symbolizes the isolation of the South from the rest of the nation. It is a romanticized community of leisure-slow-paced and without African American characters. The cartoons are, therefore, not unlike *The Andy Griffith Show*, which was set in the peaceful, all-white town of Mayberry. No stories in either series focus on civil rights or on opposition to the Vietnam War.

On the other hand, the southerners of "Possible Possum" have some similarities to earlier African American characters. They speak in the same dialect, although the "Possible Possum" characters have more of a twang to their voices. In addition, old black figures and the "Possible Possum" cast are desexualized. All of the characters of the series are male, and no stories involve romance.

A new director at Terrytoons took a different approach to illustrating the poor. Ralph Bakshi separated poverty from morality for his cartoons. His "Sad Cat" series spoofed the children's story *Cinderella* but eschewed the practice of giving the poor character a happy ending. In the episodes the ragged, overworked Sad Cat tries and fails to escape the harassment of his brothers, even with the help of an "apprentice good fairy." The series attacks the optimism of the fairy tale genre popularized by Disney while simultaneously offering a moral that more seriously addresses poverty as President Johnson declared war on it: magic does not stop oppression or make people rich.

In his initial "Tom and Jerry" cartoons for Metro-Goldwyn-Mayer, Chuck Jones presented the rare theme of compassion towards the poor. He uses poverty as a means to develop Jerry Mouse as a sympathetic character. In *Pent-House Mouse*, Jerry sneaks into Tom's luxurious apartment for food and eventually removes Tom from his own place. However, *Snowbody Loves Me* places Tom in total control over his home.

Both *Snowbody Loves Me* and *Tom-ic Energy* demonstrate a transition in Jones' work towards the promotion of *philia* love. In these films the antagonistic feelings that Tom and Jerry have for each other dwarf in comparison to their underlying friendship. To be sure, Hanna-Barbera's Tom and Jerry occasionally acted in each other's best interests. However, their truces had a context of violence; the cat and mouse co-existed peacefully either after a major fistfight or before the friendship degenerated into quarreling. Jones, in contrast, did not give the characters nearly as much tension from which to make their friendship more significant. Tom and Jerry are just nice to each other.

MGM's cartoons by Chuck Jones lack the physical slapstick of the "Tom and Jerry" cartoons by Hanna-Barbera. Then again, both sets of films have completely different foci of humor. Hanna and Barbera had developed creative ways for the cat and mouse to hurt each other. On the other hand, Jones concentrated on showing Tom and Jerry thinking about what they want to do to each other, what they have done, or what has been done to them. As a result, the audience is treated to a series of smiles, frowns, looks of surprise, winces of pain, and — especially from Tom — scowls. The emphasis on facial humor extended from Jones' tendency of "cool" detachment from the slapstick in his final years at Warner Brothers Cartoons. However, this "coolness" towards the very foundation of the "Tom and Jerry" series resulted in some awkward cartoons by Jones.

His detachment manifests itself in other ways that are uncharacteristic for the "Tom and Jerry" series. In addition to the violence itself, another hallmark of the Hanna-Barbera episodes is the sound-based humor. Film editors emphasized the impact of each strike and explosion with great sound effects, and the directors themselves voiced Tom Cat's yelps of pain. In contrast, after Jones' triumph of audio in *Now Hear This*, he did not creatively exploit the possibilities of sound for "Tom and Jerry." Rather, he resorted to another trick from that cartoon: having onomatopoeia replace or emphasize slapstick scenes. In his first "Tom and Jerry" episode, *Pent-House Mouse*, Jones accompanies Tom's hits over Jerry's head with the on-screen title "Splat!"

Jones struggled to construct consistent personalities for the cat and mouse. His "Tom and Jerry" episodes usually draw unfavorable comparisons to his earlier "Road Runner" films for Warner Brothers. To be sure, Tom chases Jerry as Wile E. Coyote pursues the Road Runner, and both the cat and coyote mug at the camera with assorted smirks, scowls and frowns. However, in the first year of the new "Tom and Jerry" series, the characters borrow from several established characters of Jones' old studio.

Some of the films came from Warner Brothers cartoons starring lesser-known figures. *The Unshrinkable Jerry Mouse* owes much of its content to Jones' *Feline Frame-Up* (1954), in which Claude Cat unsuccessfully tries to remove a cute kitten from his master's house. Jones molded Tom into Claude's role for the MGM version. However, whereas a bulldog is the kitten's advocate in *Feline Frame-Up*, little Jerry Mouse defends the kitten from Tom.

The Cat Above, the Mouse Below, "a remake of the "Bugs Bunny" cartoon *Long-Haired Hare*," is significant in two aspects. First, Jones makes another attempt at squeezing Tom and Jerry into a story tailor-made for another character. In the original film, Bugs sabotages an opera concert after the featured singer attacks the bunny in his hole. For MGM, Jones made Jerry the victim seeking revenge at singer Tom's performance. Second, it is the first episode from Jones to not contain chase scenes. In fact, Tom and Jerry barely see each other except for less than ten seconds of the six-minute cartoon. Thus, Jones made a clean break from the Hanna-Barbera years of the series by removing the defining characteristics of the original cartoons.

For *The Cat Above, the Mouse Below*, Jones continued a trend from his days at Warner Brothers Cartoons, which involved fashioning his cartoons after the movie *Gaslight*. In the movie one character secretly tries to drive another insane. Similarly, Jerry remains out of sight when trying to disrupt Tom's singing, whether under the floor of the stage or on a rafter by a sandbag directly above the cat. Jerry's discreet actions further distance his personality from Hanna-Barbera's depiction of him. In most of the original "Tom and Jerry" films, Jerry faces Tom when attacking him with assorted weapons. Part of the mouse's appeal comes from his boldness in the small creature striking his giant adversary while looking at him. Jerry's cocky attitude and the element of confrontation are sorely lacking in Jones' films.

The only "Tom and Jerry" episode to vaguely resemble the Hanna-Barbera entries is *Much Ado About Mousing*. It draws heavily from *The Bodyguard*, in which Jerry rescues a dog from a dogcatcher and is rewarded with the dog's protective services from Tom; all Jerry has to do is whistle. The only difference between the films lies in setting. *The Bodyguard* takes place on city streets, while *Much Ado About Mousing* is on a waterfront.

As for Hanna-Barbera, the studio jumped on the spy bandwagon with *The Atom Ant–Secret Squirrel Show*. Secret Squirrel is visually no different than other secret agents in movies and television. He wears a trenchcoat and has access to sophisticated gadgetry. However, he has more in common with earlier studio creations than with fictional spies. The pairing of Secret Squirrel with the small, accented sidekick Morocco Mole recalls Hanna-Barbera's *Quick Draw McGraw*, which stars a tall, white cowboy horse and a squat, Spanish-accented mule.

Hanna-Barbera was not the only television studio reinventing old formulas and characters. Cambria's syndicated television program *The New Three Stooges* unsuccessfully tried to capitalize on the popularity of the rerun live-action "Three Stooges" short films with television viewers. This animated adaptation of the defunct live-action theatrical series follows its predecessor's format of having three men act as violent stumblebums. They fail to perform tasks and accomplish goals. As a result, they are hardly a collective image of strength and confidence as the U.S. military enters the Vietnam War. The awkward and clumsy stooges mark a significant contrast to the increasingly popular superhero characterizations.

Another studio more successfully transformed a much younger group of famous men to the form of animation. King Features Syndicate Television made a bold decision in having icons of the counterculture as protagonists for children's fare. Ten months after securing the rights to animating the rock group the Beatles, King launched the series *The Beatles* on ABC-TV in September 1965. The appearance of the Beatles broke from conventional imagery of masculinity in the United States. They dressed in heeled boots and unisex suits and wore their hair in a long, "mop-top" style. Moreover, long hair had subversive or radical political connotations in the United States in the '60s. For example, newspaper cartoonists of the day identified protestors of the Vietnam War almost exclusively as people growing their hair past their shoulders. King found plenty of support for the series. A. C. Gilbert, Quaker Oats, and Mars Candies sponsored the series.[6]

However, the counterculture look of the group helped to contribute to their compatibility as cartoon characters. Ever since animation began, artists have aimed for visual humor by distorting body parts of figures or dressing characters in amusing clothes. The Beatles had already cultivated their "funny" look, long before King sought to animate them. The artists merely stylized them for television. The only gross physical exaggerations of the caricatures of the group are the long, triangular chin of George Harrison and the protruding nose of Ringo Starr.

Even the voices for the Beatle caricatures were "cartoony." The actors did not try to sound exactly like the characters they played. Paul Frees, for example, drew from Hollywood film stars. He used a Rex Harrison-type voice for his performance as John Lennon and sounded like Peter Lorre when voicing George Harrison's caricature. A director for the series noted that the accents of people from Liverpool would have been difficult for children in the United States to understand. Thus, Frees and Lance Percival — the voices for Paul McCartney and Ringo Starr — developed their own comical British accents for the musicians.[7]

The Beatles serves as a part of Beatlemania, which the counterculture image of the band helped to fuel. While their music attracted listeners, their unique hair and wardrobe made them a spectacle to behold. Even members speculated that people attended the group's concerts in order to see them instead of hear them. However, their look was also extremely marketable. Beginning in 1964, their "mop-topped" heads appeared on diverse items such as toys, clothes, and wrappings of loaves of bread. The King cartoon series not only rode the crest of Beatlemania but also grew popular enough to warrant its own merchandise. The first episode had a fifty-two share of the viewing audience. Within months of the show's premiere, the cartoon caricatures also popped up on assorted products.[8]

The caricatures of Africans on *The Beatles* proved that the socially conscious musicians in the band had nothing to do with the production of the cartoon. When touring the United States in 1964, the Beatles were the first group to announce that they would not perform in racially segregated venues. Such a declaration was politically risky, for at the time the federal government labeled many people who publicly spoke in favor of racial equality as communists or communist sympathizers. For example, the Federal Bureau of Investigation started files on Rev. Dr. Martin Luther King, Jr. and the Student Nonviolent Coordinating Committee — the group consisting of students who started nonviolent sit-ins at lunch counters in 1960. In contrast, *The Beatles* regularly assigned African figures the old stereotypical roles of indigenous cannibals or warriors.[9]

Ironically, the Beatles themselves acknowledged their musical debt to African Americans as they ascended to white superstardom in the mid–1960s. They claimed to have been inspired by Motown artists. Indeed, some of their earliest recordings included "Please Mr. Postman" from the Motown group the Marvelettes and "Twist and Shout" from the Isley Brothers. *The Beatles*, as a result, championed African American music. Each episode of the series features at least one of the band's songs, and the "Sing-along" part of the show displays lyrics for viewers to sing as the song plays. "Please Mr. Postman" and "Twist and Shout" were among the group recordings given a cartoon treatment.[10]

The "Motown Sound" was a perfect complement to the image of the Beatles in 1965. Motown's songs had appeal that transcended race. The music had no blatant political stands or complaints about racial tensions, unlike the wails about oppression in blues songs. Motown lyrics also lacked overt sexual content, in contrast to the blues and early rock-and-roll compositions. When the Beatles performed the label's hits, the group added to its "innocent" reputation.[11]

The "Sing-along" segment of *The Beatles* borrows from older cartoons. It is like *The Alvin Show* in that it presents rock music in a vaudeville context. The setting of each "Sing-along" is a stage. The musicians deliver rapid one-liners to one another. Ringo wears assorted costumes to illustrate the punchlines to his jokes. The series also uses slapstick humor to complement the verbal humor of Ringo's frequent puns. The purpose of the segment — audience participation — recalls Paramount's "Screen Song" cartoons of the 1920s and '30s, in which characters invited viewers to sing songs as lyrics appeared on the screen. *The Beatles*, however, did not use a bouncing ball to tell audiences when to sing certain words.

Ironically, as a U.S. television cartoon caricatured Great Britian, a British studio symbolically illustrated U.S. race relations in a manner familiar to stateside audiences. The television cartoon series *Dodo the Kid from Outer Space* borrows the "alien-integration" theme of the "Terrytoons" films starring Astronut. The series consists of a group of aliens coming to Earth and helping a scientist solve scientific problems. The extraterrestrials are akin to the "Freedom Summer" volunteers of the previous year, who had converged from across the country into Mississippi to help end segregation there. The program aired in the United States through television syndication but did not last long. Indeed, very few British imports had performed well on U.S. television. Ironically, during the 1965-66 season, the import *The Avengers* broke the curse, airing in the United States on CBS-TV until 1969.

Like *The Beatles*, the program *A Charlie Brown Christmas* was revolutionary but in production methods instead of its stars. The all-juvenile cast of the seasonal special broadcast came from "Peanuts"—one of the most successful syndicated comic strips of the twentieth century. While having only child figures in a cartoon was rare in 1965, several films—especially the episodes for Paramount's "Casper the Friendly Ghost"—had already starred only young caricatures. However, the producers made the unique decision of hiring children to voice the characters. Heretofore, professional female vocal artists had usually portrayed pre-pubescent figures in cartoons. In contrast, the voices of the child-actors lent authenticity to the characters.

When *A Charlie Brown Christmas* aired on CBS-TV in December, viewers also heard music that usually did not serve as background for television cartoons. The producers hired jazz musician Vince Guaraldi to score the film. His composition is smoother and much more relaxed than the scores of his contemporaries. The humor of the program comes mainly from dialogue instead of physical slapstick. As a result, Guaraldi did not have to write music for fast chase scenes, explosions, or blows to a character's body.

With *A Charlie Brown Christmas*, the U.S. animation industry ended the year with the same creativity they had used for the past eleven months. The studios had effectively capitalized on the resurging popularity of animation by redefining established characters and creating new, appealing ones. Film exhibitors and television network executives were pleased with the sizable audiences the cartoons attracted. The future challenge for the studios would be keeping the audiences that large for cartoons.

4

THE CARTOONS
OF 1966

The U.S. animation studios seemed to have the theme of "more of the same" for their 1966 productions. Only one theatrical studio in Hollywood offered a new star, while New York facilities introduced several new but abortive characters. Meanwhile, television studios learned from the popularity of King Features Syndicate's *Beatles* series that the right product to license for animation could result in a fortune. The only trick was to figure out which characters would adapt to the cartoon well and attract audiences.

Although adults raved over recent creations like DePatie-Freleng's "Pink Panther," film distributors had not yet learned to treat cartoons as something other than interchangeable "kiddie fare." They hardly paid attention to important differences among the series they promoted to exhibitors. For example, when Columbia Pictures reissued cartoons in 1966, the distributor grouped together its own defunct animation division's slapstick films, UPA's sophisticated work of the 1950s, and Hanna-Barbera's assembly-line product as "Favorites." Thus, a cartoon was a cartoon, no matter the content.

However, the content of the cartoons thematically began to change although studios developed similar characterizations to those of the previous year. To be sure, the majority of the cartoons of 1966 consisted of figures using their fists and explosives to accomplish their tasks. The imagery was on par with U.S. public opinion on the Vietnam War, for a majority of U.S. citizens approved of President Johnson's management of the conflict. Also, music and films glorifying militarism characterized domestic popular culture at the time. Sgt. Barry Sadler's song "The Ballad of the Green Berets" topped the popular music charts. On the other hand, some animators increasingly made films illustrating skepticism towards war. They satirized militarism but still in a lighthearted manner instead of a bitter one.

One significant change that year was the disappearance of the "alien-as-integrationist" genre. Its absence symbolized a growing backlash from Americans against the civil rights movement. After years of protests in the South, the Student Nonviolent Coordinating Committee (SNCC) and Dr. Martin Luther King's Southern Christian Leadership Conference (SCLC) angered northerners by staging demonstrations in Chicago neighborhoods against housing discrimination. SNCC also stirred up hard feelings by publicly denouncing the Vietnam War and by calling for black activists to organize only among themselves to strengthen their communities — the "Black Power" slogan. Correspondingly, cartoonists no longer promoted the idea of racial unity via symbolic imagery of immigrants from other galaxies. The British studio Halas and Batchelor did not make new episodes of *Dodo the Kid from Outer Space*, and Terrytoons did not produce any "Astronut" cartoons after 1966.

Spies and superheroes dominated animation in 1966 — a reflection of the escalation of U.S. troops in South Vietnam. Superheroes especially flooded Saturday morning network television, which meant more scenes of fisticuffs, bombs, and guns. The live-action series *Batman* (1966–68), a campy television adaptation of the comic book from DC Comics, had drawn a massive audience on ABC-TV since its debut in January of that year. To capitalize on *Batman*'s popularity, television networks demanded more superhero stories. However, a precedent for war drawing audiences to costumed crime-fighters had been set two decades earlier. In 1941, when the United States entered World War II, Max Fleischer's "Superman" cartoons for Paramount Pictures became a hit theatrical series. Imitators like Terrytoons' Mighty Mouse and such parodies as Warner Brothers' *Super Rabbit* (1943) and Paramount's own *She-Sick Sailors* (1944) immediately followed.

The Vietnam War-era heroes were different from the "Superman" cartoons of World War II. After the Pearl Harbor attack, Paramount transformed Superman from a science-fiction character into an unofficial U.S. serviceman. He began fighting Nazi and Japanese characters. These episodes were too timely to warrant successful re-releases after the war's conclusion, and they trivialized the war by having Superman dispose of the Axis figures so easily. In contrast, television cartoon studios did not concern themselves with caricaturing the North Vietnamese or the Viet-cong. The heroes did not serve as super-powered U.S. soldiers fighting in the conflict. Instead, the new cartoons were typical science fiction stories featuring characters obsessed with global domination.

The dominance of superheroes exacerbated the differentiation of television cartoons from theatrical ones. Television networks contracted with several television cartoonists to animate superheroes. Television cartoon producers were more receptive to the likes of Superman than theatrical producers were. The latter ones had survived for decades primarily by developing animal figures for short comedies. Consistently losing money since the late 1940s, they could not afford to risk deviating from their practices to capitalize on a brief trend.

Metro-Goldwyn-Mayer won only one Academy Award during the Vietnam War for Best Cartoon Short Subject. In contrast, the distributor had received three awards for cartoons released in three of the four years of U.S. involvement in World War II. Moreover, all of MGM's winning cartoons of that period were Hanna-Barbera's slapstick "Tom and Jerry" entries. But in the spring of 1966, the Academy did not give MGM an award for a "Tom and Jerry" cartoon but rather for a "Cartoon Special" titled *The Dot and the Line*. Far removed from the cat-and-mouse violence, this film marks Jones' peak in graphics-based humor. The figures are all geometric: a dot, a straight line, and a squiggly line. Jones rose to the challenge of creating sympathetic figures out of symbols and even handicapped himself by not using his familiar crutch of facial expressions. The dot and lines, in fact, had no faces at all.

Jones' Oscar victory with *The Dot and the Line* also showed how much the award mattered to exhibitors still interested in playing short cartoons in their theaters. One theater in New Orleans booked the cartoon with another film about a man-woman relationship: *A Patch of Blue*. Both films also had in common that the Academy had nominated them for awards. The theater advertised this shared trait in newspapers. After both films won in their respective categories, the theater proudly announced the achievement when continuing to show the films.

The Dot and the Line captures the conflict of culture vs. counterculture, despite Jones' mere uses of lines and a dot. In the film the straight line tries to woo the dot away from the squiggle although the dot finds the straight line dull. The straight line eventually impresses the dot by bending and twisting into impressive patterns, and the dot dismisses the squiggle as an unkempt, disheveled mess. The straight line represents mainstream, Europe-oriented U.S. culture by forming his patterns to the background of classical music. In contrast, the squiggle symbolizes the counterculture figure by squirming to and fro in syncopation with rock music. The victor of the straight line over the squiggle shows the director's embrace of the old versus the new.

This culturally polarizing cartoon won the Academy Award as the country itself polarized over the Vietnam War. *The Dot and the Line* is one of the first films to cast a counterculture figure into the role of antagonist. As such, it is a radical departure from the tendency in U.S. animation to develop such a character as "comic relief." The hippie-as-foe quickly became a staple of Hollywood filmmaking via such villains as the Groovy Guru in the television satire of espionage *Get Smart* and assorted junkies in several episodes of the cop-drama *Dragnet*.

The disdain for the counterculture in *The Dot and the Line* is an even further departure from the films of Jones' former studio — Warner Brother Cartoons — in which protagonists wore "zoot suits" and spoke in slang from World War II to the late 1950s. Then again, Jones rarely integrated that content into his cartoons. He allowed Bugs Bunny to engage in such behavior once in the 1940s (*Hare Conditioned* [1945]) and another time one decade later (*Knight-mare Hare* [1955]).

Meanwhile, the "Tom and Jerry" cartoons indirectly capitalized on the popularity of *Batman*. Although produced years earlier, the new releases for 1966 accentuate action with titles, just as the television series does. As *Batman* flashed such onomatopoeia as "Pow" and "Biff" in fight scenes, the "Tom and Jerry" episode *Ah, Sweet Mouse-story of Life* displayed the word "Honk" when Jerry Mouse stepped on a horn. Several cartoons produced in 1966 appropriated *Batman*'s gimmick, thus illustrating how ahead of his time Jones was.

Chuck Jones kept promoting *philia* in his cartoons for Metro-Goldwyn-Mayer. *Ah, Sweet Mouse-Story of Life* and *I'm Just Wild About Jerry*. In both films the cat-and-mouse chase climaxes to Tom somehow needing Jerry's assistance. In the first cartoon, Jerry blasts a horn in order to pry Tom's body from a rain gutter, and in the other the mouse pulls a switch in order to keep a train from running over his predator. Jones accentuates Jerry's goodness in the latter film by literally giving him a halo and wings. In such moments the director's episodes take themselves too seriously. Jones almost seemed to treat chase scenes with disdain, rushing through them with few strong gags in order to bring about an end to them.

The *philia* imagery is strongest and works best in his first original television production for MGM — the holiday special *Dr. Seuss' How the Grinch Stole Christmas*. Originally airing in December 1966, the show became a seasonal favorite, annually rebroadcast during and well after the Vietnam War. In the program, a creature who has stolen all of a community's Christmas gifts is moved to compassion by a young girl named Cindy Lou Who. Seuss' story is tailor-made for Jones. In earlier cartoons for Warner Brothers like *Bewitched Bunny* (1955), the image of a sad-looking character stops a villain from committing an undesirable act. In this case, Bugs Bunny slowly fills his eyes with tears to keep a witch from killing him.

After some promising but cheap "Road Runner" cartoons from DePatie-Freleng in the previous year, director Rudy Larriva took violence to extremes in manners that deviated sharply from those by original director Chuck Jones. For example, in *The Solid Tin Coyote*, the coyote builds a giant robotic likeness of himself to catch the bird so that the coyote can eat it. However, after a series of mishaps, the coyote becomes bent on destroying the Road Runner. Near the conclusion, he loses focus of his original goal by commanding the robot to eat the bird.

Films by Robert McKimson, the sole director of DePatie-Freleng's cartoons for Warner Brothers by the end of 1966, suggest his desensitization from violence. Other directors at the studio had quit, worked on other studio projects, or retired, leaving McKimson's weak direction as the signature style of the "Merrie Melodies" and "Looney Tunes" cartoons. He minimized the impact of the explosions of weapons. Several of his films for the year contain scenes involving grenades, bombs, and cannons; but the characters under attack often escape with little more than scratches. To be sure, the content of these films is consistent in terms of McKimson's style, for since his debut in the 1940s, he had directed action scenes with good comic timing but little punch. However, he had used explosion gags sparingly before the 1960s; thus, his conservative direction fit his earlier work. Still, in a sense, the new cartoons are a perfect complement to the new superhero trend, for McKimson's version of Daffy Duck comes through dynamite blasts and head blows relatively unscathed, not unlike Superman.

One exceptional cartoon from McKimson made a strong statement against the engagement in warfare. Rarely did any studio explore the social consequences of violence; usually, explosions hurt either the predator or the prey. However, in the "Merrie Melodies" episode *A Taste of Catnip*, an aggressive and destructive act by one character results in the denial of nourishment for several other figures. In addition, the destruction causes the others to attack him. At the start of the cartoon, Daffy Duck realizes that he is behaving like a cat because he is inhaling fumes from a nearby catnip factory. After Daffy drops a bomb over the factory, he momentarily savors his victory. Then, the local cats, now without catnip, proceed to pulverize him. McKimson's tacit warning that violence begets violence — especially from the initial victims of it — is timely in the context of the growing South Vietnamese Communist insurgency as the United States continued to escalate the Vietnam War.

Although most of DePatie-Freleng's cartoons for Warner Brothers feature militaristic comedy, they also criticize colonialism. The majority of the releases for the year star Daffy Duck and Speedy Gonzales together. In the films Daffy is in Mexico, keeping Speedy from enjoying life in his own homeland. For example, the *gringo* duck orders the Mexican mouse to move his go-go nightclub out of a building despite the mouse's possession of a lease in *Swing Ding Amigo*. In this episode and others, however, Speedy foils Daffy's efforts to get rid of him, and Daffy finally resigns himself to sharing space or resources with Speedy.

In addition to depicting oppressed racially subordinate characters in a sympathetic manner, DePatie-Freleng continued Warner Brothers' tradition of glorifying civil disobedience. In some of the Daffy-Speedy cartoons, the mouse steals things that either he or his fellow Mexican mice need for survival and does not suffer any punishments for his crime. Although Daffy rents a condemned house and orders Speedy to leave in *The Astroduck*, the mouse refuses to leave because he claims the right to live there as a matter of principle. Throughout the cartoon the duck tries unsuccessfully to drive him out. The sympathetic image of the trespassing mouse implies the studio's endorsement of people breaking laws on the grounds that the laws are immoral. As Warner Brothers released the cartoon to theaters, antiwar activists borrowed the civil disobedience tactics of the civil rights movement but opposed U.S. involvement in the Vietnam War. They claimed that the conflict was one in which the United States did not belong and conducted sit-ins, burnings of draft cards, and other illegal activities to show their commitment to their views.

Some of the "Merrie Melodies-Looney Tunes" episodes by DePatie-Freleng illustrate militant ethnic minorities, which dovetailed with the call for "Black Power." To be sure, the studio did not produce any films starring African American characters. However, Speedy Gonzales becomes a more physically confrontational figure against antagonist Daffy Duck. In *A Squeak in the Deep*, the Mexican mouse hits the duck repeatedly on the posterior in order to subdue him and to coerce him to enter into a business partnership. Speedy had never before resorted to violence but had frustrated adversaries by running too quickly for them to catch him. He counted on his pursuers to simply give up because of fatigue. Now, as Stokely Carmichael of SNCC increasingly called for blacks to replace non-violent civil disobedience with self-defense, Speedy stopped dashing away from his opponents and began retaliating.

However, Speedy is not a wholly sympathetic character. He still appears as a peon caricature, and Mel Blanc continued to give him an exaggerated Mexican dialect. Moreover, the racial humor used by Freleng in *The Pied Piper of Guadalupe* (1961) appeared frequently in McKimson's cartoons of 1966. In *The Astroduck*, as Speedy pleads with Daffy for shelter by saying "You don't understa-a-and," Daffy mimics, "No, *you* don't understa-a-and." *Feather Finger* concludes with Speedy asking the duck, "You need some help, Senor Duck," to which Daffy replies, "No, I don't any help, Senor Mouse" in Speedy's nasal delivery.

Even the poverty of the Mexican figures served as fodder for comedy in the "Speedy" series that year. Just as the racial humor demonstrated insensitivity towards the country's racial problems, the jokes about the impoverished mice were out of step with the nation's concern for President Johnson's "War on Poverty." In *Mexican Mousepiece* Daffy tries to entrap mice into a "care package" by telling them that despite their poverty, they could aid others who have even less. After realizing that Daffy has imprisoned them, one of the mice suggests that they play dead, to which another mouse replies, "Are you kidding? Some of U.S. don't have to pretend."

In addition, *Mexican Mousepiece* satirizes social activism itself by reducing it to a plot device like Mexican poverty. The film starts with Daffy having sympathy for foreign starving cats. He is moved to feed them. However, in order to do so, he imprisons another impoverished group — the poor Mexican mice. The film is timely, for Daffy's pitting oppressed groups against one another is not unlike the power of the United States in recruiting the South Vietnamese, Thais, Cambodians, and Laotians to fight their fellow citizens in the military conflict against Communism.

For the final "Road Runner" cartoon, *Sugar and Spies*, McKimson integrated the images of ineffective militarism with the spy craze. As usual the coyote fails to catch the bird. But instead of trying to subdue the bird with "Acme" products, the coyote uses devices from a spy's satchel. The coyote dresses in a stereotypical black overcoat while operating the gadgets of espionage. The technology he uses is hardly different than the props of earlier episodes. Rather, the spy gimmickry distracts from the chases and makes the coyote a far cry from Chuck Jones' depiction of it as a genius. After all, wearing an overcoat in a hot desert does not display genius.

Despite the anti-militaristic message of *Sugar and Spies*, Warner

Brothers Pictures used the cartoon's weaponry to promote its animated releases. Although the distributor did not issue any "Road Runner" cartoons after 1966, it advertised its releases for the following season in the trade periodical *Film Bulletin* with a picture of the coyote dressed as a spy. *Sugar and Spies* was the only recent Warner Brothers cartoon to capitalize on a popular trend. In the illustration the coyote chases the bird in a car equipped with machine guns. Without a description of the film in the magazine, however, the anti-militarism of *Sugar and Spies* is lost.[1]

Like Speedy Gonzales, the "Pink Panther" series has a new political context in 1966, reflecting the radicalism of the student-activists of the civil rights movement. The panther goes to violent extremes to have his color respected in *Pink Punch*. In the film he displays a sign with pink letters and a pink asterisk, but the asterisk insists on becoming green. The panther and the symbol battle over their color-based disagreement. By the time the cartoon ends, the cat is in crutches.

However, *Pink Punch* does not reward the aggression of the Pink Panther. At the end of the film, the protagonist loses his color war for the first time. He limps off the screen, thinking that he has kept his asterisk pink. But seconds before the film fades to black, the asterisk turns green. This new type of "Pink Panther" ending corresponds to the nation's backlash against the civil rights movement during the year. A growing number of U.S. citizens opposed not only "Black Power" but also SCLC's northern marches against housing discrimination. Just as the movement lost mainstream support, the panther's color adventures started to wear thin.

The directors of DePatie-Freleng's new "Inspector" series for United Artists drew more humor from the effects of grenades and bombs than McKimson did for Warner Brothers. The title-character is a French police officer based on the "Inspector Clouseau" character of the live-action movies *The Pink Panther* and *A Shot in the Dark*. The officer role allowed DePatie-Freleng to employ the usual slapstick violence for the Inspector as he struggled to catch criminals. Gerry Chiniquy, a longtime animator for Freleng, had directed only two cartoons at Warner Brothers as the studio closed, and his style was as low-key as that of McKimson. However, the Inspector was a new character, and Chiniquy sharpened his comic timing as if inspired by the novelty of the figure. Unlike his reserved treatment of earlier characters in his earlier films, he allowed the Inspector to become charred from explosions and scratched to pieces by wild animals. Chiniquy's colleague George Singer similarly gave punch to militaristic gags, as did McKimson himself in his four "Inspector" episodes.

Although the studio's cartoons for Warner Brothers depict violence in a negative context, the films for United Artists do not criticize militarism. *Unsafe and Seine*, one of the most violent cartoons of the year, offers the moral, "Might makes right." A militaristic antagonist defeats the hero — a rare ending for a theatrical cartoon. In the film an insurance agent drops bombs wherever the Inspector agrees to meet him. However, when the Inspector finally catches up to him and lunges towards him to fight, the agent beats the officer into submission.

DePatie-Freleng's cartoons for United Artists also continued its promoting of European culture from last year. White figures dominated the studio's cartoons of 1966. The theatrical series "The Inspector" is set in France. Adversaries of the title-character speak in British accents in *Ape Suzette* and *Unsafe and Seine*. The latter cartoon even features a scene in Picadilly Circus.

DePatie-Freleng did not creatively use rock music in its stories for cartoons. The studio's films for Warner Brothers suffer especially, because neither the animators nor the distributor made significant strides towards modernizing the popular characters. Only *Sugar and Spies*, by poking fun at the current popularity of secret agent characters, makes good use of the genre in the "Merrie Melodies-Looney Tunes" series. The rock music by Greene is most jarring in the films pitting Daffy Duck against Speedy Gonzales. Both characters, having long passed their primes, are products of earlier periods — World War II for Daffy and the late 1950s for Speedy. Unlike the brassy swing music that complemented Daffy's loud hoots and frenetic hops across the screen in the 1940s, the electric guitar clashes with the duck's old-hat slapstick.

The juxtaposition of imagery to music does not diminish the creativity of studio composer Walter Greene's scores. He excelled in giving traditional tunes of the public domain a contemporary sound. Moreover, he was versatile in his choices of songs to modernize. The guitar gives punch to his variation of the French National Anthem in *Unsafe and Seine* and to the classical work in *Sugar and Spies*.

After years of resisting the popularity of rock music, theatrical studios caved in and began consistently incorporating the style into the scores for cartoon shorts. For example, music directors Walter Greene at DePatie-Freleng and Jim Timmens of Terrytoons wrote compositions that spotlighted the electric guitar. As studios continued to lose money, they had tighter budgets for musicians, thus creating the need for small bands. Greene and Timmens constructed imaginative scores with the few musicians they utilized. They rarely composed works that required more than trumpets, a flute, a guitar, a saxophone, and drums.

Terrytoons used rock music most effectively in its "James Hound" series, which stars a canine contemporary to Hanna-Barbera's *Secret Squirrel*. The scores by Timmens and the direction by Ralph Bakshi complement each other in the espionage-themed episodes. The music alternates between fast-tempo rock for chase scenes and slow-paced, jazzy music for scenes of James Hound strolling or relaxing. Meanwhile, for the opening sequence, Bakshi visually accented the score by having the background change colors to the beat and making the camera zoom in and out as a trumpet's notes jumped from high to low.

Taking a cue from DePatie-Freleng, Terrytoons started producing more topical cartoons, too. Most of the relevant films came from the studio's youngest director, Ralph Bakshi. For example, his film *The Monster Masher* pokes fun at the long hair of counterculture men by having werewolves form a rock music group. The contemporary content in "James Hound" occasionally extends beyond militaristic espionage into references to modern social issues. The episode *The Phantom Skyscraper* indirectly addresses President Johnson's War on Poverty. Professor Mad, Hound's enemy, convinces random people to board a space-bound rocket by disguising it as an apartment complex and by renting apartments for free; he advertises it to the people as his solution to "the housing shortage."

The "James Hound" series exhibited some timely hawkish, colonialist imagery through its premise. Just as the United States invaded a foreign land to stop the spread of communism, James Hound went to different countries in order to stop evildoers from ruling the world. The story formula was on par with the growing U.S. military role abroad in South Vietnam. The diversity of settings also set "James Hound" cartoons apart from other theatrical offerings from Terrytoons. Each "Possible Possum" film was set in the swamp, and Astronut always traveled to Oscar Mild's suburban home.

On the other hand, in some ways James Hound was a typical Terrytoons character. As a fairly nonviolent spy, he corresponds to the studio's reluctance to use excessive violence in its cartoons. The dog only has a gun for a weapon and rarely uses it. In addition, the studio hid most of the scenes of fights and explosions by cutting to screens displaying suggestive onomatopoeia like "pow," "crash," and "boom." The live-action series *Batman* popularized this technique, but the program used the words to accentuate the impact of blows instead of censoring them.

In addition, the "James Hound" series borrows significantly from Mighty Mouse's World War II-era cartoons despite its production during the Vietnam War. Similar to James Hound caricaturing James Bond,

Mighty Mouse — originally called Super Mouse — parodied Superman. Even the timing of their debuts is similar in relation to military conflict. Mighty Mouse first appeared ten months after the Pearl Harbor bombing, which ushered in major U.S. involvement in World War II. Then in January 1966, ten months after the first U.S. Marines arrived in South Vietnam, Terrytoons introduced James Hound to audiences.

Later that year Bakshi branched beyond theatrical cartoons to superhero series for television. His series *The Mighty Heroes* (1966–67) replaced *The Mighty Mouse Playhouse*, which had aired on CBS-TV since 1955. The program stars costumed human figures with super powers. The series has little comical content; the most humorous aspects of the episodes are the unique names and powers of the heroes such as Ropeman, Cuckooman, and Diaperman. The adventures are fairly standard and conservative in politics. Similarly to other superhero programs from other studios, a montage of split-second patriotic images — the Statue of Liberty, the American Flag, and the colors red, white and blue — appears when the narrator introduces the characters in each episode.

Paramount Cartoon Studio stressed newness and color for its shorts. The distributor finally dropped "Popeye" after thirty-two years of distribution — the last eight in reruns. Ironically, Paramount promoted in 1966 exactly the same things as during World War II. When introducing the "Noveltoons" series, advertisements boasted the "novelty" and "color" the cartoons offered.

Paramount developed its first antiwar character after a long history of cartoons centered on military service. Two of the studio's most successful stars were Popeye and Superman, both of whom frequently fought foreign enemies in the films of World War II. Now, in 1966, Paramount combined militaristic imagery with the urbane humor of UPA for its last recurring star. A nearsighted Medieval knight named Sir Blur is a combination of novelist Miguel de Cervantes' fictional character Don Quixote and UPA's Mister Magoo. Blur, like Don Quixote, has an inflated sense of heroism about himself. And similarly to Magoo, the knight is oblivious to the destruction he causes. This variation of the concept of the incompetent warrior is sympathetic because of his friendly manner, old age, bravery and poor vision. However, his overzealous nature and destructive clumsiness speak to the growing concerns of U.S. citizens about the duration of the Vietnam War. Still, Blur is an atypical heroic figure among the animated superheroes of 1966, most of whom were young, strong, and not clumsy.

Disney became soft and slow-paced with *Winnie the Pooh and the*

Honey Tree. With this cartoon the producer sadly sunk to the level of his competitors in the final year of his life. First, he looked outside of his roster of stars to license another person's characters for animation. *Winnie the Pooh and the Honey Tree*— Disney's only cartoon of 1966 — stars the stuffed-animal characters of children's literature author A. A. Milne. Second, like made-for-television cartoons, the film is heavily reliant on dialogue, which the cast of stellar actors like Sterling Holloway, Sebastian Cabot, and Paul Winchell perform. Most of the rare slapstick moments come from an overeager and carefree stuffed tiger named Tigger — the only Disney-created character in the cartoon. Otherwise, the vocal talents carry the film. Ironically, the studio did not even need the vocal crutch, for it had money to animate characters fully; excessive talk in cartoons usually overcompensated for the limited movement of television cartoon figures.

Vocal performances were crucial to the production of a very cheaply made television cartoon. The Grantray-Lawrence Studio offered *Marvel Superheroes*— its adaptations of superheroes from DC competitor Marvel Comics. The studio produced ten-minute episodes of "Captain America," "The Incredible Hulk," and "The Sub-Mariner" for television syndication; meanwhile, Paramount Cartoon Studio produced entries of the component "The Mighty Thor." The films largely consist of reproduced comic-book panels and the most minimal of animation. *Batman*-inspired exclamation titles appearing on screen to accompany sounds of fisticuffs and firing tanks are more animated than the characters. As a result, narration and character voices carry each episode.

Of all the stars of *Marvel Superheroes*, the Incredible Hulk is most relevant to the Vietnam War. Marvel Comics had resumed producing "Captain America" and "The Sub-Mariner" after both series had folded earlier. However, the Hulk was an original Marvel character and was created in the 1960s. His powers come from a source having to do with the Cold War — an accidental nuclear explosion. In addition, in the '60s Marvel carved out its niche in the industry by creating heroes atypical in looks and behavior. Such characters became a sort of counterculture-type to the traditional likes of Captain America and Superman. The Hulk slouches, wears torn clothes, is green and ugly, and talks in "broken English"— a far cry from the standard poised, uniformed, white, eloquent superhero figure.[2]

The Filmation studio had much more success with only slightly better animation than Grantray-Lawrence for its version of DC Comics' character Superman. The studio smartly capitalized on the character's durable popularity, and *The New Adventures of Superman* became a ratings hit on CBS-TV as a result. The show contains several gimmicks to catch the attention of young viewers. Unlike Max Fleischer's earlier adaptation, Filmation's show features villains from the comic book issues. The program also repeats famous catchphrases from earlier filmed series of the hero such as Fleischer's "Faster than a speeding bullet." In addition, Superman was already a familiar superhero to viewers, having appeared in comics for nearly three decades by then. And DC Comics often paired Superman with Batman, whose popularity as a live-action television figure sparked the superhero craze of the 1960s.

Still, *The New Adventures of Superman* was a very unlikely hit series. Superman had not emerged from the comic books in years. The most recent filmed version of the "Man of Steel"— the live-action *The Adventures of Superman*— ceased production in the late 1950s. Also, Fleischer had made expensive, high-quality cartoons that made Filmation's limited and constantly reused animation look cheap and primitive by comparison.

On the other hand, the studio's character designs for the program corresponded to current social divisions. Long hair on men no longer was associated merely with the Beatles by 1966 but also with the "subversive" activity of outspoken opposition to the Vietnam War. Similarly, in *The New Adventures of Superman*, hair length serves as a barometer for morality and intelligence. Male characters with short hair — Clark Kent, reporter Jimmy Olsen, and newspaper editor Perry White — are "good guys." However, male figures with extreme hair length, whether bald or long, are Superman's nemeses. In addition, the extreme lengths correspond to different characterization stereotypes. Lex Luthor, Superman's bald adversary, is a brilliant scientist bent on megalomania. On the other hand, the Prankster — a criminal with shoulder-length hair — is a mildly dangerous practical joker who speaks in a New York accent.

Filmation was not the only studio illustrating politics via superheroes. In its third season, *Underdog* turned into a pioneering television cartoon show because of the new political images it featured. Leonardo-Total Television dropped the previous supporting components of the series and created new ones for the 1966–67 year. *Underdog* then began satirizing violent heroism by transforming standard heroic characterizations into foolish ones. Also, in contrast to the comic imperialism in "The World of Commander McBragg," new components of the series illustrate the practice of invading and overpowering another land as a negative one. *Underdog* still followed its contemporaries in relying on standard slapstick comedy, which helped to keep juvenile viewers tuned in on Saturday mornings. However, the series now stood alone among both television and theatrical cartoons in having a decidedly left-wing bias in its humor.

For "Klondike Kat," Leonardo-Total Television makes a foreign character the "bad guy." In each episode the title-character, a Canadian Mounted Police officer, stops the pillaging of a small French mouse named Savoir Faire. Klondike Kat is a clumsy animal who always catches his fugitive purely on accident. Thus, the studio makes a stooge out of an authority figure. On the other hand, his apprehension of the mouse suggests the moral that crime does not pay. The foreign character was punished for coming into another country and breaking its laws for selfish reasons.

In contrast, for another component of *Underdog*, the studio designated the United States as an imperialist enemy. The "Go Go Gophers" episodes consist of the abortive efforts of two U.S. Cavalry soldiers in exterminating two lone Indians — the title-characters. Leonardo-Total Television developed unsympathetic figures in the military officers. The Cavalry outnumber the two Indian characters, thus placing the gophers at a military disadvantage. Also, the failure of the soldiers to wipe out the indigenous pair implies that their mission was improper. Moreover, despite the progressive image of Indians defeating the U.S. Army on a weekly basis, the studio displayed bad taste in trivializing the practice of ethnic cleansing.

"Go Go Gophers" cartoons are some of the most blatantly anti-war of the Vietnam War era. The soldiers are incompetent, despite their strict adherence to a code of conduct. To help establish a context of time, the studio designed U.S. Cavalry Colonel Kit Coyote as an animalized Theodore Roosevelt, himself a Cavalry officer. However, the studio makes fun of Roosevelt's impetuous personality by having Kit act on impulse and suffer consequences as a result. Also, Kit and his subordinate officer utter tongue-in-cheek lines like "You're in the Army, Sergeant. You're not supposed to think" and "The Army requires blind obedience."

Meanwhile, Hanna-Barbera gave colonialism more of a serious depiction than that of "Go Go Gophers." The studio's *Space Ghost and Dino Boy* exploits the fads of superheroes and space-themed science fiction. Space Ghost and two teenage assistant astronauts fight crime as they travel by rocket through space. These white Earthlings exemplify the outer space colonialism of the studio's own *The Jetsons* by defending other planets from indigenous enemies. The only source of humor is a pet monkey who causes mischief for the heroes.

Space Ghost and Dino Boy was one of several new Hanna-Barbera series starring human crime-fighters for the 1966–67 season. To be sure, the year meant a shift for the studio away from funny animals. On the other hand, the superhero shows share the same politics as programs like

The Magilla Gorilla Show. Both kinds of series promote the maintenance of the social status quo. The contexts for social order differ. For example, Magilla himself leaves his proper "place" and later returns to it, but super-heroes restore order only after *others* have disrupted it.

Hanna-Barbera also introduced the youngest animated crime-fighters of the Vietnam War in September 1966. In the series *The Space Kidettes*, four elementary school-age children in outer space foil the evil plans of nemeses Captain Skyhook and his sidekick Static. The program lampoons its own premise by having Static warn his boss not to hurt the Kidettes because of their small sizes and young ages. While amusing, the reluctance of the studio to develop violent scenes leaves each episode with very little action. More disturbing, however, are the scenes in which the children inflict violence upon their adversaries. However, the offensive attacks by the children artistically yet exaggeratedly illustrate a facet of U.S. military involvement in the Vietnam War: the young age of the typical soldier overseas. Men between the ages of eighteen and twenty performed a significant share of the fighting; they were old enough for war but not for the right to vote.

For *The Space Kidettes*, Hanna-Barbera followed its winning formula of appropriating situation-comedy material with some animated embellishments. Just as *The Flintstones* is *The Honeymooners* as cartoon, Stone Age figures, *The Space Kidettes* greatly resembles the television adaptation of Hank Ketcham's comic strip *Dennis the Menace* (1959–63) — the outer space setting notwithstanding. In both series a man's life is made miserable by the presence of young children. Captain Skyhook tries more directly than Dennis' crotchety neighbor Mr. Wilson to rid himself of the tykes. However, both adult figures have a soft heart for their young acquaintances, as demonstrated in Static's precautions against harming the Kidettes. Also, the episodes of *The Space Kidettes* have little to do with outer space. The space setting is a futuristic variation of the suburban neighborhood of *Dennis the Menace*— complete with a rocket-as-clubhouse. The main difference between the two entities is that the Kidettes do not cause calamities for Skyhook, unlike Dennis' well-intentioned but disastrous attempts to help Mr. Wilson accomplish tasks.

The domestic situation comedy genre from which *The Space Kidettes* borrows had fallen out of favor with audiences by 1966. In recent years situation comedies had begun to focus on such characters as Frankenstein-monsters and vampires (*The Munsters* [1964–66]), witches and warlocks (*Bewitched* [1964–72]), and genies (*I Dream of Jeannie* [1965–70]). The writers developed humorous situations from their eccentricities such as magic powers gone awry. *The Space Kidettes*, while gimmicky in its outer space setting, offered few eccentricity-oriented jokes. The series did not last beyond its first season on television.

Another formula winding down was that of "anachronistic suburbia" in *The Flintstones*. In its final season (1965–66), the series lost focus. No longer mimicking *The Honeymooners*, the program began to resemble such escapist situation comedies as *My Favorite Martians* and *Bewitched*. The show dealt less with domestic squabbles and more with stories containing significant amounts of science fiction. Throughout the season a small, green, alien conscience named the Great Gazoo gives Fred Flintstone advice on how to act. Concerning stories, Fred turns into an ape in one episode; and in another, prehistoric caricatures of the cast of *Bewitched* perform magic spells on the people of Bedrock.

Hanna-Barbera sought to pump new life into the flagging cartoon sitcom by adapting it to several contemporary film genres. As *The Flintstones* ended its prime-time run in the fall, the studio's feature-length animated spy parody *The Man Called Flintstone* circulated in theaters. The cartoon is a comedy, only slightly punctuated by the fisticuffs and weaponry of the contemporary superhero television series. However, Hanna-Barbera did not completely trust in the strength of the characterizations of Fred Flintstone and others from the defunct program to carry the film. As a result, several jokes have to do with outrageous gadgetry. Also, the movie is a musical — a rarity among the "spy movies" of the '60s — and features many songs complementing the developments in the plot. Thus, *The Man Called Flintstone* oddly attempts to have figures resembling characters from *The Honeymooners* sing while dealing with international intrigue.

The Man Called Flintstone shares with *The Space Kidettes* the absence of experimental characterization. The film shows that Fred is not an appropriate choice for a spy, because he merely pretends to be one. Therefore, Hanna-Barbera is less risky with its star than other studios were with theirs. After all, in *Sugar and Spies*, Wile E. Coyote actually becomes a secret agent. Despite the movie's respectable box-office response, the studio produced no sequel and, in fact, did nothing with Fred Flintstone and company for the next five years. Moreover, it was the last commercial animated film distributed by Columbia Pictures after thirty-six years of bringing cartoons to theaters.

Another series from Hanna-Barbera had much better potential for huge ratings because it explored several popular film genres. In *Frankenstein, Jr. and the Impossibles* (1966–68), three secret agents with superhuman powers battle villains together when they are not disguised as a rock group. The Impossibles were a clever attempt by the studio to cash in on the success of *The Beatles, Batman*, and the "James Bond" movies. The songs resemble popular recordings of the day; for example, the episode "The Bubbler" features a song borrowing riffs from "Sugar Pie, Honey Bunch" by the Motown group the Four Tops. The characters had interesting powers: Coil Man's bouncing, Fluid Man's shifting of form, and Multi-Man's cloning of himself several times over.

The musical agents only appeared for two seasons, however. While the combination of genres was original, the episodes themselves are of standard fare. The individual members of the Impossibles do not have distinct characterizations. In addition, the Hanna-Barbera studio makes the powers of the superheroes too comedic for the figures to be on par with Superman. On the other hand, the episodes hardly have the witty, campy humor of *Batman*. Finally, the limited animation undercuts the drama and/or comedy of each scene.

Still, the Impossibles broke new ground as long-haired superheroes during the Vietnam War. The length of each member's hair is similar to that of John, Paul, George, and Ringo. The Impossibles also wear uniforms resembling those of the counterculture Beatles, including the high-heeled boots. However, King Features presented the Beatles merely as slapstick globetrotting musicians. In contrast, Hanna-Barbera took a risk in associating "mop-topped" rockers with the defense of truth and justice. After all, contemporary television depicted people with that hairstyle as criminals. For example, live-action series like *The F.B.I* (1965–74) and *Dragnet* (1967–70) frequently featured officers wearing close haircuts and business suits pursuing hippie lawbreakers. Before the Impossibles, neither live-action nor animated shows starred counterculture heroes. Thus, the duration of *Frankenstein, Jr. and the Impossibles* for two seasons on network television during the mid-'60s is no small accomplishment.

The new Leonardo-Total Television series *The Beagles* capitalized on the popularity of the Fab Four in a completely different manner. The program, consisting of the exploits of two rock musician dogs, only shares with *The Beatles* the role of the rocker as protagonist. Also, the words "beagle" and "beatle" sound alike. In all other ways, the dogs are dissimilar to the famous rock group. The Beagles interact with each other like Dean Martin and Jerry Lewis had before the comedy duo separated a decade earlier. In addition, the dogs are hardly countercultural, lacking the hairstyle and wardrobe of the Beatles. In contrast to Hanna-Barbera, Leonard-Total Television borrowed as little from the Beatles as possible.

As for *The Beatles*, the series lost ground in 1966. Competing studios produced more superhero series in the wake of *Batman*'s popularity than copycats of *The Beatles*, which had just delivered unprecedented, blockbuster ratings for ABC-TV on Saturday mornings the pervious year. The producers assumed that children wanted to watch crime-fighters instead of musicians. Their decisions were validated by the ratings in the fall of 1966. Week after week, *Space Ghost and Dino Boy* won higher ratings for CBS-TV than *The Beatles* on ABC-TV.

King Features Syndicate had trouble keeping pace with the increasingly political music of the band that year. One of the earliest songs of this new direction was "Nowhere Man," which criticizes apathy towards the status quo. The cartoon episode featuring this song does not concern an apolitical person but rather an old hermit content to stay in his cave. King's refusal to visually complement the message of "Nowhere Man" marked one of the first attempts by the studio to keep intact the fun-loving personalities of the movie *A Hard Day's Night* although the Beatles had evolved since then.[3]

The treatment of "Nowhere Man" is akin to the methods used by *The Smothers Brothers Comedy Hour* to take the bite out of political songs by guest performers. Just as King compromised protest for comedy, so too did comedians Tom and Dick Smothers in their series, which debuted in the 1966–67 season. When the rock group Buffalo Springfield sang the antiwar anthem "For What It's Worth" in one episode, the Smotherses popped up periodically to perform sight-gags in reference to some of the lyrics. The major difference, however, between *The Beatles* and *The Smothers Brothers Comedy Hour* is that the cartoon, although preceding the Smotherses by over one year, continued to subvert politics with slapstick. The brothers, in contrast, increasingly gave political commentary top priority over comedy.[4]

The decline in viewers of *The Beatles* also corresponds to the winding down of Beatlemania. As the series started its second season, the band suffered a severe backlash. An interview in a British periodical in which John Lennon remarked, "We're more popular than Jesus now," had recently reached the U.S. media. People staged angry demonstrations, demolishing records and other merchandise bearing the "Beatles" name and the likenesses of the members. Lennon apologized before the end of the year, but the damage had been done.

As 1966 ended, the studios survived their staff disruptions, and the militaristic story formulas weathered another year of the Vietnam War. U.S. popular culture had remained militaristic throughout the year, and animation producers capitalized on the trend via more violent slapstick and new superheroes. However, the reliance of the animators on tried-and-true characters and formulas hinted that all was not well in U.S. animation. In addition, the satirical content of some films demonstrated a willingness on the part of some animators to experiment with their past successes. The next major test of the U.S. animation industry lay in its ability to survive dramatic changes in popular culture in the immediate future.

5

THE CARTOONS
OF 1967

During 1967 the theatrical animation industry in the United States changed the politics of its imagery in tandem with shifts in public opinion on the Vietnam War. At the start of the year, animation studios caricatured militarism. When the year ended, the same facilities were illustrating antiwar themes in a good-natured manner. Meanwhile, for the first time, a majority of U.S. citizens opposed President Johnson's policy concerning the war. The theatrical studios were the most daring animation houses, exploring topics that implied concern with the course of the U.S. campaign in Indochina.

In contrast, the facilities producing for television remained committed to images combining either patriotism or white superiority with violence. For example, the most successful television cartoon of the 1967-68 season was a three-year-old colonialist series. *The Adventures of Jonny Quest* returned after having previously appeared only during the 1964-65 year. The new run of the show lasted five years, staying on the air as U.S. combat in South Vietnam peaked and then gradually disappeared. The network did not order new episodes but rather was content to air the same twenty-six episodes between 1967 and 1972. The longevity of the series was a testament to how appealing the premise of white characters exploring countries of people of color was to viewers during the Vietnam War.

Another original program from Hanna-Barbera was not nearly as successful as *The Adventures of Jonny Quest*, despite having a similar format of white figures in non–Western locales. The series *Shazzan* (1967-68) features children transported to the Arabian Nights. They summon a brown genie to fight their battles. However, he does not send them back home; first, they have to return his ring to his master. The third world is treated as exotic, as in *The Adventures of Jonny Quest*. The genie is a servile figure of color. *Shazzan* is one of the first Hanna-Barbera series to have the format of an endless quest. Many subsequent programs borrow from *Shazzan* in that regard.

The glorification of violence in *Shazzan* works to the detriment of the program. The series has little suspense, because the genie always rescues the children from danger immediately after they summon him. He has no vulnerability, unlike the mineral Kryptonite to Superman. In addition, the series was now one of many superhero cartoons on Saturday mornings in 1967 and did not distinguish itself from its competition. As an original character, for example, he does not have the built-in popularity of comic book characters brought to animation.[1]

Filmation had only middling success in capitalizing on the popularity of its hit series starring Superman. The studio teamed the "Man of Steel" with fellow DC Comics hero Aquaman for an hour-long show. One component of the show places the violence of the superheroes in a nationalist context. In "Justice League of America," a group of costumed figures fought criminals together.

DePatie-Freleng's *Super President* blended the superhero craze with patriotism in an awkward manner. To be sure, national symbolism contributed to the appeal of heroes like Marvel Comics' "Captain America" or DC Comics' "Justice League of America." However, *Super President* took the unprecedented step of giving a federal politician superhuman powers. The character's existence serves as escapism.

In the spring DePatie-Freleng experienced a critical "last hurrah" with its cartoon *The Pink Blueprint* (1966). The Academy nominated it for an award for Best Cartoon Short Subject, but it lost. It is one of the few films written by John Dunn that lacks the usual slapstick hits and bombs. Despite this validation of Dunn's original nonviolent approach to the panther, explosions and strikes remained the order of the day for "Pink Panther" and "The Inspector."

If nothing else, the Oscar nomination raised the stock of the film's director, Hawley Pratt, within the studio. Freleng's former assistant director at Warner Brothers, Pratt received the duty of supervising "Pink Panther" when Freleng retired from directing in 1965. Pratt directed the bulk of the episodes, and the studio entrusted him to launch every theatrical series except "The Inspector" and "The Ant and the Aardvark." Working on cartoon shorts to 1974, his ability to draw humor from old violent gags in fresh ways allowed him to make some of the funniest cartoons of the Vietnam War.

Pink Posies is the last "Pink Panther" episode to promote the color-validation theme. In the cartoon the feline secretly replaces the yellow flowers of a neighbor's garden with pink ones. The death of the "color war" story formula represents the waning mainstream support of the civil rights movement in 1967. For the first time, civil rights demonstrations receive less coverage than inner-city riots, Rev. Dr. Martin Luther King, Jr.'s controversial opposition to the Vietnam War, and the gun-toting members of the Black Panther Party for Self-Defense. In this context DePatie-Freleng no longer made color a central part of the panther's identity, although the title of every installment still contained the word "pink."

Meanwhile, "Pink Panther" distributor United Artists tried to directly associate the panther with the civil rights movement. Near the end of the year, a trade advertisement for cartoons distributed by United Artists contained the phrase "Pink Power," thus linking the figure with the controversial "Black Power" slogan of SNCC. However, the radicalism of the slogan was counterbalanced by the image of a friendly handshake between the cat and a police officer from France (the Inspector). Moreover, Carmichael's rallying cry had begun to lose its edge. By late 1967, several conservative African Americans had adopted the "Black Power" phrase, tailoring it to their agendas. The parodying of the phrase for a cartoon character demonstrated how toothless those two words had become.[2]

Pink Outs provides one of the Vietnam War era's most blatant attempts to extract humor from war. The cartoon is vague only identifying the war used as the setting. Otherwise, explosions in the sky and a helmeted Pink Panther holding a rifle in a foxhole comprise the signifiers of military conflict. Playing on the tallness of the Panther and the tiny size of an enemy centipede, the cartoon unexpectedly allows the centipede to kill the Panther by shooting guns drawn from each of its legs. The scene implies a warning against underestimating an enemy. It corresponds with the war because, just as the panther considers the centipede an insignificant enemy, the United States thought little of the Vietnamese and predicted a quick victory in the war. However, no matter what or how many bombs the United States dropped over North Vietnam over the past year, the North Vietnamese persisted in their campaign to conquer South Vietnam.

A similar story formula in the "Merrie Melodies-Looney Tunes" entries — Daffy Duck's underestimating of the intelligence of Speedy Gonzales — was the most consistent aspect of the cartoons released by Warner Brothers in 1967. The distributor issued animated films from three different studios that year: DePatie-Freleng (in January), Format Films (April through June), and a new Warner Brothers Cartoons (July onward). The duck and the mouse were the only established Warner stars still appearing in new cartoons. No matter which studio produced the episodes, Speedy always outsmarted Daffy by escaping various traps and even fooling Daffy into falling victim to them.

However, in the films of that year, the characterizations of Daffy and Speedy dramatically stray from their original conceptions. For example, Speedy does not engage in civil disobedience in any of the releases for the year. By this time the civil rights movement, which had popularized the tactic, was suffering a backlash from the general public. Most U.S. citizens disapproved of Rev. Dr. Martin Luther King, Jr.'s attempt to desegregate housing in the North (Chicago) instead of lunch counters in the South in 1966. They also balked at his outspoken opposition to the country's military role in the Vietnam War, which he announced on April 4, 1967.

Warner Brothers also downplayed the colonialism of the Daffy-Speedy films, in contrast to some of DePatie-Freleng's episodes. Of the duo's releases for 1967, only *Fiesta Fiasco* hints at colonialism, because Daffy trespasses on Speedy's land in order to crash a party from which the mouse has excluded him. Most of the year's cartoons are set outside of Mexico, and some are in the United States. In addition, unlike so many DePatie-Freleng entries, the new cartoons do not focus on land ownership.

In other ways the studios animating for Warner Brothers struggled to make Daffy and Speedy relevant to modern audiences. By doing so, however, the stars lose their personalities. In *The Spy Swatter*, Daffy is a spy using weapons to persuade Speedy to relinquish a secret document. In the end, the mouse uses the munitions against the duck, stops the pursuit, and keeps the secret. For this cartoon, the studio has changed Daffy into a gadget-dependent figure like Wile E. Coyote.

In poking fun at espionage, the animation industry demonstrated its tendency to milk trends long after their popularity has peaked. The secret agent remained a frequent role for animated characters like Daffy Duck in 1967. An unfortunate result was that theatrical animation became the last medium to actively capitalize on the spy craze, with the exception of the "James Bond" movie feature franchise from United Artists. Even Bond himself did not appear in a new movie that year. Television studios did not create new spoofs or imitative programs of Bond. Moreover, some "spy" series like *Secret Agent* and *Amos Burke—Secret Agent* had already been canceled, and the 1967-68 season was the last for *The Man from UNCLE*.

Despite the waning appeal of fictional spies, 20th Century–Fox invested heavily in the popularity of espionage by releasing only "James Hound" cartoons from Terrytoons that year. The studio's fascination with the secret agent reflected its confidence in Ralph Bakshi. By 1967 he had become the supervising director of the studio. He stopped directing "Sad Cat" cartoons, and the studio dropped the other series "Astronut" and "Possible Possum," neither of which Bakshi had ever directed. When he left Terrytoons to run Paramount Cartoon Studio later that year, Terrytoons resumed "Possible Possum" and "Sad Cat" (without Bakshi).

As the United States underwent its last year of escalation of forces in South Vietnam, MGM's violent "Tom and Jerry" series remained the top short subject draw for the final time. The reissues of Hanna-Barbera's episodes still contained more slapstick humor and explosions than the new entries by Chuck Jones. However, one of the episodes presents the imagery of the cartoons in a completely new context. A joke about global destruction in *Guided Mouse-ille* warns about the escalation of arms and the futility of war. It is one of the first episodes of the series to use violence to criticize it and not merely as a means of humor. Moreover, the depiction of conflict as endless despite the use of powerful weapons corresponds with the growing concern among U.S. citizens about the duration of the Vietnam War in 1967. After some gags consisting of laser-gun blasts and blows to the head, the film ends with Jerry dropping a bomb that literally explodes himself and Tom back to the Stone Age. There, they resume the conflict but with the figures wearing now leopard skins and eating bones.

Not all of *Guided Mouse-ille* is original. The story is similar to Hanna-Barbera's World War II episode *Yankee Doodle Mouse* (1943). In both cartoons Tom and Jerry battle each other with weaponry and have their own military headquarters. As a result, the films have in common a trendy capitalization upon current conflict. Jones made his film even trendier, however, by setting the cartoon in outer space, in contrast to the earlier cartoon's house setting.

Television animation also offered complex illustrations of violence and heroism. To do this, studios adapted the superheroes of Marvel Comics to animation. Marvel's heroes tend to struggle in deciding how to use their superhuman powers. They also have troubled interpersonal relationships. In addition, as Dow — a maker of weaponry used for the Vietnam War — promised "better living through chemistry," many of Marvel's figures gained their powers via freak scientific accidents.

ABC-TV exhibited a great deal of faith in airing shows starring Marvel characters. The syndicated *Marvel Superheroes* series had disappointed viewers when it first aired in the previous season. However, the network had little to lose. Its series *The Beatles* was steadily losing viewers. In addition, ABC-TV needed superheroes in order to compete with the hit superhero programs of other networks — CBS-TV's *The New Adventures of Superman* and NBC-TV's *Space Ghost*. Unfortunately for ABC-TV, CBS-TV broadcast all the programs starring the more established DC Comics characters. Marvel, in contrast, was a newer company with less proven comic book stars.

Hanna-Barbera developed a successful adaptation of *The Fantastic Four*. The series aired for three seasons. The characters received their unique powers after having suffered in outer space. The studio used past comic book issues of the super group for stories. As a result, the episodes had more substantial action and drama than the in-house creations like *The Impossibles*.

The Fantastic Four was one of the most unconventional series made by Hanna-Barbera. The characters themselves were radical, as conceived by creator Stan Lee. He wanted them to be imperfect and vulnerable. In contrast to juvenile sidekicks like Robin to Batman, Lee developed the youngest of the team as a young adult figure. The most popular team member among fans was the Thing — the fruit of Lee's desire to make a sympathetic figure out of someone offbeat, physically unattractive, and antisocial.[3]

Hanna-Barbera exercised a significant amount of progressiveness in adapting the *Fantastic Four* character Sue Storm to animation. She is a heroine of equal standing with her three colleagues. As such, she is unlike contemporary heroines in television cartoons. Most of the offerings from the studio for the 1967-68 season feature only male super-figures. Competing studio Filmation was not as bold as Hanna-Barbera. For the *Aquaman* component "Teen Titans," Filmation animated the lone teenage heroine among adolescent boys — a figure named Wonder Girl. However, it did not include the adult character Wonder Woman in its adaptation of "Justice League of America" — DC Comics' grouping of its popular heroes together in the same comic book series. Ironically, she is a member of the league in the comics.

Producer Steve Krantz also enjoyed success in bringing a Marvel property to television. Like *The Fantastic Four*, the *Spider-Man* series also lasted three seasons. The title-character gained spider-related powers after a radioactive arachnid bit him. As a Marvel character, Spider-Man possesses quirks that typical superheroes lack. He is a teenager and has no financial stability, unlike the reporter Clark Kent (Superman's identity) or millionaire Bruce

Wayne (Batman's identity). He is neurotic and cocky, and he incurs the wrath of the city he saves instead of its thanks. For example, newspaper editor J. Jonah Jameson reports the hero's acts of vigilante justice as criminal behavior.[4]

Spider-Man is one of the last protagonist cartoon characters to be defined by civil disobedience. To be sure, he is not like Robin Hood. Spider-Man does not break the law in order to save lives. However, because Jameson publicizes him as a criminal, the web-slinger becomes a social pariah for following his convictions. Nevertheless, in the 1960s his identity as a slandered hero or antihero attracted comic book readers previously exposed solely to superheroes regularly congratulated by police officers and mayors for jobs well done.

The least typical television cartoon series of the 1967-68 season satirized superheroes via witty dialogue instead of comical powers and costumes. Jay Ward returned to animation with *George of the Jungle*, which pokes fun at Edgar Rice Burrough's novel *Tarzan*. Much of the humor from the title-character comes from his verbal gaffes. The component "Super Chicken" comes the closest to resorting to silly powers for laughs; the bird gains extraordinary strength by drinking a sauce. However, each episode features funny lines. In contrast, the component "Tom Slick," starring a racecar driver, has the most conventional humor of the series, although the cartoons are on par with contemporary movies *The Great Race* (1965) and *Grand Prix* (1966). Many of the jokes are racial puns.[5]

While unique among its Saturday morning contemporaries via its sharp verbal humor, *George of the Jungle* is one of Ward's least outwardly political ventures. The show does not have a Cold War villain like Boris Badenov. Some images of colonialism exist, however. For example, no matter where Tom Slick races, he wins, thus defeating the indigenous competitors. In addition, although the "George of the Jungle" episodes are set in Africa's Mbwebwe Valley, the only stars are talking animals and white, British human figures. Moreover, some of the animal figures speak in a British accent. Vocal artist Paul Frees patterned his voice for a jungle District Commissioner after British actor Eric Blore and the voice for an ape after Ronald Colman.[6]

U.S. animation took heavy-handed but significant steps towards illustrating the counterculture. Studios did not break new ground in terms of characterization, for cartoon hippies followed the lead of beatniks in doing little more than spouting contemporary slang. Even the words the new figures spoke — "groovy," for example — were not new. On the other hand, animators took novel approaches in casting hippie figures as both sympathetic characters and leading ones. Studios, thus, began selling cartoons on the strength of the popularity of the counterculture images appropriated by the animators.

The reopened Warner Brothers Cartoons especially took a gamble by promoting a beatnik character as a new star despite having never cast him in previous cartoons. Television and movies had not presented beatniks in a sensitive manner, nor had beatniks figured as central characters in films. In addition, Cool Cat—a tiger wearing a beret and necktie—was the studio's first new star since Speedy Gonzales in 1953. The studio also made a daring risk by featuring the cat in his own adventures. Because Cool Cat appeared without established characters like Daffy Duck and Speedy Gonzales as co-stars, Warner Brothers could only promote the new character via the reputation of the studio. The distributor printed an advertisement that featured Cool Cat and another new character walking on a path toward the older, more famous Warner Brothers characters. The distance between the proven and new characters illustrated the "generation gap" between the characters and underscored that Cool Cat had not yet become a famous star.

Some of the music in *Cool Cat* has a hipper sound than the scores of other cartoons. The contemporary pop group The Clingers sang the title song, and their performance plays over the opening credits. Music director William Lava accentuated the parts of the bass guitar, keyboard, and bongo drums in the score, whereas composers traditionally highlighted horns and violins to correspond with the action of the cartoons.

Still, Cool Cat himself does not contribute much humor to his own cartoon. As a result Warner Brothers sabotaged its own character's potential for stardom. The punchlines of most of the gags consist of a hunter falling off cliffs and falling victim to his own weapons. The cat provides some amusement by mistaking a mechanical pink elephant for a living creature. However, the character mostly utters trivial lines, some of which, like "Let's split the scene," are slang expressions.

Warner Brothers Cartoons borrowed from its past in producing the cartoon. Aside from the updated music and vernacular, *Cool Cat* is little more than a recast "Bugs Bunny" episode from the 1940s or '50s. British stereotype Colonel Rimfire—the tiger's hapless hunter—plays the "Elmer Fudd" role. Cool Cat, meanwhile, imitates Bugs' unflappable demeanor and resourcefulness in outsmarting Rimfire. The hunter even quotes from the character Tweety Bird upon first seeing the tiger: "I tawt I taw a putty tat—a tiger-type putty tat." Only Cool Cat's beret and slang and the cheap animation from the studio suggest that the film first appeared in theaters in 1967.

The studio drew from the past to develop another new "hip" character. Merlin the Magic Mouse made his debut one month after the release of *Cool Cat*. The star is a caricature of comedian W.C. Fields. At the time the late humorist had become an icon of the counterculture. The animators capitalized on the fad and on the familiarity of Fields' image and voice. However, the anarchist personality that had endeared him to hippies is absent in Merlin.

Thanks to the real-life Beatles's embrace of counterculture ideas and music, the animated Beatles began to look passé after only two years. The *Hard Days Night* story formula that King Features Syndicate used for *Beatles* cartoons worked against the series, as the group developed a psychedelic sound. Many of the Beatles songs serving as centerpieces for new cartoons carry the themes of utopia and love. The animators interpreted the music by producing an increasing number of episodes featuring multicolored dream sequences or surreal worlds. Such imagery, however, was incongruous with the old images of the mop-top, conservatively attired band members. Moreover, the backgrounds became more visually interesting than the band—a sad fate for a group once known for its visual uniqueness.

Another problem with the 1967-68 season of *Beatles* episodes lay in King's awkward juxtaposing of contemporary trends. The studio borrows from *Batman* in having more on-screen words accompany sound effects, and the band caricatures still occasionally appear as soldiers and fighter-pilots. Such militaristic imagery, while attractive to children as U.S. involvement in the Vietnam War escalated, clashed with the group's new songs and with the "head" graphics that the studio developed for the music. For example, in the new opening sequence for the series, John Lennon appears as a World War I-era fighter pilot shooting down a German plane, and George Harrison appears as soldiers of various eras. However, all titles appear in a contemporary wavy, distorted script, superimposing a background of swirling, flashing colors. Moreover, this pro-war montage came on the heels of the real-life group's historic live worldwide broadcast, in which they wore mustaches and love beads while singing "All You Need Is Love."

Still, some of the actual experiences of the Beatles helped King to modernize the program. In the episode "Got to Get You into My Life," the caricatures practice transcendental meditation as a means of escape from screaming fans. The film cites Harrison's actual interest in India when his caricature tells his cartoon band-mates that he once read a book about the country. In real life Harrison introduced Indian culture to the other

Beatles. By the airing of this cartoon in the fall of 1967, he had already learned to play the sitar from the renowned Indian musician Ravi Shankar and had recorded songs with the instrument. To establish an Indian setting for the episode, the soundtrack briefly features Harrison's use of the sitar in the 1966 song "Love You To." In addition, although produced earlier in 1967, "Got to Get You into My Life" remarkably aired only a few weeks after the conclusion of the first meeting of the Beatles and Maharishi Mahesh Yogi in late August.[7]

The counterculture also influenced the cinematic style of *The Beatles*. Years after *A Hard Day's Night* had dazzled U.S. audiences by integrating non-sequiters, speeded-up and slowed-down scenes, and other techniques into the same film, Hollywood movie and television directors copied the style for their own works about rock musicians. One of the most popular of the derivations was the Screen Gems television show *The Monkees* (1966–68), which concerned four long-haired rock musicians. King adapted the gimmickry to animation for *The Beatles* in 1967. However, such filmmaking was not in the episodes but in the "Sing-along" segments. Although the regular stories strive for laughs from viewers, the "Sing-alongs" merely call for audiences to sing titled lyrics as a song plays. Consequently, King did not have to develop a plot for every "Sing-along." The entry for the song "Rain," for example, merely features several quick successive cutaways to different still images to correspond with Ringo Starr's rapid drumming.[8]

King tried not to alienate juvenile viewers while making so many references to the counterculture. "Strawberry Fields" does the best job of integrating both elements. To be sure, the song has a progressive sound, using a slowed-down recording of Lennon's voice and sounds played backwards. Also, much of the episode moves at a slow pace, keeping in tempo with the song. However, the lyrics to the song illustrate a simplistic and happy place, which suggests a child-like quality. In addition, the cartoon shows lots of children having fun — first by misbehaving, throwing things at the Beatles, but then by playing in their orphanage after the group members change the building's color from gray to psychedelic.[9]

However, King's efforts could not lure back viewers who had left for the superheroes. Exhibiting little faith in the program, ABC-TV did not help to save it. The network requested only a few new episodes, leaving audiences to watch mostly reruns for the balance of the year. Consequently, ratings kept dropping throughout the 1967-68 season.

Of all the commercial cartoon studios operating in 1967, only Paramount produced cartoons that suggested a "revolution" in terms of graphics and content. The studio's new producer, veteran animator Shamus Culhane, was responsible for the revamping of the facility and its product. His cartoons feature creative, abstract stylization reminiscent of the animation studio United Productions of America (UPA) in its heyday of the '50s; the studio even redesigned its only major "star"—the juvenile sorceress Honey Halfwitch. Some people associated Paramount's new artistic direction with current radical artistic trends. According to studio animator Doug Crane, an older colleague named Al Eugster called the changes "the new 'Peter Max' craze"—a reference to the successful pioneer of "pop art" during the '60s.[10]

The visual changes were radical in U.S. animation, especially on the East Coast. Both Paramount and Terrytoons lagged behind the Hollywood studios in adopting contemporary methods of animation, but Terrytoons updated its practices one decade before Paramount began. Culhane required that animators receive training in the new methods of animation. Gailzaid noted, "It was a short-lived program. Nick [Tafuri] was one of the guys teaching it. It lasted for a bit, until they closed the studio." Initially, few of the senior illustrators were willing to change their methods of animating. Most of the older illustrators, according to Crane, considered the graphics either "totally revoltin'" or "disconcerting." However, in time, "Some, probably most, sincerely tried to turn their thinking around and understand the mindset of these young whippersnapper designers."[11]

Under Culhane's tenure, the stories for Paramount's cartoons subversively tackled modern social and political issues. The producer highly prioritized scripts of superior quality. He dropped all recurring characters except for Honey Halfwitch and avoided physical slapstick humor. He strove for funnier dialogues and strong personalities for characters. As a result, Paramount Cartoon Studio eventually moved beyond its customary puns and violent slapstick towards sophisticated topical humor.

My Daddy the Astronaut couches humorous commentary about patriotism and colonialism in dialogue and designs suggesting a juvenile point of view. The narrator considers his father's planting of the U.S. flag on the moon as a sign of the nation's ownership of the moon. In addition, the artists designed the figures and backgrounds in the style of a young kindergartener and used actual crayons for the cartoon. Crane recalled that Eugster animated this film with a disposition of "almost childish glee."[12]

The innovative and topical cartoons from Culhane could not save Paramount Cartoon Studio from its financial woes. The conglomerate Gulf + Western had recently purchased Paramount Pictures Corporation and saw the animation department as a financial liability. Crane stated that rumors spread that the facility would soon close. In order to keep Culhane from leaving as morale among the artists dropped, Paramount named Culhane the executive director of the studio. However, within weeks, he departed for good to open his own animation business: Shamus Culhane Productions. "Shamus Culhane was way too sophisticated for Paramount," former employee Vicki Gailzaid opined. "He was there for a short time."[13]

Paramount boldly continued to produce radical "message cartoons" instead of traditional slapstick animation — a bold move, considering the studio's shaky future. Culhane's replacement, Ralph Bakshi, made witty films that discussed relevant social issues. These developments underscored Bakshi's commitment to making art instead of commercial product. As someone essentially hired to shut down the studio, he did not waste time trying to invent cartoon stars. For example, only one of his five Paramount films features new animal figures. However, he had ideas about the kinds of characters he preferred. Crane revealed that Bakshi brought to Paramount "[a] bag of characters that he'd been developing while at Terrytoons." The distributor, meanwhile, hoped that Bakshi would bring new life to the studio.[14]

One major difference between Bakshi's films and those of Culhane is in urban imagery. Culhane frequently set cartoons in cities, even moving Honey Halfwitch's house from the countryside to the top of a skyscraper when taking over Howard Post's character for a few episodes. Such graphics suggest escapism, which conflicts with contemporary images of cities in 1967. Riots and other violent demonstrations in urban areas appeared frequently on nightly news broadcasts throughout the year; people burned and looted buildings to express frustration over police brutality, joblessness, housing discrimination, and other pressing problems in cities. Unlike Culhane's scenes of sunny metropolitan areas, Bakshi's cartoons present a very gritty city, full of run-down tenements and dimly lit streets at night. His foreboding depictions of urban settings are very similar to those of Max Fleischer's cartoons during the Great Depression. However, Bakshi's city also reflects the urban turmoil of the 1960s.

Bakshi also criticized U.S. society more bluntly than Culhane did. Unlike Culhane's humorous asides about owning the moon, Bakshi's figures angrily address the issues that infuriate them. His film *Marvin Digs* presents the problem of the generation gap and places it in the very relevant context of conservative adult versus hippie. However, the older adult characters criticize the behavior of young adults in vague terms. They use the words "ingrate" and "troublemaker" without outlining specific problematic actions. They lament, "After all we've done for them," without saying what they have done for the youth. Only a frustrated police officer goes into some detail, "All this love, love, love, hair, hair, hair — that's all they've got to show for themselves."

Psychedelic graphics serves as a means to an end in *Marvin Digs*. They figure very minimally in the cartoon. They exist merely to provide evidence for Marvin's father to criticize contemporary youth. The only surreal moment in the film arrives immediately after the opening credits in a brief dream sequence in which Marvin imagines swirling colors and three longhaired female "flower children."

Despite the theme of the "generation gap" in *Marvin Digs*, both the younger and older artists at the studio embraced the counterculture references. Crane, a young animator at Paramount, welcomed the new style of illustration: "I found myself very comfortable with animating the 'psychedelic graphics' of cartoons such as *Marvin Digs* for Paramount Studios in 1967. It was an era of change, stylistically." The veteran animators also raised little objection to working on these images. Crane remarked about one of his older colleagues,

> Veteran Paramount animator Nick Tafuri (incidentally, one of the nicest and funniest men I've ever met...) thought it was for sure that all of the designers of the day had gone to drugs. But his attitude was, "It's work, it pays, and it's a hell of a lot easier drawing a bunch of purple, green and polka dotted orange flowers popping on and off screen that it is to animate Popeye and Bluto wrestling in a sea of man-eating alligators!!"

Vicki Gailzaid, the head of the ink and paint department, stated, "They got a kick out of that — Nick and all those old-school animators. They were smiling, laughing." While under threat of closure, the studio rarely had such a positive atmosphere. "It was pretty staid there the last two years," Gailzaid remembered.[15]

As with the animators and modern design, the studio's musicians worked well with "acid rock" musicians to make the score for *Marvin Digs*. The rock group The Life Cycle provided the instrumentation to studio composer Winston Sharples' score. Meanwhile, the lyrics to the title-song, which describe the character Marvin, came from an unlikely source: the ink-and-paint department. Gailzaid — in her words, a "love hippie" at the time — explained, "They [the studio staff] were having trouble with the *Marvin Digs* song, and I said, 'That's a piece of cake. I can write that.' It was about a love hippie." This figure, according to the song, was "just a groovy guy with love to share" and believed that "pleasures are found in poems."[16]

Despite the antiwar implications in the film's calling for love, *Marvin Digs* instead shows how conservative the animation industry had become by the middle of the Vietnam War in 1967. To be sure, Marvin not only spread flowers to neighbors but also, to Gailzaid, opposed the war. She defined a "love hippie": "What this meant for me at the time was that I was against the War in Vietnam as I believed, as many others did (and which I still do), that there must be a better way to work things out." In referring to Marvin as a "love hippie," she associates opposition of the war with him. Still, the film did not exploit the politics of Gailzaid's song; no characters mention war at all. The content was a far cry from MGM's cartoon *Peace on Earth* (1939)—an overtly antiwar cartoon in which forest animals recall humanity exterminating itself completely through war.[17]

Bakshi was completely uninterested in politicizing the content of *Marvin Digs*. He later told Michael Barrier of wanting Marvin to be a truly counter-cultural character but in behavior instead of political viewpoint. He hoped to have the hippie figure engage in sexual intercourse and to use profanity. However, the Hays Code still existed, and such content broke the rules. Also, Paramount executives balked at radical and unique content in cartoons, preferring to have the cartoon studio work on creating new "funny animal" stars. After all, years earlier the same illustrators had produced very popular child-friendly series "Casper the Friendly Ghost" and "Little Audrey."

For all its counterculture signifiers, *Marvin Digs* focuses on a father's search in finding his values in his son. Thus, the film promotes social conformity and offers a one-sided view of the current "generation gap" between the "baby-boomers" and their parents. Marvin and his friends paint city buildings in psychedelic patterns only after hearing the mayor tell citizens to "treat your city as you would your home." Also, Marvin only receives his father's respect after the mayor congratulates Marvin for his "drive, incentive and originality."

In *Marvin Digs* civil disobedience takes place. The studio even borrows the language of the civil rights movement. The hippies dub the beautification of their city a "paint-in." Such phrasing was still daring in 1967, for similar phrases "sit-in" and "teach-in" carried political connotations.[18]

Marvin is only a counterculture image like the swirling colors of the opening sequence. The studio does not develop a characterization for him. The cartoon does not explore the hippie's feelings about his estrangement from his father. Whereas the father calls him "that ball of hair" and "fuzzy," Marvin does not answer him with retorts or with any words or any change in facial expression. Rather, he seems oblivious to his father's hostility towards the counterculture.

In contrast to the flowers and hearts in *Marvin Digs*, the final cartoons from Paramount use militaristic imagery in fatalistic contexts. Bakshi drew from war by using images of mass destruction from bombs to end his cartoons. In *The Fuz*, a superhero's chasing of a ball of hair (later revealed as a little girl) climaxes into a mushroom-cloud explosion not unlike one from an atomic bomb. *Mouse Trek* illustrates a military cat's efforts to kill a giant mouse with various munitions. In the end the planet blows up, leaving the cat and the mouse with barely enough room to stand together on a small rock. Cartoons had rarely joked about global destruction, and Bakshi himself had not directed films with such content at Terrytoons. However, an incident recounted by Crane proved that the Vietnam War especially devastated Paramount Cartoon Studio employees:

> One of the girls in the Ink and Paint department was quietly told one beautiful morning that she had a call on the phone in the corridor. A supervisor and a lady friend walked with her to answer it, and moments later we heard the scream. The call was from her mother who had the sad duty of telling her that her fiance had been killed in action in Viet Nam the day before. It brought the war home to all of us ... no one would be quite the same again....[19]

By November, Gulf + Western made no secret of its plans to terminate the animation studio. Paramount promoted the planned short-film releases of 1968 as all live-action. "This is what exhibitors, prompted by their customers want," Mario Ghio told *Film Bulletin*. Strangely, however, despite this ominous declaration, the cartoon studio had not yet closed.[20]

Finally in December 1967, after a four-decade association with animation, Paramount shut down its cartoon division. Bakshi's films did not make enough money to convince Gulf + Western to keep the studio open. Crane remembered returning from lunch one day and seeing a crowd of workers gathering around on the sidewalk outside the Paramount building on West 44th St. The door was chained, and the Manhattan Sheriff's Department taped a note to the glass door telling them that the building would be opened for them to go in one at a time the next day, a Wednesday, in order to collect their personal belongings. "I never did go back on Wednesday to retrieve my sweater," Crane said. He then saw the saddened, speechless ex-employees saying their goodbyes on that sidewalk:

> "Oh ... don't worry ... our paths will cross again, I'm sure...."
> "Hey give me your number...."

"You stay well, now, y'hear??"

"Catch you around, Al," Nick Tafuri said to Al Eugster ... his friend of 45 years ... before Paramount was Famous Studios ... before Famous was Fleischers...

"Catch you around."[21]

After the studio closed, no other cartoon producer dared to take creative risks with their theatrical and television series. The remaining commercial animation producers on both coasts remained content in making cartoons in which figures merely performed slapstick gags or defeated villains. Small wonder that Crane had trouble leaving the spot outside where he had just been fired:

I stood there for a long while ... watching my friends walk away ... to the north ... to the east....

It was a long time ago.

Paramount studio ... and all of them ... all gone now....

I remember them with fondness.... [22]

6

THE CARTOONS
OF 1968

The year 1968 marked a turning point in U.S. animation in terms of violence. For the first time, slapstick gags involving gunshots in cartoons coincided with graphic television footage of images of several assassinations. In Vietnam photographer Eddie Adams took a picture of the exact moment a South Vietnamese official fired into the head of a member of the Vietcong; the picture became one of the most famous images of the conflict. Domestic events, meanwhile, were just as gruesome. In April the scene of Martin Luther King, Jr. lying on a motel balcony floor, blood flowing from a gunshot wound to the head, saturated the airwaves and made front-page news. Similar media coverage took place two months later when Senator Robert F. Kennedy, a presidential candidate that year, was shot in the head and neck. Horrified Americans saw similar scenes in cartoons that year; DePatie-Freleng's film *G.I. Pink*, for example, features a soldier accidentally shooting himself in the face.

While most television studios subsequently ceased production on "superhero cartoons" in response to the events, Filmation initially tried to sustain the genre while making some concessions to nonviolence. For *The Batman-Superman Hour*, the studio allowed Batman and Robin to use their fists to fight opponents. However, no criminals shoot the heroes with firearms. The villain Mr. Freeze carries a gun, but it discharges ice instead of bullets.

The Batman-Superman Hour was one of the last series to capitalize on the live-action *Batman* series. By then, ABC-TV had cancelled the program. The cartoon did not duplicate the campy humor that had made the live-action show popular. Voices in the cartoon were overacted, but minimal animation stifled the characterizations. Filmation used neither "fight words" nor famous guest stars.

Filmation's show merely resembles its live-action counterpart in its stylization of urban violence. The backgrounds of the cartoon are nowhere nearly as foreboding as those of the final Paramount cartoons from the previous year. However, more criminal activity takes place in Gotham City than in the neighborhoods of *Marvin Digs* and *The Fuz*. The live-action and animated depictions of Gotham City are of clean streets and economically healthy businesses. The only dangerous parts of the city are the hideouts of the villains but only became the villains are there and have weapons.

With war abroad and killings at home that year, television networks sought animated series with stories devoid of punches and explosions. The new programs that debuted in September 1968 were mostly comedies containing more dialogue than action, and almost all the characters had no super powers. Filmation found a receptive response to its adaptation of the comic-book teenagers Archie, Jughead, Betty, and Veronica in *The Archie Show*. Meanwhile, superheroes and slapstick animals were on borrowed time. Only one new superhero emerged that fall on network television, and CBS-TV banished its popular but violent "Tom and Jerry" series that fall to Sunday mornings, where it languished for four seasons.

Meanwhile, in theaters Metro-Goldwyn-Mayer's cartoon *Duel Personality* (1968) returned the "Tom and Jerry" series to its militaristic roots after years of understated, personality-oriented gags. Unlike Warner Brothers, MGM had gained a reputation in the 1940s for violent cartoons instead of socially satirical ones. When Chuck Jones took over the series in the mid–1960s, he decidedly made episodes with less slapstick humor. The cat and the mouse still chase each other, but Jones makes them stare and each other or at the audience with various facial expressions instead of having them strike each other. *Duel Personality*, full of scenes involving cannons, pistols, and slingshots, is Jones' only exception to the rule.

Duel Personality's presentation of violence as cyclical or perpetual corresponds with the developments in the war in Vietnam in 1968. It is one of many cartoons to depict war as endless or without conclusion. The film begins with Tom chasing Jerry in a mansion, then proceeds to several duels in which the adversaries try to kill each other, and finally ends with the same chase as in the opening. The plot thus presents a warning of the futility of escalating weaponry to resolve a dispute.

MGM also awkwardly balanced traditional cartoon humor with counterculture imagery in 1968. The "Tom and Jerry" cartoon *Rock 'n' Rodent* places Jerry Mouse in a jazz band consisting of beatnik mice. The psyche-delic parts are mild, mostly featuring Jerry and the mice absorbing the colors of the strobe lights on stage and one scene of the band members superimposed over each other. Tom Cat's slapstick attempts to sabotage the band and his facial reactions to his mishaps comprise the bulk of the film. More strangely, at the end of the film, Jerry walks to his home by imitating silent-film comedian Charlie Chaplin's gait.

Rock 'n' Rodent is simultaneously a typical and unique Vietnam War-era film from Chuck Jones. It is standard in that he does not draw much from the counterculture for the film. As beatniks embraced the gritty and melancholy rock music of Jefferson Airplane and the Doors, MGM's music director Carl Brandt scored a cheerful jazz number for Jerry's band to play. However, although the mice serve as mere props, their appearance is unique to Jones' work. After all, in *The Dot and the Line* (1966), the hippie squiggle plays the nemesis. In contrast, the beatniks of *Rock 'n' Rodent* are neither enemies nor comic relief. They only establish a setting that Jones had previously rarely employed.

Although MGM made an animated film about a counterculture environment, the studio also produced a short subject that implied support for the segregation of beatniks from mainstream society. Jones' cartoon *The Bear That Wasn't* tells the story of a bear mistaken for a white-collar worker. Wherever the animal goes, people mistake him for a man needing a shave. Here, long hair is simplistically dismissed as a similarity to the appearance of an animal.

Instead of exotic character looks, Walter Lantz presented exotic locales and white superiority. As the Hanna-Barbera series *Shazzan* left the airwaves in 1968, Lantz depicted West Asia as a land full of riches and mysticism for white characters. In the episode *A Lad in Bagdad*, the bird is the "white" protagonist served by a West Asian genie. Another West Asian plays the role of the villain. Woody is less an invader than a tourist of a foreign land. However, the film still shows colonialism via the woodpecker's conquering of one indigenous figure while becoming the master of another one.

Even among the indigenous figures, however, Lantz uses race to differentiate "good" from "evil." The imagery implies white superiority. The genie has blond hair and speaks as if from the urban East Coast, whereas the villain lacks these European traits. Lantz, however, was not unique in doing this. In the Warner Brothers cartoon *A-Lad-in His Lamp* (1949), a West Asian warlord has a thick indigenous accent, while a genie speaks like the character Thurston Howell II from the television series

Gilligan's Island (courtesy Jim Backus, who played both the genie and Howell).

The only theatrical cartoons to bring military conflicts to definite ends in 1968 were anti-colonialist films from Walter Lantz. After years of having Chilly Willy the penguin search cold climates for fish, the studio unveiled a new story formula involving unflattering caricatures of the U.S. Armed Forces. In these new episodes, the U.S. government builds a disruptive military base near the penguin's igloo, and the bird eventually drives the officers away by using explosives and other weapons.

Lantz, however, was not consistent in his imagery of political radicalism. In contrast to the anti-government theme of "Chilly Willy," protest receives heavy-handed comic treatment in the "Beary Family" cartoon *Jerky Turkey*. Junior Beary disguises a turkey as a "protest singer" to keep father Charlie Beary from killing the bird for food. When asked to perform, the turkey simply sings about how people should eat other meats besides turkey. Thus, the film depicts protest as self-serving, which was a complaint directed by several people towards the anti-war movement.

Unlike Lantz, Warner Brothers-Seven Arts Cartoons did not offer mixed messages in 1968. It abandoned colonialism for its last Daffy-Speedy films. Neither film features Daffy in a position of power over Speedy, nor are the Mexicans in the films depicted as poor and uneducated. *See Ya Later Gladiator* stars a Mexican scientist, who has created a time machine. In *Skyscraper Caper* Speedy keeps Daffy from accidentally killing himself while sleepwalking.

Skyscraper Caper is also notable in that it is one of the first theatrical cartoons to depict an American figure and a Mexican character as friends. They share not only a house but also a bedroom. Instead of Daffy chasing Speedy in anger, the mouse pursues the duck to save his life. The relationship marks a change from their usual antagonism. In addition, the film provides some of the first progressive images of racial integration in a Hollywood cartoon. After all, the film's release predated by one month the passage of the Civil Rights Act of 1968, which called for the federal government to prevent housing discrimination. The legislation was approved within days of the assassination of Rev. Dr. Martin Luther King, Jr. in April.

The Warner Brothers-Seven Arts cartoon *Feud with a Dude* gives a fabled battle a Vietnam War context. For decades cartoon studios had illustrated the gunfire exchange between the Hatfield and McCoy families of the mountains. In most cartoons after both sides resolve one argument and cease firing on each other, they start another disagreement and resume shooting. Most animated films made before the Vietnam War conclude with an intervening party helping both families to come to peace terms for good. In Warner Brothers' own *Naughty Neighbors* (1939), Porky Pig and Petunia Pig negotiate a cease-fire. However, *Feud with a Dude* ends with the departure of wanderers Merlin Mouse and his assistant Second Banana, both of whom are escaping the bullets from the families. By leaving the shooters to continue an endless war by themselves, Merlin and Second Banana dramatize the opinion that the United States needs to leave the Vietnam War.

Another Warner Brothers-Seven Arts offering, *Flying Circus* illustrates the military stalemate of the Vietnam War via the setting of World War I. Unlike earlier cartoons about war, this one does not end with an enemy soldier dying but rather with the soldier humiliated in a nonviolent manner. In the film a German pilot and an American pilot fight each other in the air. Although the German accidentally wanders into a U.S. military camp and is surrounded by U.S. soldiers, he does not surrender.

Flying Circus illustrates how differently the theatrical studios conceptualized hero figures during the Vietnam War from the heroes of World War II cartoons. Good-looking, physically fit, and tall heroes and unattractive, out-of-shape, short enemies appear in *Flying Circus*. These designs mark a change from the usual theatrical protagonist as a small but clever figure. Even the physically strong older characters like Popeye or Metro-Goldwyn-Mayer's dog Droopy are still shorter than their opponents. Smaller protagonists are underdogs in films, thus attracting sympathy from viewers. Immediately after Japan bombed Pearl Harbor, small but victorious protagonists dominated new cartoon releases. In contrast, by the Vietnam War, the United States had become a superpower, and hero figures correspondingly grew in size. Thus, the film promotes nationalism instead of sympathy for the underdog.

Another aspect of the Vietnam-era cartoon hero is his use of offensive warfare instead of defensive tactics. Unlike World War II cartoons, in *Flying Circus*, the U.S. pilot shoots at the enemy first. He even brags about doing so. Not only does the hero look strong but, in attacking first, operates from a position of strength or advantage.

The image of the larger protagonist is on par with the superheroes in cartoons for television. The U.S. pilot is as muscular as Filmation's Superman or Batman but lacks superhuman strength. However, the theatrical artists chose to poke fun at the "good guy" persona instead of cashing in on the phenomena via faithful adaptations of comic-book stars. The U.S. pilot does not even throw a single punch at the German, unlike the blows delivered by the aforementioned crime-fighters.

Meanwhile, the depiction of the enemy figure had not substantially changed in two decades. Ever since the silent era, mustaches had appeared only on antagonists, not protagonists. Likewise, the mustache on the German pilot of *Flying Circus* signifies his immoral personality. Like the shorter body size and the different uniform, the facial hair was a visual contrast between him and the U.S. pilot. Except for DePatie-Freleng's character the Inspector and King Features Syndicate's detective figure Cool McCool, the animated protagonists of 1968 did not have facial hair.

Warner Brothers-Seven Arts gave many of its cartoons the theme of anti-colonialism in 1968, reflecting public distaste for the Vietnam War. The studio had formerly espoused colonialism in cartoons about safaris. In films like *The Major Lied Till Dawn* and *Africa Squeaks*, white characters explore the animals and plants of the African continent while served by indigenous blacks. However, by 1968, the war had soured the public from engaging in literature and film that showed rainforest areas as attractive and exotic. Thus, in that year the cartoon studio made the white explorer a bumbling antagonist instead of a comic hero.

The "Merrie Melodies" cartoon *Chimp & Zee* offers mixed messages on colonialism. To be sure, the episode features a white hunter chasing a blue-tailed simian monkey throughout the jungle but failing to catch it. The story is exactly like that of Warner Brothers-Seven Arts' own *Cool Cat* from the previous year. On the other hand, the predator fails because a white boy wearing only leopard skin is protecting the animal. As a result, the images of white people as both Africa's protector and exploiter clash. Moreover, the cartoon presents an image of white superiority. A white figure preserves the environment of a continent populated largely by blacks, yet no indigenous blacks appear in the film with the whites and the animals. With colonialist imagery on the wane, *Chimp & Zee* is the last theatrical cartoon to offer a white protagonist figure in the mold of Tarzan.

Meanwhile, the "Cool Cat" cartoons from Warner Brothers blend anti-colonialism with the "endless conflict" theme of *Feud with a Dude*. In the episodes Cool Cat continues to outwit British hunter Colonel Rimfire in the jungle. The films, however, do not end with the tiger causing the marksman to sulk away in defeat, nor does the animal kill his predator with explosives or other devices. Rather, the films end as they begin — with Rimfire chasing the cat. In the conclusion of *Big Game Haunt*, the two adversaries stop to take a breather after having run for a distance, but they resolve to resume the chase. Such endings are a far cry from films starring Bugs Bunny, who frequently blew up hunters via dynamite or goaded them to wave a flag of surrender. Still, unlike the bunny,

Cool Cat belongs to the Vietnam War era, which fostered films lacking resolute ends to conflicts.

Warner Brothers slightly dabbled in psychedelic animation and camerawork for *Bunny and Claude*. The techniques do not add to the humor and have nothing to do with the plot but rather serve as superfluous visual frills. The camera zooms in and out in several scenes. Objects rapidly and repeatedly pop on and off the screen. To some extent, the cartoon approximates the visual style of *Bonnie and Clyde* (1967).[1]

The co-opting of the film techniques of *Bonnie and Clyde* for *Bunny and Claude* is a testament to the versatility of the often-underrated director Robert McKimson. A director for over two decades by 1968, most of his films offer little visual exaggeration. His characters tend to retain their appearance despite very physical gags — very little stretching of bodies, barely any alteration after a dynamite explosion, and almost no unique poses of figures or camera angles. However, the title-characters of *Bunny and Claude* were the first starring characters he had created in years. The opportunity to work on his own stars seems to have invigorated his creativity.

In addition, *Bunny and Claude* employs slapstick comedy, just as *Bonnie and Clyde* had done. Many of the gags in the feature originated in "Keystone Kops" films of the early days of moviemaking. Thus, the popularity of *Bonnie and Clyde* legitimated the continued use of slapstick in cartoons. However, Warner Bros-Seven Arts Cartoons did not want to merely stop at *Bunny and Claude* for that type of humor. Rather, the studio made plans to begin yet another new series — an animated adaptation of the "Keystone Kops" series.[2]

Bunny and Claude, like *Bonnie and Clyde*, is a product of the new ratings system established by the Motion Picture Association of America. The rabbits escape the police at the end of the cartoon, despite having robbed banks and having fired shots at the sheriff. As a result, they suffer no consequences for their antisocial behavior. Both the cartoon and the movie legitimize violent social disorder, which Hollywood films had not previously done. In the historical context of 1968 — urban rioters protesting police brutality, joblessness and poverty, and antiwar demonstrators opposing the Vietnam War on the grounds of immorality — the actions of the radical or outlaw have connotations of social reform. *Bonnie and Clyde* does a better job of establishing the motives for the robberies than the cartoon, because the feature shows the impoverished, hopeless lives of Parker and Darrow. Through heists, they gain the money they have always wanted. Bunny and Claude, on the other hand, do not convey that same sense of need.[3]

An advertisement for *Bunny and Claude* in the trade magazine *Film Bulletin* foreshadows the cartoon's playful attitude on the movie's gory humor. Whereas posters for *Bonnie and Clyde* declared, "They're young, they're in love, and they kill people," the rabbits instead say, "We're young and in love, and we'll kill 'em at the box office." In addition to displaying a great deal of faith in unproven characters, Warner Bros-Seven Arts Cartoons shows in its flyer that *Bunny and Claude* does not take seriously the original feature's artistic images of violence. For example, in the cartoon the sheriff emerges from explosions and gunshots with only minor scratches, in contrast to the somewhat orgasmic death throes of Bonnie as bullets enter her body in *Bonnie and Clyde*.[4]

The last female lead protagonist in theatrical animation, Bunny is one of the most progressive female figures in Hollywood films — live-action or animated. In an era when few female characters in movies deviated from the "housewife" characterization or subordinates to men in the workforce, Bunny traveled across the country with her beau. Moreover, as animation studios started to decrease slapstick content, Bunny by default became one of the most violent cartoon characters — male or female — in 1968. She shoots at the sheriff with a machine gun. She also uses a gun to rob banks with Claude. She also displays behavior formerly reserved for male cartoon characters. In the opening sequence, she smokes a cigar. Before her, the cartoon characters who most often smoked tobacco were Popeye, the Pink Panther, and assorted cowboy figures.

Bunny's somewhat feminist persona does not result merely from her role as a parody of Bonnie. Rather, her characterization has roots in other female characters from Robert McKimson. Bunny's independent streak was first exhibited in an elderly bird named Prissy, who lived alone and chased after Foghorn Leghorn in some of the director's films the 1940s and '50s. Also, McKimson's cartoon *Wild Wife* (1955) consists of a white housewife telling her husband why the work she does to manage the household is important. Similarly, Bunny is no sidekick to Claude but an equal partner. She is as bold as Claude in robbing carrot patches and firing at the police.

Despite Bunny's unique female characterization, the studio applied some gender stereotypes to her. She bats her eyelashes when wanting something; she does so as she asks Claude for more carrots. She wears jewelry and makeup. In the only time she thinks independently (asking for carrots), Claude shames her. The music also degraded women, for the lyrics to the theme song identify Bunny as a "broad."

Also, Bunny is not as developed a character as her cinematic counterpart Bonnie. In *Bonnie and Clyde*, Bonnie evolves as a character. In contrast,

Bunny remains one-dimensional throughout *Bunny and Claude*. To some extent, the six minutes of the cartoon do not allow ample time for deep characterization. As a result both Claude and the sheriff share Bunny's lack of depth. However, due to the absence of development for female cartoon figures throughout the history of theatrical animation and the scarcity of such characters in cartoons, Bunny's simplicity is especially poignant.[5]

As a result of the minimal characterizations of Bunny and Claude, their relationship also lacks substance and meaning. *Bonnie and Clyde* is the story of lovers condemned to die. *Bunny and Claude* does not have any sense of tragedy. The title-characters do not display any affection towards each other, except when Bunny calls Claude "honey" when asking him for more carrots. The couple does not appear doomed, because the sheriff constantly fails to capture them. They exist merely to lampoon another fictional relationship.[6]

The Warner Brothers-Seven Arts cartoon *Norman Normal* is a "message cartoon" in the tradition of *Marvin Digs* (1967). Both cartoons discuss social issues with minimal reliance on swirling colors. However, *Norman Normal* goes beyond Bakshi's exploration of the generation gap by tackling other topics like bigotry, alcoholism, and social conformity. Whereas Bakshi tried to balance traditional cartoon comedy with political themes, *Norman Normal* uses animation as means to an end of exploring domestic cultural values of the late 1960s.

Animated commentary on social conformity was not novel in 1968, but the means by which *Norman Normal* critiqued society was. In the 1950s United Productions of America (UPA) made cartoons in which characters struggled to fit into society despite their quirks. For example, nearsighted figure Mister Magoo caused havoc by making mistakes brought upon by his poor vision, but he was oblivious to his errors and staunchly believed that he did fit in. In contrast, Norman Normal is critical of the poor behavioral choices of the people in his social circle and chooses not to conform. In one of the first animated attacks on racism since *The Hole* (1962), he interrupts a character, "Is this a joke you're gonna tell me of a minority group, and after you tell it we're all gonna laugh and feel superior?" Whereas *The Hole* breaks from traditional black stereotyping by having black and white figures as social equals, *Norman Normal* uses an all-white cast to challenge the complacency of whites towards racist actions like the telling of derogatory jokes.

The film was one of the last theatrical cartoons to showcase a musical celebrity: Noel Stookey of Peter, Paul and Mary. *Norman Normal* continued the animation industry's practice of exploiting performers. However, despite the success King Features Syndicate had with *The Bea-*

tles on television, theatrical studios stuck with their established series starring animal figures instead of taking a risk with an individual short cartoon. The popularity of Stookey's music made *Norman Normal* an attractive project for Warner Brothers. In a letter written in a unique style, Stookey recalled, "In the mid sixties, based to a large extent on peter, paul and mary's musical success, i sold warnerbros. on the idea of producing a contemporary cartoon based on 'everyday life.'"

Unlike the musicians caricatured in previous cartoons, Stookey had creative control over *Norman Normal*. When Paramount Pictures distributed Max Fleischer's cartoons in the 1930s, the company arranged for prominent musicians to sing in live-action segments of Fleischer's films. Sometimes the animators illustrated cartoon figures singing the performance. However, they had no influence over story construction; even the Beatles were out of the loop for the episodes of their cartoon three decades later. In contrast, Warner Brothers-Seven Arts trusted Stookey with his vision of *Norman Normal*: "i think the film was attempting then as it does now to question some of the attitudes that society values as 'normal.'" Stookey, in turn, left a significant amount of work for the studio to do. He noted, "once i'd done the audio work it was done. i probably would have stayed more involved if my first choice as a lead designer (milt glaser) had been accepted by the company."

Warner Brothers-Seven Arts recognized the uniqueness of *Norman Normal*. The distributor marketed the film as a different entity from the usual cartoon releases. Instead of a "Merrie Melodies-Looney Tunes" episode, it was a "Cartoon Special." To be sure, it differs from the other studio offerings in important ways. It is the product of a contemporary performer instead of an in-studio writer. The music score is authentic rock from Stookey, as opposed to William Lava's mildly jazzy compositions. The visual humor comes largely from surreal metamorphosis — not violent slapstick. Indeed, the cerebral and reserved Norman Normal is hardly the same kind of cartoon figure as the broader Daffy Duck or Speedy Gonzales.

Aside from Stookey's contributions, *Norman Normal* looks similar to the other Warner Brothers-Seven Arts cartoons released in 1968. The character designs are stylized in the manner that director Alex Lovy brought from Hanna-Barbera to Warner Brothers-Seven Arts. The direction itself is low-key, which was the case for all of Lovy's cartoons for the studio. Stookey was gracious in his appraisal of the aesthetics: "though i was hopeful for more of a disney production (3-D), the cartoon as drawn has a classic abstract quality to it."

The abstract images in *Norman Normal* are minimal and are, in fact, segregated within the cartoon. The psychedelic effects and the long-haired figures singing the title-song appear only in the opening sequence and the conclusion. The rest of the film focuses on a white, bespectacled, white-collar figure struggling to relate to his boss, co-workers, and his father — also a white-collar character. A few surreal visual effects punctuate the narrative. Explaining the importance of conformity, Norman's father blends into his office wall, and Norman and his employer transform into children while having an argument. Nevertheless, most of the humor comes not from visual gimmickry but instead from dialogue, not unlike offerings from other studios as rising costs in animation led to figures moving less and talking more.

The most avant-garde antiwar film from Warner Brothers-Seven Arts came from beyond the studio. The distributor released the independent short film *The Door* and, as with *Norman Normal*, dubbed this outside film a "Cartoon Special." *The Door* consists of a montage of live-action images of war and urban life juxtaposed with animation of two Native Americans witnessing the footage. The film displays for viewers instead of entertaining them. It has no plot to interest audiences. More importantly, it does not offer different imagery than content on contemporary television news reports on riots and the Vietnam War. After *The Door* Warner Brothers-Seven Arts did not release further "imported" cartoons.

By the end of the year, Warner Brothers-Seven Arts was in a creative tailspin. The studio initially followed in the footsteps of UPA in experimental animation but eventually morphed into the Paramount Cartoon Studio of the 1960s — a studio without bankable characters and constantly testing new stars in old story formulas. Even the characters introduced by the studio to audiences resembled those from Paramount's defunct studio. In *Big Game Haunt*, a friendly ghost named Spooky — very similar in personality to Casper the Friendly Ghost — pursues Cool Cat and Colonel Rimfire. And, as in the "Casper" cartoons, Spooky unintentionally scares his co-stars while trying to befriend them.

In contrast, DePatie-Freleng had no such problems with originality in 1968. The studio managed to mix politics with slapstick humor in several shorts. Richard Schickel identified the studio as the only one currently and consistently making interesting cartoon shorts. His comment is telling, because at the time Walter Lantz Productions, Terrytoons, and Warner Bros-Seven Arts made those films, too. However, those other studios — animating for nearly four decades — had settled into producing formulaic characters and stories. In contrast, five-year-old DePatie-Freleng had not been in operation long enough to fall into a creative rut.[7]

The one exception is the "Inspector" entries of the year. DePatie-Freleng revamped "The Inspector" but removed the creativity from nearly every remaining episode in the process. The studio experimented with stories beyond the officer's chasing of crooks. Unfortunately, many of the new plots were merely borrowed from much older cartoons and did not fit the series. For example, *Transylvania Mania* concerns a vampire trying to kill the Inspector in order to remove the officer's brain and place it in a Frankenstein monster. Warner Brothers Cartoons had made a similar film starring Bugs Bunny over a decade earlier. Also, in *Bear de Guerre* the officer takes on an Elmer Fudd-type role. In this cartoon the Inspector goes on a hunting trip, in which he targets an anthropomorphic, talking bear instead of a human criminal. When the Inspector does chase criminals, he does not always catch them in the conclusions — a stark contrast to his accidental, clumsy apprehensions of crooks in the earlier episodes.

DePatie-Freleng satirizes several aspects of war in *Hawks and Doves*. The cartoon — the debut of the new theatrical series "Roland and Rattfink" — caricatures the division of the homefront over the war. Roland is a pacifist from Doveland, antagonized by war-loving Rattfink from Hawkland. After a series of dogfights in World War I–era planes, Roland defeats him. However, the film does not end with Rattfink's surrender but rather with Doveland's government making Rattfink rich by paying reconstruction funds to Hawkland. Considering that the "Inspector" series had lost its freshness, DePatie-Freleng launched this new series at an opportune time.

Unfortunately, *Hawks and Doves* starts the trend in the "Roland and Rattfink" series of problematically depicting "good" and "evil" according to color. In the film Roland, the "good" figure, is a white, blond-haired, blue-eyed figure; but Rattfink, the "evil" figure, is green. In addition all of the characters are white, except for Rattfink and his equally evil, green mother. Almost every episode over the next three years stars white characters — playing either sympathetic roles or incidental ones — and the only evil and non-white figure, Rattfink. In that same period, Hollywood significantly moved away from all-white movies and television shows and started presenting sympathetic images of racial minority groups. As a result the "good-versus-evil" imagery in "Roland and Rattfink" is very regressive.

Also regressive is one of the few colonialist cartoons of the year from the studio. The "Pink Panther" episode *Pink Sphinx* depicts the cat as an explorer for treasure in the Middle East. The only indigenous figures in the film are veiled women, a seller of camels, and a police officer. Furthermore, the women and the businessman have brown skin, but the officer is a white male figure. Even in a remote desert setting, brown people lack power or social control.

The "Pink Panther" cartoon *G. I. Pink* borrows from very old caricatures of army life but illustrates them in a Vietnam War-era context. The image of the clumsy soldier dates back to blackface minstrelsy as a crude and inaccurate statement about black ineptitude in the armed forces. During World War II, the Disney Studio revived the characterizations for its star Donald Duck, as did producer Sheldon Leonard for the live-action television series *Gomer Pyle U.S.M.C.* in the '60s. *G. I. Pink*, however, is a product of the late 1960s, because the panther's mishaps during basic training involve the typical explosives of contemporary animated films. He accidentally throws a live grenade at his sergeant, shoots him in the face and tosses him onto a land mine.

DePatie-Freleng stopped producing cartoons promoting civil disobedience in 1968. *Pinkcome Tax*, for example, shows civil disobedience gone awry. The cartoon is a unique variation of the "Robin Hood" legend and stars the Pink Panther as one of Robin's Merry Men, but in the end both the panther and the famous robber are incarcerated. Never before had an animated adaptation of Robin Hood failed to escape the sheriff of Nottingham. However, by this time, the civil rights movement had experienced a backlash. Presidential candidates that year vowed to bring "law and order" upon civil rights and antiwar demonstrators. Also, after the death of Dr. King, no new civil rights figure had stepped in to promote nonviolence and peace as dramatically as he had. More militant movement groups like the Black Panther Party for Self-Defense and the Student Nonviolent Coordinating Committee received more media coverage by then.

DePatie-Freleng's *Les Miserobots* from the "Inspector" series links violence to contemporary social problems more clearly than *Pinkcome Tax*. The Inspector becomes a victim of automation, losing his job to a robot police officer. The dismissed cop then turns into a corrupt vigilante, vowing to kill the robot in order to regain his job. Over the course of the film, he fires both a pistol and a rocket launcher at the machine and attempts to fire a cannon at it. In a scene corresponding to the actions of current urban rioters, the Inspector throws a brick into a random building in order to draw the robot into a trap. His de-evolution into a murderous vandal due to his firing results in yet another cartoon capitalizing on the popularity of justified violence in *Bonnie and Clyde*. To be sure, the story deviates from the original concept of the series but does so in an original and provocative manner.

In addition to addressing topical themes, DePatie-Freleng followed the lead of movie and television producers by cashing in on the most superficial aspects of Haight-Ashbury: hippies and psychedelic design. Some of the year's feature films about the counterculture—*Skidoo*, *Wild in the Streets*, and *Psych-Out*, for example—depict its members as one-dimensional, longhaired, musical, and incoherent partygoers. Co-producers George Schlatter and Ed Friendly had the greatest television success with this imagery in their series *Rowan & Martin's Laugh-In*. *Come on in! The Water's Pink* ends not with the standard shrinking of a scene in a circular shape but rather with the final scene diminishing in size in a shapeless form. The focus blurs in *Pink Sphinx* when the Pink Panther begins to hallucinate in the desert heat. Over the next six years, the studio prints the on-screen titles of episodes in psychedelic script.

The "Pink Panther" episode *Psychedelic Pink* owes more to the silent-era "Felix the Cat" animated films than to San Francisco art trends. To be sure, the DePatie-Freleng cartoon presents more counterculture imagery than other short cartoons released in 1968. *Psychedelic Pink* has backgrounds consisting of hearts and flowers enveloped by swirling colors, the camera focus blurs to add visual distortion, and the panther's costar is a hippie. However, the film also borrows from the earlier series in developing unlikely dual purposes for objects. In one scene the panther grabs a light bulb from over his head—the typical visual representation of a brainstorm—in order to change the bulb in his lamp. Later, the cartoon concludes with gags from letters of the alphabet; the cat uses the letter "j" as a golf club, and the hippie holds the letter "f" as a gun and fires it at his feline customer.

Psychedelic Pink also distorts music to add to the visual surrealism. The studio had started to splice together parts of various scores after music director Walter Greene left for Walter Lantz's studio in 1966. Some cartoon scores consist of bits of music from as many as seven earlier episodes in order for certain scenes to have appropriate music to complement the action. *Psychedelic Pink* does not borrow from as many scores, but in three scenes, a quiet and jazzy five-beat section of the score from the episode *Rock-a-Bye Pinky* repeatedly plays, sounding like a broken record. The repetition was a creative way for DePatie-Freleng to musically illustrate a drug hallucination, especially considering that all of Greene's scores for the studio predated the exploitation of the counterculture by mainstream media.

The ending of the film, in which the hippie shoots at the panther, serves as a symbol of the passing of San Francisco's counterculture, as it had existed in the "Summer of Love" of the previous year. In 1968 several bands having formed and honed their sound in San Francisco over the past few years found success on the *Billboard* charts and left for Los Angeles and other large cities. At the same time, violent crime escalated in the Haight-Ashbury area. Meanwhile, in *Psychedelic Pink*, Pink Panther accidentally wrecks the hippie's bookstore, which frustrates the proprietor to the point of picking up and using a weapon.

United Artists, the distributor of the DePatie-Freleng cartoons, cemented its reputation as a source of "head" animation with the feature-length cartoon *Yellow Submarine*. King Features Syndicate produced the movie, in which caricatures of the Beatles fight invaders of the area of Pepperland with music. The film is much more surreal than *Come on In! The Water's Pink* and contains more creative uses of color and design than *Psychedelic Pink*. Then again, DePatie-Freleng and King approached the counterculture from completely different angles. The former studio made gags out of the graphics, but the latter made a narrative of them.

King used Beatle songs and specific colors to tell the story of *Yellow Submarine*, because the animators did not have much of a script delivered to them from their producer. The story is a retooling of the episode "Strawberry Fields Forever" from the defunct *Beatles* cartoon series, in which the musicians add color to a drab orphanage by playing the title-song. In the movie, the music restores color to Pepperland after attacks by the enemy Blue Meanies removed it. The animators had the challenge of illustrating fifteen songs in ways that connected them to the story. Moreover, most of the chosen tunes came from the album *Sgt. Pepper's Lonely Hearts Club Band*, which had a completely different plot than the movie. The artists accomplished their task by using more graphics and colors than usual for various scenes.[8]

An immediate legacy of *Yellow Submarine* upon its release was its counterculture suggestiveness. The media reported concern about drug abuse by both the artists and the viewers. However, the psychedelic images in the movie came from the creativity of the illustrators. The artists did not use hallucinogenic drugs. Still, critics noted that the feature lacked a coherent story. *Time* magazine ran two articles on the movie, saying first that it was "schizophrenic" and then calling it "less a coherent story than a two-hour pot high" one month later.[9]

Yellow Submarine, in fact, marked the debut of psychedelic animation from the United Kingdom. Based in London, the artists of TVC had minimal exposure to the graphics of Haight-Ashbury. Also, the United Kingdom had not yet embraced the "pop art" of Peter Max. Thus, King's ambitious animating of counterculture icons via its initial foray into "head" animation was a baptism of fire.[10]

Although the same studio that had produced *The Beatles* for television made *Yellow Submarine*, the animators revamped the designs of the band members. The cartoon likenesses resembled how the musicians looked on the cover of *Sgt. Pepper's Lonely Hearts Club Band*, instead of the mop-topped figures of *A Hard Day's Night*. To be sure, the Beatles of 1968 wore their hair differently than four years earlier and had long abandoned their matching outfits for a more psychedelic wardrobe. However, the swirling colors on the new clothes of the *Yellow Submarine* Beatles better fit the surreal animation, just as matching, monochrome outfits had made animation of dozens of short *Beatles* television cartoons over two years easier for the studio.[11]

For all its progressiveness, *Yellow Submarine* retains several traditional aspects of animation, many of which illustrators still practiced during the Vietnam War. The film represents a continuation of the distributor's formula for success in animation — acquiring cartoons based on established properties. Just as DePatie-Freleng had borrowed the characters Pink Panther and the Inspector from Blake Edwards' movie *The Pink Panther* (1963) for cartoons released through United Artists, King still had legal permission to animate the rock group for the distributor. Many gags from old cartoons abound as well. In one scene a cigar explodes in a character's face, and in another psychedelically designed Indians battle U.S. Cavalry soldiers emerging from the submarine.

The verbal humor in *Yellow Submarine* recalls the cartoons produced by Warner Brothers during the 1940s and '50s. Many of those cartoons feature inside jokes about the stars of the films and modernize story formulas in original ways. For example, after years of having Bugs Bunny say "What's Up Doc" to hunter Elmer Fudd, Warner Brothers added variety to the routine by having the two characters switch roles in *Hare Brush* (1955) and by constructing a seven-minute opera out of Fudd's pursuit of the bunny in *What's Opera, Doc* (1957). Similarly, *Yellow Submarine* features a character crying for help by shouting the lyrics from the Beatles's song "Help." Also, to poke fun at the group's signature "yeah yeah yeah" lyrical catchphrase, the Meanies answer all questions affirmatively by saying "no." This awareness by the studio of the musical trends set by the Beatles helps make *Yellow Submarine* a much more convincing imaging of the group than King's *Beatles* series.[12]

The film's storytelling via the soundtrack similarly updates one of the oldest techniques of animation for the Vietnam War era. Before studios first made sound-synchronized cartoons in the 1920s, animators had timed their drawings to songs and had developed gags from the lyrics. In the early twentieth century, cartoons tended to have nineteenth century minstrel songs as centerpieces. Although *Yellow Submarine* exploits "head" tunes by the Beatles instead of tunes glorifying slavery and insulting African Americans, many of the techniques of imaging music are similar. When lyrics appear on screen, *Yellow Submarine* distorts the words in some of the same ways that Max Fleischer had done for the songs in his theatrical "Screen Songs" cartoons (1928–37). In both cases, letters shrink, enlarge, and transform into objects. The only difference is that King also used Technicolor to play with the words, whereas Fleischer only made black-and-white episodes.

Although the band's music had matured beyond the love songs of the mid–'60s, King made *Yellow Submarine* very attractive to children. Many of the songs of the psychedelic music soundtrack catered to the sensibilities of minors. To be sure, the film showcases such complex songs as "Lucy in the Sky with Diamonds." However, others like "Yellow Submarine" and "When I'm Sixty-Four" have simple melodies and lyrics for juvenile viewers to enjoy. For example, "Yellow Submarine" expresses its theme of utopia in a repetitive chant-like chorus — very easy for children to follow. The movie's success led to a diverse array of toys displaying the cartoon's caricatures of the Beatles, and their sales boosted the band's marketability for the first time since Lennon uttered his infamous "Jesus" comment in 1966. The *New York Times* praised the movie as entertainment for everyone in the family to enjoy.[13]

Despite *Yellow Submarine*'s general message about love, the movie presents many images of warfare. At first, the people of Pepperland practice nonviolence, refusing to fight back when the Meanies attack. Then, when the Beatles arrive, they use not only their music but also physical force to battle the Meanies. For example, the group members hit enemy figures over the head with apples. In addition, the aforementioned Cavalry-versus-Indian scene shows the Beatles engaging in military conflict; drummer Ringo Starr leads the officers into combat and returns to the submarine with arrows stuck all over his body.

The character Chief Blue Meanie is himself a product of an actual war. According to Heinz Edelmann, he devised much of the figure's personality by borrowing from Adolf Hitler. Edelmann studied old World War II-era newsreels of the Nazi dictator to use his gestures and mannerisms for Chief Blue Meanie. The character especially walks very similar to Hitler's stride in the old films.

The release of *Yellow Submarine* marked the last opportunity for the public to see a contemporary image of the Beatles as united, carefree hippies. In the movie, all of the members lived in the same house and, as in the television show, did not have wives or children. The soundtrack for the film consisted of apolitical songs, mostly about love. However, by the fall of 1968, the group had already started to splinter and become more socially conscious. For example, when recording "The White Album" earlier that year, each member worked more on individual tracks than on collaborative songs. Moreover, John Lennon had begun to write overtly political songs like "Revolution." He put his views into practice with his new partner Yoko Ono by demonstrating against human prejudice and the Vietnam War. *Yellow Submarine*, thus, captured the calm before the storm of dissension tore the group apart two years later.[14]

Few psychedelic images appeared on Saturday morning television cartoons in 1968. Unlike the theatrical cartoon industry, which allowed for isolated films on the counterculture like *Marvin Digs*, television networks wanted weekly series. However, the studios had yet to create hippie characters for the medium. They usually restricted "head" graphics to main-title sequences and hardly explored the values of the counterculture in those series. The opening to DePatie-Freleng's violent superhero program *Super President* presents flashing colors and the title of the series written in the trendy swirling lettering. Meanwhile, Hanna-Barbera's *The Wacky Races* has a unique opening of cars driving in front of a screen filled with multiple writings of the show's title in shapeless fonts.

Ironically, the characters who most closely espoused the utopian rhetoric of the Beatles in *Yellow Submarine* looked the least like the group. In the fall of 1968, Filmation adapted the stars of Bob Montana's comic strip *Archie* to animation. The characters dress conservatively; the closest of the cast to resemble a nonconformist is Jughead, who slouches and always has his eyes halfway closed. Also, most of the music that the cast performs (as the Archies) is typical fare about budding romance. However, some exceptions, such as the lyric "The lesson for today is love," echo the sentiment of "All You Need Is Love." Filmation visually complements the tunes with flashing colors and scenes of flowers and hearts sliding across the screen.

The Archie Show can be best described as a "bubblegum cartoon" for reasons transcending the genre of the music the series promotes. "Bubblegum music" of the late 1960s and early '70s was a popular style that had complex production arrangements beyond the typical rock ensemble (drums, lead guitar, bass guitar, and vocals). However, the lyrics were apolitical, unlike the year's "soul" songs of black pride from the Impressions and James Brown or the antiwar music of Jefferson Airplane and the Beatles. Similarly, Archie and his friends do not hit each other over the head or blow each other up, unlike the slapstick theatrical cartoons or televised superhero series. Nor do the characters discuss the political topics of race and war, as in the Hubleys' cartoons of the early '60s. Indeed, the inoffensive content of *The Archie Show* lies somewhere in the middle.

The music of the series especially helped Filmation to modernize an otherwise anachronistic series. Archie had originally emerged during World War II and starred in milquetoast adventures on the homefront in high school. Filmation left the comic-strip format alone and even had the students "hang out" at a malt shop after school. In addition, while the female characters wear the fashionable mini-dresses of the '60s, the male figures wear clothes from the '40s. As clean-cut teenage figures, the boys contrast with current long-haired "teen idols" like actor Bobby Sherman or musician Davy Jones. However, the series takes on a contemporary feel primarily when the cast comes together as the rock group the Archies and "performs" songs by session musicians. The characters play modern instruments like the electric guitar and keyboard, and their songs sound like those of contemporary "pop" radio.

Still, Archie and his friends are hipper in their comic book appearances than on television. In addition to depicting the teenagers as a rock band, the periodicals feature the characters in contemporary clothes. In contrast, in the ten years that Filmation produced animated adaptations of Archie, the studio never changed the wardrobe of the characters. Then again, studios rarely altered the clothing of their characters. *Yellow Submarine* was an exception, in that King gave the Beatle caricatures psychedelic duds instead of the uniforms they had worn through all three years of *The Beatles*.

Ultimately, Archie was a more appropriate Saturday morning cartoon protagonist that year than the Beatles were. The Archies' bubblegum sound better suited the typical cartoon-viewing age group. The psychedelic Beatles, in contrast, made songs too sophisticated for pre-teens. The Archies were more popular on television that year, too. As the teenager figures began a decade-long run on television, the 1968-69 season of *The Beatles*—consisting entirely of reruns—was the last for the series.

The year 1968 was also the last in which new theatrical Terrytoons cartoons appeared in theaters. With Ralph Bakshi's departure from the studio the previous year, remaining directors Art Bartsch, Cosmo Anzilotti, and Dave Tendlar moved away from urbanity for the studio's films that year. Tacitly admitting that no one but Bakshi effectively handled the

"James Hound" cartoons, the directors dropped the series to return to "Sad Cat"—now set in the suburbs—and the rural "Possible Possum." Moreover, in the wake of years of riots in cities like Watts in 1965 and Newark in 1967, romanticized city settings had briefly fallen from favor in Hollywood. Thus, the last Terrytoons cartoons dovetailed with trends in modern U.S. filmmaking and current social events.

In 1968 discourse about Disney cartoons had become political instead of artistic. Richard Schickel's new book *The Disney Version* changed how people viewed the films from Walt Disney Productions. Schickel represented the counterculture, lambasting the studio's messages, values, and imagery. For example, he disliked Walt Disney's formulaic filmmaking, considered the late filmmaker resistant to change, and claimed that Disney did not make artistic films. In contrast, the mainstream loved Disney. Readers either loved or hated the book—a metaphor for the polarization of the country over the Vietnam War at the time.[15]

Walt Disney Productions did not capitalize on all of the attention it received by releasing new animated films. The studio's only cartoon for that turbulent year was *Winnie the Pooh and the Blustery Day*. Released that December, it is an understated film starring A. A. Milne's popular characters; no slapstick appears, aside from the frenetic bouncing of Tigger. The cartoon is also typical of the studio's work of the 1960s, for it is longer than the usual seven-minute theatrical short and features off-screen narration. Some scenes and advertisements feature contemporary "head" imagery like psychedelic distortions of letters, but it is minor and does not terribly distract from the conservative tone of the film. Schickel unflatteringly likened the tone to that of a 1950s television situation comedy.[16]

As the year ended, U.S. animation entered a paradox. As people became critical of Disney's low-key and "wholesome" films, animation studios began producing the same kind of cartoon, or at least very nonviolent cartoons, in the wake of the rising domestic and foreign casualties of the Vietnam War. Animators sought to directly address social issues without alienating their juvenile and less politically knowledgeable audience. In the next year, they struck a balance by appropriating counterculture trends.

7

THE CARTOONS
OF 1969

A new motion picture ratings system, having its first full year of operation in 1969, affected filmmaking in the United States. The Motion Picture Association of America (MPAA) devised the ratings in order to counter the decline in theater attendance that had taken place in recent years. The new classification guidelines allowed more profanity, violence, and sexual content in films than the Hays Code had permitted. However, movie studios ran the risk of earning the usually unprofitable "X" rating for a film if the MPAA found it too explicit. Most studios, therefore, aimed at making movies within the guidelines of the "Parental Guidance Suggested" ("PG") or "Restricted" ("R") ratings; the latter designation prohibited minors from viewing the film without an accompanying parent or guardian. The theatrical animation industry, meanwhile, retained its family audiences from the Hays era by making cartoons for the "General Audience" ("G") rating, which meant that the cartoons contained a bare minimum of violence and no profanity or sexual situations.

The MPAA ratings made irreversible the differences in content between the theatrical cartoons and those for television. One aspect theatrical animation and television animation shared in common lay in their changes in content as a result of the assassinations and war-escalation of the previous year. For example, both kinds of cartoon studios set more films in domestic locales instead of foreign ones. Fewer theatrical shorts featured fisticuffs and bombs, especially for gags; however, some such content remained because the "G" rating for theatrical cartoons did not forbid them. Meanwhile, advertisers and network executives pressured television cartoon studios to cease production of superhero cartoons because of their scenes of fistfights and gunfire. The studios complied but adapted their successful story formulas promoting colonialism to nonviolent network standards. Instead of invading other countries to fight their corrupt leaders, figures now toured foreign lands and stumbled upon intrigue.

Feature-length cartoons offered some deviation from these patterns. The first animated theatrical movie from Mendelsohn-Melendez offers a very sophisticated allegory of the Vietnam War as of 1969. In *A Boy Named Charlie Brown*, the title-character wins a series of local spelling bees but loses the national one. However, Charlie Brown is not the typical "loser" cartoon character. Studios usually depicted animated losers as figures whose flaws lead them down destructive paths. Some imperfections like Daffy Duck's exaggerated cockiness are behavioral, while others such as the German pilot in the previous year's *Flying Circus* become losers because of their ethnicity. In contrast, Charlie Brown does not have any glaring flaws except nervousness. As a result, he is a more sympathetic loser. Also, his loss is not treated comically, for when he returns home from the big contest, his friends welcome him without teasing him. Previous television holiday specials starring the character contain a few scenes in which he experiences misfortune, but the movie is the first adaptation of Charles Schulz's comic strip to focus on Charlie Brown's hopes of winning and reality of losing. It had a timely message; as the United States stopped pursuing military victory in Vietnam in favor of a gradual withdrawal from the conflict, *A Boy Named Charlie Brown* assured audiences that a person could lose with dignity.

Throughout animation history, illustrators embraced various kinds of stylization. In the 1930s, realistic graphics from Disney were the standard. Then, in the '50s, United Productions of America (UPA) started the new trends of limited animation and flat-color backgrounds. The studios did not adopt another common type of stylization for most of the '60s. With cartoon facilities recently shutting their doors for good, the surviving cartoon producers had little incentive to experiment with their films. But before the decade ended, the next fad in cartoon graphics came from outside the animation industry.

Yellow Submarine and *The Archie Show* ushered in a wave of cartoons starring young adult musicians. To be sure, animation producers and television networks sought the success of the movie and the series by borrowing from them. Competing studios either found other rock groups besides the Beatles to caricature, or they hired musicians to make songs for phony groups not unlike the Archies. However, the cartoon bands did not look exactly like *The Archies*; for example, Filmation's rock-band interpretation of Franklin W. Dixon's stories of the Hardy Boys included an African American figure in the cast — the first in Saturday morning television animation.

In 1969 American animators adopted the designs and film techniques from movies and television shows about the counterculture. They had several mainstream works as models that year. *Easy Rider*— a movie about motorcycle-riding drifters — became a surprise-hit film. In television *Rowan & Martin's Laugh-In* reigned as the most watched series, and ABC-TV scored a new hit program with the underground "hippie cop" characters of *The Mod Squad*. Although animation, as usual, stumbled upon these visual trends after live-action filmmakers had, the cartoonists enthusiastically appropriated the gimmickry for their films. They, in fact, carried the torch of psychedelic filming after live-action Hollywood had started to tire of it.

Instead of adapting to "head" animation, the Disney studio told audiences that it was ahead of its time. Buena Vista reissued the feature-length cartoon *Fantasia* (1940). The film contains plenty of scenes involving transformations of figures and frequent color changes for backgrounds and characters. Borrowing modern slang to help the thirty-year-old movie appeal to a young generation, the studio promoted *Fantasia* as "the ultimate experience." However, it was a completely different film than *Yellow Submarine*. The soundtrack to *Fantasia* was classical music conducted by Leopold Stokowski, and the designs for characters and backgrounds were more intricate than the shapeless stylizations in *Yellow Submarine*. Nonetheless, the re-release of *Fantasia* was a financial success. Journalist David Rider reported that the film did "excellent business." In relation to the movie's attraction to the counterculture, he wrote, "I'm told that it [*Fantasia*] has been taken up by the hippies who, after a few drags on a marijuana fag, are drifting along to blow their minds on Bach and Beethoven."[1]

Another Disney film released in the same year as *Fantasia*'s reissue appealed to fans of avant-garde cartooning in a different manner. In *The Disney Version*, Richard Schickel lamented that Disney removed a talented director named Ward Kimball away from animation-related projects and that the studio had yet to implement some modern filmmaking touches as in *A Hard Day's Night* into its cartoons. The studio granted both of his wishes in 1969 via Kimball's theatrical short cartoon *It's Tough to Be a Bird*. Kimball had made another cartoon that deviated from Disney's usual look in 1953, when he designed *Toot, Whistle, Plunk and Boom* in the heavy stylization found in UPA's cartoons. Although the cartoon won the year's Academy Award, Disney did not approve of the style and discouraged Kimball from directing further films. With Disney dead, however, Kimball returned to animation. *It's Tough to Be a Bird*— the company's most overtly psychedelic film since *Fantasia*— pokes fun at the evolution of flight via numerous juxtaposed animation styles. Clips of older Disney cartoons and visible pencil sketches in otherwise inked figures exemplify such aesthetic clashes. The psychedelic tone of the film lies in its incoherence, unlike *Fantasia*, which employs more surrealistic imagery such as characters and backgrounds changing colors to the rhythm of music.[2]

It's Tough to Be a Bird was an atypical Disney short not only for its graphics but also for its cast and story. In the last few years before his death, Disney made animated films with established characters from literature, popular studio stars, and recognizable celebrity voices. By doing so, he broke no new ground in animation. Kimball's cartoon, however, stars a new figure — a bird — with the relatively unknown actor Dick Bakalyan voicing the character's narration of an original story.[3]

Kimball's offbeat methods of production and direction did not hinder the success of his film. To be sure, the lack of a "star" figure meant that the studio could only sell the cartoon to exhibitors on the strength of the Disney name — a strength now tested with Disney's death. However, *It's Tough to Be a Bird* won the year's Academy Award for Best Cartoon Short Subject. On the strength of this victory, Kimball used his directing style on major Disney projects over the next four years. Moreover, his films were often the only new images of Disney animation circulating in theaters or television for much of that period. Thus, his psychedelic filmmaking *was* Disney animation at the time.

Kimball's freewheeling approach appeared in films of other studios but with much less originality than *It's Tough to Be a Bird*. For example, Warner Brothers' "Cool Cat" episodes of the year borrow significantly from *Rowan & Martin's Laugh-In*. In *Bugged by a Bee*, for example, the tiger utters the show's catchphrase: "Sock it to me." Other characters from the studio had previously appropriated established catchphrases, such as rooster Foghorn Leghorn's "Pay attention, son," from comedian Kenny Delmar. However, the animators had always given the figures strong personalities of their own. In contrast, Cool Cat lacks a dynamic characterization.

In addition to gags, the format of *Rowan & Martin's Laugh-In* creeps into "Cool Cat." For the last episode *Injun Trouble*, the studio crammed numerous stereotypical jokes about Native Americans into six minutes. Many of the jokes consist of quick one-liners — not unlike those of the popular television series. To be sure, in the 1940s and '50s, director Fred "Tex" Avery often constructed cartoons with several brief gags. However, his gags were usually visual puns that defied cinematic conventions and stretched cartoon figures into unrecognizable forms. For example, in his film *Lucky Ducky* (1948), a dog is knocked down and lies on the ground with his upper body in a Technicolor background and the lower body among black-and-white scenery. No such invention appears in the "Cool Cat" cartoons of 1969, as evidenced by such tiresome puns as "pail-face" and the old "how" greeting.

The reliance on Native American generalizations in *Injun Trouble* shows that the "message film" genre that Warner Bros.-Seven Arts had embraced the previous year was merely a passing fad. In 1968 the studio's landmark *Norman Normal* had challenged the acceptance of racial humor in U.S. society. Now in 1969 the studio endorsed it in *Injun Trouble*. Thus, *Norman Normal* is more influenced by the input of Noel Paul Stookey, contracted by the studio to write and co-produce that one film, than by the studio itself.

On the other hand, *Injun Trouble* reveals how integral racial humor was to the existence of the studio. Back in 1930 the first cartoon ever distributed by Warner Brothers starred an African American caricature named Bosko. He survived until 1933, but the studio continued to draw humor from minorities. The studio held onto the one-dimensional Mexican figure Speedy Gonzales for an unusually long time for a minority character — fifteen years (1953–68). Thus, it is almost poetic for the swan song of Warner Bros-Seven Arts to contain racial jokes just like the debut had.

The references to *Rowan & Martin's Laugh-In* in *Injun Trouble* barely conceal the old story formulas that continued to plague the "Cool Cat" cartoons. To be sure, the "hunter-prey" focus and the co-star Colonel Rimfire were gone. However, Cool Cat followed in the footsteps of several cartoon characters in his final cartoon *Injun Trouble* by performing hoary jokes at the expense of indigenous Americans. Some of the gags dated back to cartoons of the 1930s. Even the title was unoriginal, for at least four other cartoons — including an earlier one from Warner Brothers — shared it. In addition, the slang made Cool Cat more of a hippie caricature than a hip character. One line from *Bugged by a Bee* was, "Are you kidding, baby? Baseball is my *bag*. It's not just a *happening*. It's my *thing*."

Closing for good in 1969, Warner Brothers Cartoons never managed to create inventive and irreverent films during the Vietnam War. To be sure, other studios in their waning years also failed to produce animated social satires, but Warner Brothers had established its own identity in the 1940s by making witty sociopolitical cartoons. The studio hit its stride during World War II by producing films about serious topics ranging from meat shortages and blackouts to the military draft. The writers effectively used popular catchphrases from radio and movies for cartoon characters but also developed sayings that also widely circulated. The studio also embraced swing music before it had mainstream appeal. In the 1960s, however, the cartoons lost their edginess. The few attempts at catchphrases like Colonel Rimfire's "Tally ho" did not register with audiences. The studio neglected to attempt to illustrate contemporary issues like urban poverty and the Vietnam War in a humorous context. The staff had stopped trying to adapt older characters to changing times and retired Daffy Duck and Speedy Gonzales in 1968. However, the studio still broke no new ground, for Cool Cat and other new characters performed the same slapstick jokes as their predecessors.

Theatrical audiences still embraced the Warner Brothers humor above that of other studios but wanted only the old cartoons. "Road Runner" cartoons were the most popular among exhibitors that year, which is unsurprising in the age of drifter flicks like *Bonnie and Clyde* and *Easy Rider*. Warner Brothers-Seven Arts Cartoons borrowed from its own heritage via *Rabbit Stew and Rabbits Too*. Director Robert McKimson reused several "Road Runner" gags from his former colleague Chuck Jones—substituting a fox and Rapid Rabbit for the coyote and the speedy bird. McKimson even recalled the Road Runner's "beep beep" chirp by having the rabbit honk a bicycle horn. The distributor eventually noticed that the "classic" cartoons fared better with exhibitors than the new releases. When the Kinney Corporation bought Warner Brothers-Seven Arts Pictures and renamed it Warner Brothers Pictures in 1969, the cartoon department did not survive the transition.

Likewise, a change in ownership of Metro-Goldwyn-Mayer (MGM) that same year left the "Tom and Jerry" cartoons lost in the shuffle. Kirk Kerkorian bought the film company and immediately started downsizing it. Thus, after 1969, MGM stopped distributing new "Tom and Jerry" cartoons. The series ended without having adapted to the cultural trends of the '60s. Although Tom Cat surfs in *Surf-Bored Cat* (1969) and Jerry Mouse plays a spy in *The Mouse from HUNGER* (1969), the stories for both films do not develop strong personalities for the cat and mouse. As a result, they are cartoons in which any small and tall figures could have starred—not just Tom and Jerry. The strongest attributes of the episodes are the scores by new music director Dean Elliott. His uses of the keyboard and electric guitar complement the topical stories of surfing and espionage.

Still, MGM did not help "Tom and Jerry" by releasing the violent episodes from directors Abe Levitow and Ben Washam as the public started to sour towards brutal animated slapstick. For example, the genre of espionage was dying in 1969. The television series *Get Smart* entered its final season, and the latest "James Bond" movie *On Her Majesty's Secret Service* (1969) performed worse than previous entries. However, MGM introduced *The Mouse from HUNGER* to theaters that year, which was one year after the television show it parodies — MGM's own *The Man from UNCLE* — was cancelled. In addition, the standard, violent humor in *The Mouse from HUNGER* contrasts with the public's backlash against militarism in cartoons. The episode features explosions from bombs and land mines, shots from guns, and the falling of a guillotine blade.

In many episodes MGM illustrates the folly of war via militaristic imagery. *The Mouse from HUNGER* features as many gags about the deployment of weapons as explosions from those munitions. Tom raises rifles, barbed wire, and land mines up through streets and floors — merely to try to destroy one small mouse. In *Catty-Cornered* two cats, separated by a wall, unwittingly attack each other while trying to catch a mouse. They start with flyswatters but end with grenades. One of the most foreboding warnings about war since *Guided Mouse-ille* (1967) is another futuristic cartoon: *Advance and Be Mechanized*. The latter film reuses some scenes from the former, which feature a robot cat chasing a robot mouse. The conclusion to *Advance and Be Mechanized*, however, consists of the robot cat and mouse rebelling against Tom and Jerry, respectively, and turning them into zombies walking like machines.

Surprisingly, MGM produced psychedelic animation that year by giving a twist to a routine story formula. In 1949, MGM started using clips of earlier cartoons to serve as the bulk of animation for a "new" cartoon. This kind of cartoon was cost-efficient, because it called for less new animation, which continued to climb in cost. *Shutter Bugged Cat* (1969) is such a film, in which Tom looks at old scenes of himself to study his mistakes in chasing Jerry. However, unlike other "cheater" cartoons, *Shutter Bugged Cat* plays with the footage by employing distorted images and sounds. In several scenes, new animation of figures is superimposed over the older clips. The frames of the film clips often flicker rapidly on and off in succession in order to create the illusion that Tom is watching them from his projector. In addition, the stock footage moves in reverse. Dean

Elliott's rock score correspondingly plays backwards, creating an uncharacteristically psychedelic effect in a "Tom and Jerry" episode.

Terrytoons also contributed to the shift in antiwar imagery, although the studio no longer made new films. Between 1969 and 1971, 20th Century–Fox theatrically released Terrytoons cartoons originally broadcast on CBS in the mid–'60s. Whereas "Hector Heathcoate" and "The Mighty Heroes" related to romanticized images of war when they first appeared on television in the early Vietnam War, the characterizations of these stars as flawed heroes were similar to those of such contemporary icons as Spider-Man or the Incredible Hulk of Marvel Comics. Meanwhile, after the Tet Offensive convinced more U.S. citizens to support peace in Vietnam instead of military victory, reissued "Astronut" episodes presented the peaceful coexistence of beings from two different planets. However, Marvel's heroes had emotional flaws, but Terrytoons's stars had a physical one — clumsiness. Also, the comic-book characters starred in serious adventures, but Terrytoons cartoons were comedies.

Walter Lantz made completely different films conveying antiwar sentiment, and they were ironically some of the most violent cartoons criticizing militarism. His cartoons featuring unsuccessful military ventures in 1969 corresponded to the growing aggressiveness of antiwar protests in the late 1960s. In some "Chilly Willy" cartoons, military caricatures stationed in polar areas disrupt the penguin's life. In *Project Reject*, a pilot burns his home with jet exhaust. The penguin retaliates by bombing the military headquarters. His sabotage of the government facility appeared in theaters as demonstrators picketed draft boards and various army, naval, and air force bases across the country. In the following year, real-life antiwar violence mirrored cartoon content when students bombed the Sterling Hall building of the University of Madison at Wisconsin, killing one. They had intended to destroy the facility's Army Math Research Center.

Not all of Lantz's films contained such anti-government content. For example, he took Woody Woodpecker in a new nonviolent direction in 1969. The producer returned Woody's old nemesis Buzz Buzzard to the series after fifteen years. Buzz had started as a gun-toting western outlaw in 1948 and played other sinister roles like pirates and highway robbers into the 1950s. When Lantz revived the character, however, he revamped Buzz as an urban confidence artist. This characterization had appeared in comic-book adaptations of "Woody Woodpecker" by the Dell and Gold Key companies throughout the '50s and '60s. Woody's comic adventures were typically milquetoast in comparison to the animated cartoons because of a heavy emphasis on dialogue. Buzz's new mellow demeanor is a perfect fit to the cartoons, because by 1969 they too are laden with dialogue and milquetoast because of parental complaints about violence.

In 1969 DePatie-Freleng overhauled its theatrical product but linked the new series to the old ones by reusing tried-and-true militaristic gags. The "Pink Panther" series went on hiatus for two years, but "The Inspector" never came back. Joining "Roland and Rattfink" were two "chase cartoon" series: "The Ant and the Aardvark" and "Tijuana Toads." These series carry the torches passed by "Tom and Jerry" and "Speedy Gonzales" via the content of long chase scenes punctuated by fistfights, explosions and gunshots. However, DePatie-Freleng's cartoons differ from the older films, because due to rising costs in animation, these new characters talk more in their films than their predecessors had.

The unpopularity of the Vietnam War affected how DePatie-Freleng depicted Mexicans in the "Tijuana Toads" series. The studio used colonialist imagery in the first film *Tijuana Toads*. As a result, the cartoon shares more with the "Speedy Gonzales" episodes than the Mexican stereotypes of sombreros, laziness, and the expression "Holy *frijoles!*" In the first episode, a Texan grasshopper beats up Mexican frogs on their own land. This "ugly American" insect behaves similarly to Sylvester Cat and Daffy Duck — American characters imposing themselves upon Mexican mice to the point of physical harm. Further episodes lack this imagery. Responding to the audience fatigue toward films in which American characters overpower foreign characters, especially those of color, DePatie-Freleng instead switched the focus of the "Tijuana Toads" cartoons away from cultural clashes and towards the interplay between the bossy, overweight Toro Frog and his skinny pushover friend Pancho Frog.

The studio blended old and new modes of cartooning for its use of celebrity caricature. The film *Tijuana Toads* draws from John Wayne for the grasshopper's characterization. Wayne was known as a right-wing, pro–Vietnam War figure, which makes his personality appropriate for the colonialist insect. To be sure, studios had caricatured Western stars for years; Warner Brothers played Bugs Bunny as a Gary Cooper-type against Yosemite Sam on several occasions. However, the parody of Wayne was unique to animation. In *Tijuana Toads* his image is of a Texan who cannot handle Mexican food. The characterization is on par with guest appearances the actor made on *Rowan & Martin's Laugh-In*, which mercilessly tweaked his "tough-guy" persona.[4]

Meanwhile, in the "Pink Panther" film *Pink-a-Rella*, Elvis Presley is caricatured for the first time without any references to his songs or to rock music at all. He is lampooned as a celebrity. By this time, he had become a movie star and only recently returned to music. He also became politically conservative, which may contribute to the lack of mean-spiritedness in his new animated representation. The days of the rocker depicted as a loud, pompadour-topped guitar-strummer were long gone.

Before shelving "Pink Panther" in late 1969, the studio produced an episode that corresponds to the theme of violence-as-survival in *Bonnie and Clyde* (1967). Just as the poverty-stricken Parker and Darrow shot people in order to rob banks, the cartoon *Extinct Pink* focuses on four figures trying to kill each other for one bone to eat. In addition to stealing the bone from each other, they roll boulders and chop down trees towards one another, and they strike each other with mallets. However, one major difference between the films is that Bonnie and Clyde become victims of the violence they inflict on others. The cartoon characters do not suffer as much from their brutality towards one another as from their disunity. While fighting for the bone, they lose it entirely.

Thus, *Extinct Pink* shares *Bonnie and Clyde*'s unhappy theme for an ending. To be sure, Bonnie and Clyde are shot dead in one film, and the cartoon characters accidentally drop the bone into an alligator's mouth in the other film. The cartoon concludes with the quarrelers still hungry. Still, both films illustrate the moral that violence does not yield long-term constructive results. On the heels of the backlash against both the Vietnam War and animated physical confrontation, the message in *Extinct Pink* is very relevant.

Another DePatie-Freleng cartoon, the "Roland and Rattfink" film *The Deadwood Thunderball*, borrows from *Bonnie and Clyde*'s theme of survivalist violence. In the cartoon stagecoach owners hire Rattfink to hijack a new locomotive driven by Roland. Upon accepting the offer, Rattfink revealingly sneers, "There's only one reason I stoop to these lowdown schemes. It keeps me off welfare." Thus, in contrast to most of the other entries of the series, the character has a motivation for a life of brutality and crime.

In addition, Rattfink's "welfare" statement is timely. The United States had just elected Richard Nixon to the presidency the previous year. In so doing, U.S. citizens rejected opponent Hubert Humphrey — a liberal politician in the tradition of President Franklin Roosevelt, whose New Deal policies had created the dole. Also, the media increasingly reported the rise of illegal drug sales and the dire conditions of urban areas in the late 1960s. Rattfink's comment symbolically acknowledges that a significant number of people view criminality as a viable alternative to welfare.

Through that series, DePatie-Freleng became the first studio to use "flower children" to illustrate war. Heretofore, hippies were characters in stories that offered no direct commentary on war. In contrast, the "Roland and Rattfink" episode *Hurts and Flowers* satirizes the domestic division over the Vietnam War. Rattfink embraces conflict but is frustrated when he fails to antagonize the hippie Roland to fight him. A political cartoon, *Hurts and Flowers* preaches that violence leads to self-destruction; Rattfink literally kills himself trying to stop Roland from spreading flowers. However, the film also professes that "flower power" is not the answer, either, because no amount of flowers from Roland can stop Rattfink from hating him. This pessimism toward the idea of a hippie utopia runs counter to United Artists' film *Yellow Submarine* (1968) as well as DePatie-Freleng's own *Psychedelic Pink* (1968). As a result, the writer of *Hurts and Flowers*, John Dunn, bit the hand that fed him.

Dunn's *Hurts and Flowers* satirizes the counterculture but in a much different manner than in the stories in *Psychedelic Pink* by Jim Ryan, who had left DePatie-Freleng by 1969. Instead of drawing gags from psychedelic graphics, Dunn poked fun at the philosophy and lifestyle of hippies. Surrealistic imagery such as swirling colors and flowers is very minimal in this film. Rather, the film employs the traditional Warner Brothers humor of action-based gags. *Hurts and Flowers* exaggerates Rattfink's anti-counterculture sentiment by having him shoot one of Roland's flowers with a pistol. On the other hand, the cartoon caricatures pacifism by making Roland respond to each blow from Rattfink not only with a smile and a flower for him but also without confronting the bully about all of his attacks.

In addition, *Hurts and Flowers* superficially addresses drug abuse. The references to characters becoming "high" provide novelty to otherwise routine physical humor. The first drug-related scene draws humor from fisticuffs. The blurring of the camera's focus symbolizes Roland's entrance into an aggressive "trip" after having sniffed a strange gas. He transforms into a hate-filled character and pummels Rattfink to a pulp. Another joke about drug usage is a pun serving as a punchline to an old setup in filmed comedies. In the climax of *Hurts and Flowers*, Rattfink, while carrying nitro glycerin, falls after slipping on a banana peel. After the container of nitro glycerin falls on him and explodes, a hippie bystander declares, "Man, like, he had a bad 'trip.'"

By the time of the release of *Hurts and Flowers*, drug-related humor had entered family entertainment. The television show *The Smothers Brothers Comedy Hour* (1967–69) had paved the way. However, the series had to be clandestine in order to do so. In the recurring skit "Share a Little

Tea with Goldie," the program satirizes homemaking shows by having a female hippie (played by Leigh French) make humorous references to drugs in the slang of the day. Censors later edited the jokes after discovering the coded language of the program's writers. The "trip" reference in *Hurts and Flowers* is tame in comparison to the one-liners cracked by Goldie. Thus, DePatie-Freleng failed to fully capitalize on the new topic of humor pioneered by the Smothers Brothers.[5]

The music in *Hurts and Flowers* perfectly complements the cartoon's blend of counterculture characters and old-fashioned gags. Doug Goodwin, DePatie-Freleng's new music director, played melodramatic piano melodies in the fashion of silent-movie music whenever Rattfink harmed Roland. However, other scenes involving Roland have the organ or sitar — frequently used instruments in psychedelic rock songs — as background music. Meanwhile, the electric guitar and drums are prominently featured throughout the score.

Hurts and Flowers is an anomaly among the "Roland and Rattfink" episodes. It is one of the few films in which Roland does not deliberately fight or contest Rattfink. Also, whereas other entries show Roland feeling a wide range of emotions, he is constantly happy in *Hurts and Flowers*. It is also the only "Roland and Rattfink" film without dialogue, except for the hippie's "trip" line. Despite these exceptions, United Artists used the cartoon to promote the series. The distributor's advertisement for the cartoon releases of 1970 features a grinning Roland in the same turtleneck sweater he wears in *Hurts and Flowers* and holding a flower in his hand. The advertisement was misleading, however, for *Hurts and Flowers* is the only cartoon to cast Roland as a hippie.

Hanna-Barbera followed DePatie-Freleng's lead in giving a starring role in an animated cartoon to an antagonistic character bent on mayhem. In *Dastardly and Muttley in Their Flying Machines*, Dastardly — bearing a similar handlebar mustache to Rattfink — tries to stop a carrier pigeon from carrying out missions. Hanna-Barbera's series even employed World War I imagery, just as "Roland and Rattfink" had done in *Hawks and Doves* (1968). A major difference is that Hanna-Barbera created an animal sidekick for Dastardly — a dog serving as comic relief by snickering at his master's failures. DePatie-Freleng, in contrast, presents Roland and Rattfink's fights as pure "good versus evil" without the crutch of comic animals, except for a horse in *The Deadwood Thunderball*.

Both Dastardly and Rattfink represent the lack of progress concerning U.S. military activity in Vietnam. The characters do not fail because of the strength and cleverness of their opponents. The pigeon and Roland do not actively seek to harm their antagonists and are, thus, sympathetic for merely minding their own business. Thus, Dastardly and Rattfink can rightly claim, as a U.S. colonel once told a North Vietnamese military official, that they were never defeated on the battlefield. Instead, these Vietnam-era antagonists are victims of their own mistakes, especially when taking militarism to extremes.

Dastardly and Muttley was one of the last television cartoon series to feature gags resembling those of theatrical cartoons. After 1969, cinema screens and television screens presented completely different kinds of characters and exploited their own genres. The "chase scenes," explosive props, and the plots set in wars appeared in new films from Lantz and DePatie-Freleng and old entries from Terrytoons. Television animation studios, meanwhile, abandoned funny animal characters with bombs in favor of human figures wearing contemporary fashions, performing rock songs, and driving in psychedelically painted vehicles.

These counterculture touches first appeared in the most successful of the new shows: *Scooby-Doo, Where Are You* (1969–72). Although young, the characters do not have on-screen parents. The adolescents solve their own problems and catch villains without needing the assistance of adults. After the series became a hit with viewers, Hanna-Barbera and other studios created several derivative shows featuring teenagers accidentally finding trouble while traveling on the road. In addition, other series starring Scooby-Doo followed. None of the programs, however, achieved the success of *Scooby-Doo, Where Are You*.

The character Shaggy from the series is the closest approximation to a hippie in Saturday morning animation. Ironically, his characterization hearkens back to the 1950s. He looks and behaves like the beatnik character Maynard G. Krebs from the live-action situation comedy *The Many Loves of Dobie Gillis* (1959–63). Both are goateed nonconformists. However, Shaggy's lack of conformity is superficial: long hair and an untucked shirt. The only subtlety in Shaggy's radicalism lies in his name. While the other characters have the names Fred, Daphne, Velma, and Scooby-Doo, only the name Shaggy is descriptive. When identified in each episode, his name draws viewers to his unique appearance.

Despite his superficiality, Shaggy is still a notch above previous animated beatniks and hippies in terms of characterization. He is not funny solely because of his looks. Rather, he has peculiar quirks, too. He indulges in his voracious appetite for food. He is a master of voices and disguises, especially when confronted by ghosts. Also, he avoids hard work as much as possible, proudly admitting how afraid he is to look for ghosts. His more substantial personality shows a softening by the animators towards the counterculture. Here, Hanna-Barbera were able to do with him what Ralph Bakshi did not do with Marvin of the Paramount cartoon *Marvin Digs*—develop a convincing hippie character within the limitations of family entertainment.

In addition to popularizing counterculture signifiers, *Scooby-Doo, Where Are You* also serves as the last original cartoon series on Saturday morning television to score huge ratings. By the time of its debut, series starring characters created by the studios themselves had become a rarity. When the '60s began, television animation had started with such promising, unique characters as Jay Ward's Rocky and Bullwinkle. But then the popularity of *The Beatles* and *The New Adventures of Superman* lured studios to license established properties for animation.

To make room for *Scooby-Doo, Where Are You* and other new teenager-cast series, the networks moved their most violent programs from Saturday mornings to Sunday mornings. For the 1969-70 season, CBS-TV placed *The New Adventures of Superman* and *The Adventures of Batman* in the new day. ABC-TV did the same with its superhero series *The Fantastic Four* and *Spider-Man*. None of these shows survived past the end of the season.

Still, *Scooby-Doo, Where Are You* is not far removed politically from Hanna-Barbera's funny animals of the early 1960s. This new series has the theme of "law and order," which corresponds not only to a major component of Richard Nixon's successful campaign for president the previous year but also to the maintenance of the status quo in old Hanna-Barbera shows like *Wally Gator*. The major difference between both kinds of programs is in the actions of the protagonists. In *Wally Gator* the title-character always schemes to disrupt the status quo by leaving the zoo for freedom. In contrast, the teenage detectives actively seek to restore order after various people disguised as apparitions and monsters cause chaos.

In addition, the television cartoons of 1969 are similar to those of the start of the 1960s. Superheroes, funny animals, music offerings, and theatrical packages still comprised the animated offerings to viewers. *The Bugs Bunny Show* and *The Bullwinkle Show* were yet airing on network television although in perpetual reruns, and *The Archie Show* bore a striking resemblance in format to *The Alvin Show*. While trends remained fairly consistent over the decade, some of the older funny animals and slapstick characters had gradually lost their viewers. *Underdog* and *The New Casper Cartoon Show* disappeared at the end of the 1969-70 season.

On the other hand, studios animating licensed characters ran the risk of having critics note the popularity of the figures instead of commenting on the merits of the animation. When the rock song "Sugar Sugar" by session musicians billed as the Archies became a hit, the group's producer Don Kirshner received all the glory. Filmation, who animated the series that promoted the song on television, hardly received any notice. The *New York Times* did not examine the characterizations or animation of the Archies. They were mere drawings without feelings, thoughts, or complexity. The group "doesn't exist" but is rather a "nongroup." The article congratulated Kirshner for his savvy use of the medium of television to promote his music. Months later the periodical *Variety* related Kirshner's musical exploitation in *The Archie Show* with his work on *The Monkees*. This article also concentrated on the formula of creating a studio group to make songs for both television and radio airplay.[6]

The cartoons of 1969 proved that the counterculture aesthetic could not save animation studios from its creative slump. Rather, tried-and-true formulas kept studios afloat. Lantz, after all, did not survive into a sixth decade of independent cartooning by being trendy. In the '50s he had refused to animate in 3-D and for the wide-screen process CinemaScope. At the same time, he also avoided making artsy stories of the UPA variety. By taking few risks, he won no Academy Award nominations during the Vietnam War. However, he was still in the business of theatrical short cartoons at the end of 1969, whereas MGM — the Oscar winner for *The Dot and the Line* — and Warner Brothers — nominated for four cartoons in the first two years of the war — were defunct. Still, children's tastes were changing, and Lantz struggled to keep his old characters relevant in the 1970s. After all, as the new decade began, the "Woody Woodpecker" theatrical series turned thirty years old, and "Chilly Willy" became fifteen. Meanwhile, television studios in search of new characters learned not to prioritize originality. Hanna-Barbera especially began to prioritize cashing in on the most profitable and hip names in U.S. entertainment by adapting them to animation, whereas Filmation merely continued to exist as a licensing studio — not having a completely original series for another three years.

8

THE CARTOONS OF
1970–1971

Although the United States continued to pull out of the Vietnam War as the 1970s dawned, the war and civil rights issues presented new frustrations to U.S. citizens. In spring 1970, after a brief lull, fervent antiwar activism resumed when President Nixon broadened U.S. ground troop placement beyond South Vietnam into neighboring Cambodia. Meanwhile, communities across the country debated over the practicality of busing black children to white schools and vice-versa in order to achieve racial balance in the institutions.

In 1970 and 1971, diverse opinions on the war filtered into American popular culture. Americans demanded it after years of escapist entertainment that shied away from illustrating domestic problems. Contemporary music drifted away from psychedelic, utopian messages to blatant antiwar rhetoric. Edwin Starr's "War" and Freda Payne's "Bring the Boys Home" were among the top-selling singles of this period. Movies alternated between patriotic, pro-military films like *Patton* (1970) and copycats of *Easy Rider*. Meanwhile, on television, audiences watching the situation comedy *All in the Family* (1971–79) on CBS-TV chose whether to side with the conservative bigot character Archie Bunker or his longhaired liberal son-in-law Mike Stivic over social issues like racial integration and the Vietnam War.

The emergence of relevance in popular culture further drew a wedge between theatrical and television animation. Theatrical shorts stuck with slapstick but offered more political commentary than in recent years. In contrast, television cartoons were apolitical yet trendy. They exploited contemporary music and cast already established characters in nearly every new series of the 1970-71 and 1971-72 seasons.

The only contemporary issue that television cartoons addressed more seriously than theatrical cartoons was racism. The short films from DePatie-Freleng and Walter Lantz in 1970 and 1971 completely avoided the subject. Both studios were content in continuing Latino, Asian American and Native American stereotypes and leaving African American figures out of cartoons. For example, DePatie-Freleng introduced the "Tijuana Toads" series, which stars sombrero-topped frogs speaking like Speedy Gonzales, for the 1969-70 season. In contrast, for the 1970-71 season, television studios offered more series with African American main characters but shunned the other ethnic groups of color. These programs did not comment directly upon the topic of racism. However, the ways in which animators developed black characters and in which writers constructed stories revealed specific political viewpoints on the issue.

In 1971 the "Tijuana Toads" series picked up where the Daffy Duck–Speedy Gonzales films of the mid–1960s ended. In the previous year, the studio had mostly pitted Mexican antagonists against the frogs. However, the new episodes feature some *gringo* figures, not unlike Sylvester Cat and Daffy Duck chasing Speedy in Mexico. The cartoon *Snake in the Gracias* features two such characters — a clumsy yellow crane and a lisping blue snake. In many cases the American characters provided opportunities for the studio to reuse stories from previous films. *Croakus Pocus*, in which a sorceress chases the toads, recalls pairings of Bugs Bunny with Witch Hazel in *Broomstick Bunny* and other cartoons. These episodes continue the anti-colonialist theme that DePatie-Freleng promoted throughout the duration of the Vietnam War, for the toads usually outsmart the American figures after their own interests in Mexico.

As Mexican imagery languished, new and bold statements on African American characterization came from an unlikely source in the fall of 1970. On the heels of Filmation's success with *The Hardy Boys*, Hanna-Barbera broke from traditional means of caricaturing blacks by developing unique personalities for animated black figures. Ironically, when they were directors of shorts at MGM in the 1940s and '50s, the team had relied heavily on jokes concerning the "mammy" stereotype and explosions leaving characters in blackface. Hanna and Barbera stopped making fun of African Americans when the pair formed their own studio in 1957 but only offered images of animals and white people for the next thirteen years. Hanna-Barbera finally returned to black representation for the series *The Harlem Globetrotters* and *Josie and the Pussycats*. Hanna-Barbera did not create the

African American figures of these series; they were licensed from others. Still, the studio adapted the characters to animation without the broad stereotypes.

Hanna-Barbera had few precedents as models for *The Harlem Globetrotters*. The first network television series with African American leading characters since the cancellation of *Amos 'n' Andy* in 1953, did not debut until 1968, but even that show —*Julia*—featured more white regular characters than black ones. The next such show — an all-black, sitcom adaptation of Neil Simon's play *Barefoot in the Park*— lasted only one season (1970-71). A basketball team had never been the focus of a comedy series. In addition, cartoon studios had previously poked fun at the sport for six-minute shorts, not for half an hour.

The Harlem Globetrotters emerged when frequent images of blacks on television were of civil rights demonstrators, soul singers, and soldiers fighting in the Vietnam War. In this context, audiences would not find the old stereotypes relevant, and civil rights groups like the NAACP would not accept them. "All we were concerned about was making a funny show," Hanna-Barbera writer Ken Spears recalled. "We did treat everything on the show with the utmost degree of respect." This respect involved developing characters in manners reflecting the social gains made by African Americans as of 1970, instead of hearkening back to the caricatures of the '50s. For example, avoiding accusations of minstrelsy, the studio hired black actors to voice the Globetrotters figures. An African American husband-and-wife team served as "instrumental and helpful" consultants to Hanna-Barbera. "There are things we cannot do," Spears remembered the couple saying. "We can't stereotype the ways that blacks are 'supposed to' sound like. Let the actors be themselves, and do not encourage them to sound 'too ethnic.'" He also said that they worried, "We didn't want the *Amos 'n' Andy* thing."[1]

Hanna-Barbera gave *The Harlem Globetrotters* especially special treatment by creating new personalities for the figures. Spears noted, "We talked to the players and managers and inserted traits of their characters into the show." This technique differed from the studio's standard approach of appropriating characteristics of proven cartoon stars and celebrities for their new figures. One of the voice actors in *The Harlem Globetrotters* was Eddie "Rochester" Anderson — a buzzsaw-voiced character-actor famous for playing Jack Benny's servant in radio, movies, and television. However, his voice was less raspy for the cartoon, and he played an energetic athlete instead of a lazy, sarcastic butler.[2]

The Harlem Globetrotters offered several new animated images of

African Americans to viewers until 1973. The plots of their cartoons often consisted of the Globetrotters catching crooks or defeating contraptions made by mad scientists. Even the scenes of the team riding on the bus was daring, for their driver was an elderly white woman named Granny. No television series had shown whites working for blacks. Moreover, while some viewers opposed scenes of integrated playgrounds on *Sesame Street*, the black Globetrotters and the white Granny traveled all over the country in the same bus. Somehow, *The Harlem Globetrotters* managed to avoid controversy for three years.

For *Josie and the Pussycats*, Hanna-Barbera, in Spears' words, "lifted the characters right out of the comic book," but developed a completely new animated African American female representation in the process. As in the magazines from Archie Comics, Hanna-Barbera's Pussycats are an integrated, all-female rock music group. Valerie, the black member, often uses her technological expertise to help the band and their crew to escape dangerous predicaments. No series on television — live-action or animated — had ever cast a black woman in a leading role as a scientific authority figure for white characters. In addition, before this series and *Julia*, African American women had only supporting roles as maids.[3]

Valerie's persona, although novel to animation, was not new to television viewers. She is somewhat derivative of the black electronics agent character Barney Collier of *Mission: Impossible*— a series from Paramount Television about agents stopping both national and international crime and corruption (1966–73). Actor Greg Morris played his character as unflappable and focused on his tasks, and voice actress Barbara Pariot did the same for Valerie. CBS, which aired both series, mandated the resemblance between the two characters. Spears remembered, "The character Valerie, they [CBS] saw her as a 'female Greg Morris'— a bright, young black girl."[4]

Another major similarity between Valerie and Barney lay in the Cold War tensions that they illustrated in their respective series. When the federal government escalated U.S. involvement in the Vietnam War, the agents of *Mission: Impossible* infiltrated foreign governments. By 1971, however, most Americans disapproved of continued U.S. combat overseas, and the program started shifting to plots involving domestic activities such as illegal drug syndicates. Likewise, in 1970, the Pussycats went to other countries. But two years later, with U.S. troops still fighting in Vietnam, all of the band's adventures took place in outer space, thus changing its genre from foreign intrigue to science fiction. The new series—*Josie and the Pussycats in Outer Space*— aired until January 1974.

Through Valerie, Hanna-Barbera made an extraordinary, political statement about images of glamour and sex appeal in 1970. She and her bandmates perform in skimpy uniforms onstage and wear miniskirts offstage. Her wardrobe deviates from the long, frumpy dresses worn by "mammies." More importantly, the animators gave her an "Afro" hairstyle, and never treated it as part of her character. Hanna-Barbera did not develop jokes at the expense of her hair, nor does the series ever explicitly address her skin color. By presenting Valerie as an attractive woman, the program challenges the notion of long, straight hair as the only kind of beautiful hair. The show also breaks from convention by placing the "Afro" in a context having nothing to do with African American militancy or left-wing politics. After all, the most televised woman wearing the hairstyle that year was Angela Davis, a Communist who was on the FBI's "Most Wanted" list for allegedly planning to kidnap prisoners in San Quentin and supplying the weapons that killed four people during the ordeal.

Like *The Harlem Globetrotters*, *Josie and the Pussycats* caused little stir in its four seasons on the air. People did not raise objections to the revealing outfits, the integration, or anything else in the series. However, Hanna-Barbera also failed to receive public accolades for their groundbreaking black images in network television. Spears for example, thought that the arrival of integrated animation was timely: "In those days, all of television was pretty white, but a black character in a cartoon was a natural evolution." To be sure, by 1970, audiences had grown comfortable to such non-servile images of blacks as nurses in *Julia* and teachers in *Room 222*. Also, newspapers only reported television cartoons when announcing their network debuts. As a result, as Spears recalled, "Nobody was coming out, saying, 'Yay, look what you're doing, you're breaking the color barrier.'"[5]

Another Hanna-Barbera series featuring teenage characters slightly differentiated itself from *Scooby-Doo, Where Are You* and *Josie and the Pussycats* through nonviolent representations of war. In 1971, the studio produced the program *The Funky Phantom*, in which a ghost of a U.S. citizen from the Revolutionary War era travels with adolescents across the country in a dune buggy. Ironically, the soldier-specter is the figure taking on Shaggy and Scooby-Doo's frightful nature, and he does not carry any weapons. His characterization was unique, for military officers had appeared in cartoons as brave, clumsy, and reluctant, but not afraid. *The Funky Phantom* demonstrates that debate about the war had not cooled, for the series equates pacifism with cowardice.

That same year the studio significantly drew from its own past in producing *Help! It's the Hair Bear Bunch*. Reviving the "survivalist animal" genre of the early Vietnam War, the program concerns a group of bears taking measures to improve their lot within their home the Wonderland Zoo. The show borrows from *Yogi Bear* in having bear protagonists struggle for agency within their place of social confinement, *Wally Gator* via the zoo setting as the place where the animals are kept, and *Top Cat* through the story formula of a gang using schemes to better themselves. As with all the previous cartoons, this new one also features human figures as the foils for the animals. But unlike recent cartoons poking fun at social protest, *Help! It's the Hair Bear Bunch* is unique in that the bears are successful in their efforts. As with Yogi Bear's status as a sympathetic protagonist engaging in antisocial behavior, the Hair Bears are also shown in a positive light. Their protests for such causes as more food are counterbalanced by the willingness of the bears to remain locked up and preserve the zoo's status quo.

Despite its in-studio predecessors, *Help! It's the Hair Bear Bunch* is also the product of a bygone television era. The story formula is similar to that of the live-action series *The Phil Silvers Show*. Daws Butler even approximated his voice to that of Silvers when playing the role of the bear masterminding the schemes. Hanna-Barbera tried to update the material by dressing the bears in counterculture apparel, some of which had become more mainstream in U.S. fashion by 1971. However, the series did not appeal to young cartoon viewers of the 1970s, born after *The Phil Silvers Show* ended its network run. The cartoon only lasted one year on Saturday mornings and later popped up on Sunday mornings for an additional season (1973–74).

Changes in audiences' tastes did not affect just television cartoon production. The animation industry's sensitivity towards complaints about violence in cartoons extended into theatrical releases starring military figures. In 1971 DePatie-Freleng constructed awkwardly censored images of the Armed Forces. The "Pink Panther" episode *Pink-In* contains clips from past series entries in order to illustrate the recollections an acquaintance describes in his letter to the panther. The film uses footage from *G.I. Pink* (1968), in which an Army officer inspects the cat's rifle. However, *Pink-In* deletes the scene's comedic climax, in which the gun fires into the serviceman's face. Instead, the inspector finds nothing wrong, and the panther merely returns to his barracks. Without another closing gag for the scene, the inclusion of the clip adds no humor whatsoever to *Pink-In*. By this time the "Pink Panther" cartoons of 1964–69 appeared on NBC-TV on Saturday mornings, and any new theatrical episode needed to be free of scenes of gunshots to characters' faces in order to air on television later.

The title *Pink-In* is also significant in that it suggests a less radical context for the language of leftist movements. Only four years earlier, NBC-TV had misgivings about airing a comedy show with the phrase "laugh-in" in the title because of its similarity to the protest tactic "sit-in." Now, in 1971, DePatie-Freleng's film title plays upon both the phrase "peek in" and the word "pink," and the hyphen separating "pink" from "in" gives the title a similar look to "sit-in," "teach-in," "love-in," and other hyphenated demonstrations ending with the word "in." By this time, activists staged fewer events as President Nixon withdrew more U.S. troops from Vietnam. Consequently, the civil rights and antiwar movements faded from media coverage.[6]

The studio also toned down militaristic gags in cartoons without representations of the Armed Forces. Very few films from DePatie-Freleng in 1970–71 have characters caught in explosions from bombs and land mines. In most of those cartoons, the aggressor is the victim because of his ineptitude in operating a weapon. The studio was very familiar with this formula, for it had produced the last episodes of the defunct "Road Runner" series, which also had the theme of faulty militarism via the coyote's mishaps with his explosive gadgets. In addition, as audiences increasingly objected to violence inflicted by characters upon one another, a figure hurting himself became the only means by which the studio could retain its traditional violent slapstick gags.

In contrast, the "Roland and Rattfink" episodes of this period comprise DePatie-Freleng's last presentations of gags involving combat. Only in this series did the studio show characters shooting at each other with guns, cannons, and other equipment. To be sure, most of the entries of this series take place outside of military battles. Bombs, mines, guns, and grenades do not even appear in a few of the films. Some of the new stories involve roller-skating, a college track meet, the Canadian Mounted Police, and a parody of Robin Hood. In some cases the studio shoehorned the characters into plots from older cartoons from other studios. *The Foul-Kin* (1970) concerned Rattfink's attempts to appease an elderly rich relative — the same premise of Walter Lantz's film *Skinfolks* (1964). Meanwhile, *A Taste of Money* (1970), which borrows the story of a man wooing a rich widow from Warner Brothers' *Honey's Money* (1962), does not even star Roland although the film is still officially a "Roland and Rattfink" cartoon.

In addition, good and evil become blurred in the latter episodes of "Roland and Rattfink." In *The Foul-Kin*, Roland feeds a selfish, wealthy relative to a pit of crocodiles for selfish and immoral revenge. In *The Great*

Overland Continental Cross-Country Race, Roland repeatedly strikes Rattfink after losing a race to him; Rattfink cheated to win. These films show that the Hays Code is dead, because the characters do not suffer consequences for their antisocial behavior. They are in the tradition of *Bonnie and Clyde* (1967). The last "Roland and Rattfink" cartoon, *Cattle Battle* is one of the few wartime cartoons that kill off both the "good guy" and the "bad guy."

Still, DePatie-Freleng did not completely abandon the original "good versus evil" format of the series. The studio produced at least one combat episode per year. *War and Pieces* (1970) consists of jokes involving cannons, as Roland and Rattfink attack each other at sea. In 1971, the studio set the cartoons in the Old West, in which the stars fire guns at each other from a far distance and toss explosive devices at one another. In *Trick or Retreat* (1971), Roland is a U.S. Cavalry officer shooting at Rattfink and Indians, and Rattfink helps the indigenous warriors attack Roland by purchasing rifles for them wholesale.

In addition to the traditional humor via bombs and bullets, *Trick or Retreat* borrows another old source of humor when illustrating peace negotiations as an exercise in futility. Back in 1949, Metro-Goldwyn-Mayer's cartoon *The Truce Hurts* concluded with animals fighting after having tried to abide by their own peace treaty throughout the length of the film. Over twenty years later, in *Trick or Retreat*, the Indians and Roland also fail to officially conclude their war. In the cartoon both sides negotiate in a tepee marked "Peace Conference," and they predictably share a peace pipe. However, the cartoon abruptly ends with an Indian accidentally filling the pipe with gunpowder, causing the pipe to explode in Roland's face. By this time, peace talks between North Vietnam and the United States had taken place for three years without any settlement in sight.

Trick or Retreat captures the political diversity of the U.S. Armed Forces in the waning years of the Vietnam War. In the early '70s, a growing number of soldiers co-opted some of the signifiers of antiwar protestors, marking peace symbols on their helmets or wearing beads. Other officers wanted President Nixon to resume bombing North Vietnam in order to convince North Vietnam through brute force to release U.S. prisoners of war, some of whom had been incarcerated for seven years by 1971. In the "Roland and Rattfink" episode, one minor character is a cavalry leader speaking like John Wayne, the star of the movie *The Green Berets* (1968) and an outspoken supporter of the Vietnam War. In contrast, Roland is a pacifist cavalry serviceman picking flowers and talking to birds and insects. At one point he even admits, "I don't like violence."

One of very few cartoons to feature an antiwar activist figure, *Trick or Retreat* taps into anti-activist rhetoric, which received more media exposure in 1970 and 1971 than in previous years. In April 1970, Vice-President Spiro Agnew likened antiwar demonstrators to the Ku Klux Klan and the Nazi Party, and he encouraged U.S. citizens to behave accordingly against them. Soon thereafter, patriotic counterdemonstrations increased, one of which climaxed with "hard hats" beating up young protesters. Meanwhile, on the aforementioned television series *All in the Family*, viewers could listen to Archie Bunker identify activists by such pejorative names as "pinko" and "commie." Similarly, DePatie-Freleng's cartoon equates antiwar activism with cowardice. In the film an Indian burns his draft card because of his reluctance to fight the Cavalry. When confronted by a tribesman, the activist flees, crying, "Me Indian brave, but me not brave Indian."[7]

Through the joke about burning a draft card, DePatie-Freleng constructed a new depiction of an old characterization. During World War II, at least two cartoons featured war resisters. As in *Trick or Retreat*, Daffy Duck literally dodges his draft notice out of fear instead of moral conviction in the Warner Brothers Cartoon *Draftee Daffy* (1945). However, Warner Brothers makes the duck a sympathetic character by balancing his timidity with patriotism. Moments before receiving his draft notice, he cheers while reading newspaper accounts of battles and fantasizes about shooting at enemy soldiers. In contrast, the Indian's act of setting his card on fire manifests his hatred of war itself. As a result, *Trick or Retreat* makes the indigenous character unsympathetic towards the pro-war "Silent Majority." Ironically, by the release of *Trick or Retreat*, public card-burning demonstrations had sharply declined due to President Nixon's withdrawals of U.S. troops from the war and his efforts at draft reform. DePatie-Freleng, thus, gave the activists a parting jibe.

Walter Lantz's similarly "anti-hippie" film *Woody's Magic Touch* (1971) is unique among studio product because of the characterization. Few of his films satirize current events or trends in contemporary popular culture. By the 1970s his idea of relevant humor consisted of characters uttering such catchphrases from *Rowan & Martin's Laugh-In* as "Very interesting." Thus, the image of a hippie in *Woody's Magic Touch* is a welcome surprise. Still, the figure is a one-dimensional stooge in the tradition of beatnik characters in *Banty Raids* (1963) and *Drum Up a Tenant* (1963). He sports some stereotypical counterculture signifiers: scruffy beard, beads around the neck, acoustic guitar, striped bell-bottom pants, and no shoes.

In addition, Lantz's hippie is a socially powerless figure, reflecting the novelty of the counterculture in mainstream U.S. society as late as 1971. He needs Woody to rescue him from a witch who had turned him into a dragon. Like the Indian in *Trick or Retreat*, the hippie is unsympathetic because he voluntarily shuns any social power whatsoever. When identifying himself to Woody through song, the hippie brags about avoiding both work and responsibility. In addition, the film presents a generation gap and sides with the "Silent Majority." Woody derisively calls the character "Junior," implying the bird's seniority and the hippie's immaturity. Also, in the film's "comedic" climax, the hippie's father disowns him, and Woody changes the "flower child" back into a dragon.

The patriotic, anti-hippie cartoons of 1970–71 were among the last of a wave of militaristic movies from Hollywood at this time. From the mid–1960s to the early 1970s, movie studios produced several films recreating previous wars; World War II was the most frequent conflict of choice. One of the most popular features of this period was *Patton* (1970). President Nixon viewed the movie about the World War II general's life more than once while deciding whether to order U.S. troops to invade Cambodia. As studios began to use war as a setting for antiwar movies like the Korean War in *M*A*S*H* (1970), *Trick or Retreat* presented a final good-natured ribbing at militarism.[8]

Surprisingly, the Disney studio offered the most diverse images of the counterculture in 1970 and 1971. Before Walt Disney died, the studio had rarely developed stories centered on characters with liberal views and tastes. Ever since using rock-and-roll music for part of the music score for *A Symposium on Popular Songs* (1962), the studio had not integrated counterculture or youth culture into its films. The recent "Winnie the Pooh" films, moreover, suggested a shift in shorts production to a pre-pubescent market. However, in the years since Disney's death, the cartoonists were more willing to explore less conservative sources of characterization. On the one hand, the staff integrated references to slang words and costuming for the feature film *The Aristocats* (1970). In contrast, Ward Kimball capitalized on the success of *It's Tough to Be a Bird* (1969) by producing and directing the short film *Dad, Can I Borrow the Car* (1970) and the television series *The Mouse Factory* in a similar patchwork filmmaking style.

The Aristocats is a conservative film with mild psychedelic touches. The cartoon follows the studio's formula for success: cute juvenile characters, mentor figures who enjoy jazz, and the theme of social acceptance. Phil Harris, voicing alley cat Thomas O'Malley, sings Dixieland songs just as he had for the figure Baloo Bear from Disney's cartoon feature *The Jungle Book* (1967). The alley cats start the film living in a slum but relocate to Duchess's mansion in the end, not unlike Cinderella's transformation from her ragged clothes to her ballroom dress in the studio's *Cinderella* (1950). The only references to contemporary popular culture are flashes of colors and a figure of a cat wearing long hair, sunglasses, and beads.

The movie's images of the counterculture are far removed from their contexts. Although the film is set in the 1910s, the alley cats speak in slang of the 1940s and play "Dixieland" music. On top of these incongruities, *The Aristocats* inserts a musical number in which the cats perform against a backdrop of floating, swirling colors, giving the effect of strobelights in discoteques of the '60s. As the figures appear to rapidly change colors, they utter such contemporary phrases as "groovy" and "turn me on."

Even the character Scat Cat is an anachronism but of African American imaging instead of hippies. To be sure, he is voiced by black entertainer Scatman Crothers and vaguely resembles jazz musician Thomas "Fats" Waller. On the other hand, he is the only alley cat not named by his ethnicity. The others have names like "Chinese Cat" and "British Cat." Thus, the Disney studio, in creating the name "Scat Cat," makes music synonymous with African Americans. While a stereotypical association, the name is still an improvement over the studio's movie *Dumbo* (1943), which stars a bird named "Jim Crow."

Dad, Can I Borrow the Car, in contrast, is one of the least "typical" of the Disney studio's animated short films. It has the same mix of several different film techniques as *It's Tough to Be a Bird*. The cartoon is about a teenager's love for automobiles. However, Kimball illustrates the story through such curious means as clips of automobiles for earlier cartoons and a new live-action scene parodying used-car television commercials starring shifty pitchmen. In addition, the cartoon is more entertaining and less educational than the studio's films of recent years — especially the previous automobile-centered cartoons *Freewayphobia* (1965) and *Goofy's Freeway Trouble* (1965).

Disney made *Dad, Can I Borrow the Car* more youth-oriented than earlier cartoons in terms of production techniques as well as content. The teenager who wants a car narrates the film, as opposed to the father recalling the story about his son. Also, an adolescent actor voices the narrator — a contrast to the standard practices of having adult actors voice juvenile characters and having adults narrate films. The studio cast its own contract player Kurt Russell — the star of Disney's live-action hit movie *The Computer Wore Tennis Shoes* (1969) — as the teenager.

One year later the syndicated half-hour series *Mouse Factory* introduced Kimball's cartooning style to television audiences. Each episode focuses on a specific theme and is hosted by a guest star. Kimball integrated film clips with new animation and new live-action scenes featuring the guest host and one or more of the famous Disney animal characters like Mickey Mouse or Goofy, for example. The series lasted for two years.

By this time Chuck Jones at Metro-Goldwyn-Mayer (MGM) had warmed to psychedelic graphics. His "Tom and Jerry" cartoons contained attractive stylization but more in line with United Productions of America's films of the 1950s instead of more modern animated works. Then, he produced and directed *The Phantom Tollbooth* (1971)—the first feature-length cartoon made by Jones and distributed by MGM. In the story a bored little boy visits an abstract world.

Contemporary graphics notwithstanding, *The Phantom Tollbooth* is standard filmmaking from Jones. Throughout his career at Warner Brothers Cartoons, he made several films about a boy escaping to surreal environments. In *From A to ZZZ* (1954), a sleepy schoolboy daydreams of battling numbers on a chalkboard and imagines himself as a chalk figure. Jones used the same boy character years later for a similar story in *Boyhood Daze* (1957). And one of his last films for the studio, *Martian Through Georgia* (1962), concerns a restless Martian leaving his planet for the excitement of Earth. Thus, *The Phantom Tollbooth* recycles the familiar formula.

Unfortunately for Jones, *The Phantom Tollbooth* suffered from distribution mismanagement. Because the film contains animation, MGM marketed it as suitable fare for weekend matinees for children instead of a major motion picture. Critics were kind to the film. However, critical pleasantries could not save the movie. Shortly thereafter, Jones and MGM parted company. The producer/director started his own animation studio, but MGM released no further new cartoons before pulling out of film distribution entirely in late October 1973.

Cartoon producers Arthur Rankin, Jr. and Jules Bass brought the psychedelic animation of the cartoon feature *Yellow Submarine* to television via the series *The Jackson Five* (1971–73). The Rankin-Bass studio was not a likely candidate for popularizing such imagery, for in the 1960s it had a niche in television animation as a supplier mostly of successful puppet-animation holiday specials like *Rudolph the Red-Nosed Reindeer* (1964). As late as 1969, it had made a cartoon adaptation of the song *Frosty the Snowman*. Two years later the studio commissioned animators in the United Kingdom to make the episodes of *The Jackson Five*. Robert Balser, the animation director for the program, had worked on *Yellow Submarine*, and he employed some of the same graphics from the movie for *The Jackson Five*. The series presents the images in a different context than the movie does. The assorted swirls and colors visually complement inoffensive songs in the "bubblegum" genre about falling in love in *The Jackson Five*, unlike the more complex compositions about utopia and surreal worlds in *Yellow Submarine*.

The Jackson Five borrows from the Beatles in other ways having to do with animation. The program is similar to the *Beatles* cartoon show in terms of format. It is based on an actual musical group, and each episode features at least two entire songs from the band. In addition, the producers even hired Paul Frees to voice incidental characters, just as he had done in *The Beatles*. Thankfully, he did not voice any of the Jacksons, in contrast to his renditions of John Lennon and George Harrison for *The Beatles*. However, just as a white actor voiced the black character of *The Hardy Boys*, Frees did play Motown founder Berry Gordy in the *Jackson Five* episode "It All Started With..." and sounded nothing like him.

Also, like the Beatles, the Jacksons had an innocent image and sound that made them very marketable. In the early 1970s, Motown still prioritized apolitical music and did not want its singers to speak out on issues. Artists like the Temptations, Edwin Starr, and Marvin Gaye managed to record "message music," but Motown president Berry Gordy watched the Jackson Five more closely than he did the others (except Diana Ross) by then. Consequently, songs like "Ball of Confusion," "War," and "What's Going On" were off-limits to the Jacksons. The songs used in the *Jackson Five* episodes focused mostly on love relationships — a somewhat mature subject for the teenagers but illustrated innocently through the "bubblegum" lyrics. In addition to the group's exposure to young fans through the cartoon and "teen magazines" like *Tiger Beat*, the brothers also appeared in television commercials on Saturday mornings to promote breakfast cereal; Post Cereals was a sponsor of their series.[9]

Unlike *Josie and the Pussycats*, the Jackson caricatures are somewhat desexualized. The brothers had no female co-stars, whereas the Pussycats interacted with two male figures. To be sure, some episodes of *The Jackson Five* contain scenes of crazed girls chasing the Jacksons. The musicians also interact with various attractive black female characters ranging from princesses to a caricature of Diana Ross from fellow Motown singing group the Supremes. However, romance is not a focus of a story, unlike many of the *Beatles* cartoons. The Jacksons, after all, were teenagers; Michael Jackson, the youngest member, turned thirteen one month before the premiere of *The Jackson Five*. Also, before 1972, none of the brothers had married. Nevertheless, network television was more comfortable in presenting sexuality through black women than black men, at least in animation.

The Jackson Five enabled one British cartoon studio to return to prominence in U.S. animation. John Halas and Joy Batchelor co-owned and co-operated an animation unit. A studio for hire, Halas and Batchelor had started the Vietnam War period by animating "Popeye" episodes for producer William Snyder and director Gene Deitch in 1961. One decade later, the studio switched from fisticuffs and spinach to teenagers and bubblegum when Rankin-Bass farmed out animation assignments for *The Jackson Five* overseas. With the success of the series, Halas and Batchelor received more opportunities to animate cartoons for the United States.

The program also shows the decline of resistance by television networks to drug references and radicalism. Michael Jackson's pet mice are named after musician Ray Charles — a rhythm and blues singer who had suffered a heroin addiction until the mid–1960s. Charles also took a political stand against racism during that time, refusing to play for segregated audiences. In further evidence of the acceptance of actions once considered unconventional, the Jackson caricatures wear Afros. To be sure, the real-life brothers wore them, but few African American artists wore them as late as 1971; the Silent Majority still associated the hairstyle with black militancy. Even Flip Wilson, television's top comedian, did not have one before the following year. However, the number of blacks wearing an Afro on television increased, and the hairstyle took on diverse contexts. While the foreboding undercover "hippie officer" figure Linc had an Afro on *The Mod Squad* (1968–73), so did the middle-class character Lionel Jefferson on *All in the Family*.

The frenetic film style of *Rowan & Martin's Laugh-In*— still popular as the series entered its fourth year — finally entered Saturday morning animation in 1970 with *Archie's Funhouse* and *Sabrina and the Groovie Goolies*. Unlike *The Archie Show*, which consists of short cartoons and a musical number, an episode of *Archie's Funhouse* features three musical performances and numerous one-liners connected by brief sight-gags and live-action clips of children laughing ostensibly at the show. To ensure laughs from the jokes, Filmation hired writers from *Rowan & Martin's Laugh-In* to develop gags for *Archie's Funhouse*. *Sabrina and the Groovie Goolies* also borrowed from the popular live-action show but used monster figures like ghosts, werewolves and a Frankenstein caricature to deliver lines.[10]

Rowan & Martin's Laugh-In revived vaudeville, as the cartoon had done over a half-century earlier. Mickey Mouse and Bugs Bunny were vaudeville comedians. Robert McKimson and Chuck Jones — directors at the now-defunct Warner Brothers Cartoons — borrowed from famous vaudevillians when developing characterizations. They use broad gestures when talking or break into a tap-dance routine upon request. *Archie's Funhouse* and *Sabrina and the Groovie Goolies* connect animation to vaudeville by aping the freewheeling style of *Rowan & Martin's Laugh-In*. Archie and the Goolies, on the other hand, do not have that same vaudevillian spirit that older cartoon characters have. They rarely conduct themselves impulsively by spontaneously starting a dance, for example. Also, perhaps because the Archies and the monsters had existed in other formats, they appear as figures plugged into vaudeville.

The following year Filmation retained the chaotic style for a portion of each installment of the series *Archie's TV Funnies*. For two or three minutes, characters from the comic strip "Smokey Stover" exchange one-liners with each other. In between the jokes are cutaways to a cat ringing a bell or holding up a sign. However, this new program has a completely different format from the others. Stars of comic strips take up the bulk of each episode, thus showing that Archie and company cannot carry a series by themselves or attract viewers on their own. Also, the teenagers are the operators of a television station instead of a band; in fact, for the first time, no new music is promoted in the series.

In 1971 the comic-strip detective Dick Tracy returned to television animation in *Archie's TV Funnies* in a much less comic manner than in his previous series. Instead of the racially stereotyped figures of UPA's episodes from ten years earlier, Filmation brought the strip's supporting cast to the "Dick Tracy" cartoons. Also, as in Gould's stories, Filmation's "Dick Tracy" entries are set in a crime-filled city. Most of the urban scenery is recycled from the studio's recently cancelled "Batman" cartoons.

The new "Dick Tracy" episodes also mirrored the comic strip in adapting to public distaste for violence in child-related media. In recent years the strip had suffered a backlash from readers aghast at the graphic content of the daily panels. Similarly, Filmation's cartoons lacked the firepower of the UPA series. No officers carry guns in the new films. Also, the guns that villains use do not have bullets but rather ropes to bind people, heat rays to melt electric wires, and other gadgets.

The prominence of character Tess Trueheart in these stories also results from changes in animation during the Vietnam War. A photographer, she is also Dick Tracy's wife and accompanies him on adventures, going undercover and following his directives towards helping him catch crooks. Unlike other wartime female supporting characters like Olive Oyl, Lois Lane or Polly Purebred, Tess does not require a man to rescue her from danger. Her independence places her on par with the female leads of *Josie and the Pussycats*.

Another new series from Hanna-Barbera helped launch a nostalgia craze in television animation in 1971. The studio revamped one of its most successful properties — *The Flintstones*, which had left the air five years earlier. *Pebbles and Bamm Bamm* aged the tots from *The Flintstones* into adolescents and cast them in stories very similar to those from Filmation's various *Archie* programs. As a result Fred Flintstone and Barney Rubble have reduced roles in this program. The look to the past was on par with the current nostalgia trend in popular culture. Popular movies like *Summer of '42* and the aforementioned *Patton* were set in the 1940s, and the musical *Grease*— a "love story" set in the 1950s — started an off-Broadway run.

The popularity of bubblegum music in television animation peaked. Filmation continued to shine in 1971, when its series *Sabrina and the Groovie Goolies* spawned the hit song "Chick-a-Boom," credited to an artist named Daddy Dewdrop instead of the fictional Goolies group. Hanna-Barbera tried to duplicate its competitor's success by incorporating songs into chase scenes in at least four of its shows produced between 1970 and 1971. The studio even hired Don Kirshner away from the Archies to produce music for *The Harlem Globetrotters*. However, none of the tunes entered the music charts. Rankin-Bass, meanwhile, was content to animate already proven songs by the juvenile Motown group the Jackson Five.

The dominance of bubblegum music in animation differentiated Vietnam War animation from that of World War II. Nearly thirty years earlier, contemporary hit songs contained lyrics that rallied troops or the homefront. Animation studios frequently made references to them in music scores or as cartoon centerpieces. In contrast, the television studios were decidedly neutral about the Vietnam War. They avoided promoting songs that either criticized or supported the conflict or the troops. By 1971, U.S. animation was largely a medium targeted at children, who would not have the political biases about the war anyway.

Despite this trend Lantz unsuccessfully tried to spice up one of his established characters. Woody Woodpecker becomes sexual in *Coo Coo Nuts* (1970). The bird eagerly anticipates watching a "peep show," rapidly furrowing his brow and slyly smiling to the audience before entering. The scene is jarring, although the new movie ratings system is two years old by then. The studio had not established Woody as an overtly sexual figure before 1970. If anything, the tameness of his adventures and the high-pitched voice supplied by Lantz's wife gave the woodpecker more of a juvenile quality than an adult one.

Lantz's "Chilly Willy" is more like television shows than the latest "Woody Woodpecker" cartoons are. Chilly models appropriate behavior in most episodes, instead of stealing food for survival. The penguin talks in complete sentences. With rising animation costs, he had to do more talking than anything else; after all, animating only a beak was cheaper than animating an entire body. Chilly also gained a gang of friends, not unlike the gangs of *Scooby-Doo, Where Are You* and *The Archie Show*. The Chilly Willy of 1971 is a far cry from his first appearances of the 1950s as a thieving, mute character living alone.

When Lantz returned Chilly to his old ways in two cartoons from 1971, the studio could not decide in which context to place his illegal survivalism. In *Chilly's Hide-a-Way*, the bird lives in an abandoned house and successfully removes its owner from the premises, who has returned after years of neglect. On the other hand, in *Airlift a la Carte*, the starving Chilly and polar bear Maxie fail to steal fish from a general store. Lantz was more consistent when giving the bird good behavior; all of those episodes have Chilly experience happy endings as rewards for his moral conduct.

The cartoons of 1970 and 1971 reveal that animators had conflicting loyalties. They largely stuck to successful formulas in terms of plot and characterization. They also ensured the popularity of new projects by adapting established properties to animation. However, the artists also demonstrated a willingness to take risks concerning race and war-related politics. For the cartoons of 1972, the studios did not retreat from their bold, new direction.

9

THE CARTOONS
OF 1972

In 1972 U.S. animation entered a period of transition. The traditional means of exposing cartoons to audiences disappeared. Meanwhile, new markets for U.S. animation emerged. In addition, studios developed new ways to present the same violent gags. Old stars made their final appearances, and new characters started major, groundbreaking trends in characterization and story.

The deaths of notable pioneers in the animation business that year symbolized the entrance of U.S. animation into this transitional state. Max Fleischer, producer of "Betty Boop," "Popeye," and "Superman" cartoons, passed away in September. Warner Brothers also lost three of its previous animation giants: director Frank Tashlin, who introduced unique comical uses of camera angles to animation; Carl Stalling, the arranger of hundreds of cartoon scores over two decades; and writer Tedd Pierce. To be sure, when each of the aforementioned artists died, they had not worked on cartoons in years. Still, with their deaths, their contributions to the industry were gone forever.

West Coast theatrical animation was on its last legs. After over four decades of active cartoon production, Walter Lantz closed his studio. He was the only producer making cartoons exclusively for theaters by that time; his sole competitor — DePatie-Freleng Enterprises — made more films for television than for the movie houses. Thanks to the cheapened state of Lantz's animated films, durable characters like Chilly Willy the Penguin and Woody Woodpecker ended their runs with whimpers instead of bangs. The producer had gradually reduced his budget over the years, which led to more simplified designs and color schemes; he even started reusing music director Walter Greene's scores from previous cartoons. In addition to technological problems, Lantz tired of reducing the physical humor of his cartoons, and he did not earn his investment in each film until nearly twenty years after its release.[1]

The "Woody Woodpecker" cartoons broke little new ground in 1972. Lantz surrounded him almost exclusively with familiar co-stars and nemeses. The major exception was a new recurring sidekick mouse named Mousie. The rodent figure possesses a comic edge that Woody has lost by this time. He speaks in a manner suggesting an urban upbringing. He receives as much time on screen as Woody does, thus suggesting the diminishing appeal of the old bird. Nevertheless, as a new and unproven character, Mousie did not warrant official "co-star" billing. Woody is the only figure named in the opening sequences to the films in which Mousie appears.

Moreover, Lantz uses Woody Woodpecker to brag about the character's longevity as a *theatrical* star. While waiting for Mrs. Meany to load her gun in *Chili Con Corny*, the bird advises the cinema patrons, "You might as well go get some popcorn, folks, while 'Mrs. Dummy' here gets some more bullets." The woodpecker was the last character influenced significantly by vaudeville. In his films he wears white gloves and has an awareness of his audience. *Show Biz Beagle* further evokes vaudeville via setting and story construction. Part of the story takes place on a vaudeville stage. The dog, in the tradition of vaudeville, performs several different acts in one show.

The last cartoons by Lantz reveal his desensitization to violence during the Vietnam War. The final episode of Walter Lantz's "Chilly Willy" series contains some of the last images of warfare in theatrical animation. In *The Rude Intruder* the penguin fires a cannon at an oil tanker captain wanting to drill where the bird lives. The captain then retaliates by dropping a bomb from a plane. However, when attacked by the cannon, he merely has scratches on his body and torn clothes after the smoke clears. Such scenes illustrate the dilemma of studios, trying to animate traditionally militaristic activity in manners acceptable to parents of the viewers. While the lack of apparent injury shows viewers that the character is not hurt, it also romanticizes violence by suggesting that bombs do not really harm people.

The air raid scene especially demonstrates how nonviolent American animation had become over the course of the Vietnam War. In the conflict's early years, animation studios produced cartoons like DePatie-Freleng's

Suppressed Duck (1965) and *A Taste of Catnip* (1966), which feature images of bombs dropping on characters and buildings. In contrast, the bomb in *The Rude Intruder* bounces off Chilly Willy's catapult and explodes in the captain's plane. The captain, thus, suffers retribution for his militarism by becoming a victim of it. Lantz's film suggests here that aggressive actions lead to dangerous consequences. Still, the minimal damage to the pilot, although caught in both the bomb's explosion and the crash landing of his plane, minimizes the impact of the anti-militarism message.

In addition to criticizing violence, *The Rude Intruder* surprisingly embraces the left-wing political concern of ecology. The content is unexpected from a Lantz film, for he had, after all, condescendingly caricatured hippies in *Woody's Magic Touch* only one year earlier. In one scene Chilly imagines a bird covered with oil as a result of the drilling that the captain wants to do. As a result, the protection of the planet is the penguin's motivating factor in shooting cannons at the oil driller. Chilly's role as a militant activist is rather timely, considering that since the start of the 1970s, domestic protests had become more deadly. In addition, his cause of environmentalism reflects the increasing mainstream acceptance of the ecology movement; in 1972 the second annual Earth Day took place, and makers of automobiles began reducing the amount of hazardous gas emissions from their vehicles.

In contrast to Chilly's pro-social vigilantism, Lantz's famous bird Woody Woodpecker resorts to violent, self-serving survival techniques. By doing so, the character recalls his debut — *Knock Knock* (1940) — in which he eats by pecking a panda's house full of holes and suffers no repercussions for doing so. However, in the 1940s, such antisocial behavior from cartoon characters was novel and welcomed by audiences as a refreshing change from the harmless stars of Walt Disney's Cartoons (Mickey Mouse, Donald Duck, Goofy, and Pluto). Over the years the woodpecker evolved into a figure attacking others merely in self-defense instead of provoking conflict. By 1972 Woody's aggressive streak was no longer novel and, worse, did not relate to an American public weary of the Vietnam War and of domestic unrest. In *For the Love of Pizza*, he breaks into Grandma's house and disguises as her in order to eat the food that Mrs. Meany (as Little Red Riding Hood) brings to her. Despite his state of starvation as his motivating factor, Woody is no sympathetic protagonist. He disposes of those discovering his deception — pecking Mrs. Meany's nose and foot and watching her inadvertently drown her grandmother.

To the very end, Lantz promoted U.S. colonialism in his films although in fewer yearly releases. As with the survivalist imagery, Lantz relies on tried-and-true formulas for colonialist imagery. In *The Genie with the Light Touch*, Woody plays "Aladdin" once again. However, his genie is not real, as in *A Lad in Bagdad* (1968), but rather a mouse wearing a fez while hiding in a lantern. Because the mouse is not an actual genie and does not serve Woody, *The Genie with the Light Touch* merely displays colonialism via symbolism. Still, by 1972, the images of interethnic servitude were so standardized that even Lantz's abstract ethnic images were "old hat;" six years earlier the Pink Panther had donned a fez and had squeezed inside a lamp to play a genie in DePatie-Freleng's *Genie with the Light Pink Fur*.

Woody's films symbolize colonialism from within the United States as well as abroad. The "Woody Woodpecker" episode *Indian Corn* stars the bird as a wanderer driving through an Indian community and humiliating the indigenous characters along the way. The film legitimizes the woodpecker's destructive presence in a tribal land. He disrupts the family of Indians trying to catch him. The film is one of the last to portray indigenous figures as morons, which further justifies the "white" cowboy Woody's triumph over them. They wear leather pants in a hot desert setting, and they mistake a buzzard wearing a rubber glove on its head for a woodpecker. In an era of movies containing more progressive, sympathetic images of Indians like *Little Big Man* (1970), *Indian Corn* is a major step backward.

Indian Corn, however, differs from Lantz's previous cartoons starring Native Americans because of the film's references to its own repetitiveness concerning the imperialist imagery. To be sure, Woody is not the first character to complain about overused story formulas in his own films; both Elmer Fudd from Warner Brothers Cartoons and DePatie-Freleng's Rattfink did so in *The Big Snooze* (1946) and *Sweet and Sourdough* (1969), respectively. However, these two figures fussed about playing antagonists. In contrast, the woodpecker's point of contention is his constant squaring off against an indigenous figure over a tribal ritual. When yet another Indian tries to hunt the woodpecker to use its feathers for ceremonial purposes, Woody complains, "Oh, boy! One of those!"

Lantz's colonialist and militaristic cartoons are the last lingering slapstick violent shorts, corresponding to the last gasps of U.S. military involvement in the Vietnam War in 1972. Throughout the summer Nixon shifted the responsibility of major combat from young, drafted soldiers to professional enlisted men. He announced in June that he would send no more draftees to South Vietnam. Two months later the last U.S. ground troops were withdrawn, leaving airmen and support personnel. Reflecting South

Vietnam's growing role in ground combat, the United States experienced no casualties for a week in September — the first casualty-free week since 1965.

The continued decline in popularity of the Lantz cartoons in 1972 was part of a growing cultural backlash against fictional colonialism and militarism. While some television programs like *Mission: Impossible* and *Josie and the Pussycats* merely changed formats and survived a few more years, other series simply folded. Animation's most colonialist television series, Hanna-Barbera's *The Adventures of Jonny Quest* ended a five-year rerun stretch on network television. Like its inspiration — Milt Caniff's "Terry and the Pirates" comic strip, which barely survived the year, the cartoon's foreign countries populated by people of color no longer made attractive and exotic settings for viewers tired of the war.[2]

The demise of Lantz's "The Beary Family" signaled the end of traditional conservative humor in animated film. The popularity of *All in the Family* showed that audiences could accept a character loudly but ignorantly espousing right-wing political views. Archie Bunker is a different kind of bumbling sitcom father, mangling his words instead of getting into freak accidents while doing physical labor for the household. As a result, the old kind of physically bumbling father, as represented by Charlie Beary, became passé. Moreover, Lantz did not take risks with his cartoons and made no attempts to change Charlie's personality. He apparently still found the Bearys a series worth the cost of production that final year, making four "Beary Family" films in contrast to only one "Chilly Willy" cartoon.

In 1972, animation studios began to soften their caricatures of hippies but still failed to sensitively depict them. The impassioned rhetoric of counter-demonstrators, illustrated in cartoons by DePatie-Freleng and Lantz from the previous year, was now absent. This development corresponds to the dwindling number of anti-war protests and the decreasing sizes of such demonstrations throughout the year. Nevertheless, the activists were still a rich source of humor for the cartoonists.

That fall, Hanna-Barbera revamped *Scooby-Doo, Where Are You* but destroyed its imagery of youth empowerment in the process. In its new format as *The New Scooby-Doo Movies* (1972–74), the teenagers solved mysteries with the aid of middle-aged guest stars. As a result, the concept of young adults solving problems all by themselves was gone. For example, in episodes featuring Batman and Robin as guests, the teenage detectives are reduced to assistants helping the superheroes capture criminals. The pairing was just as odd to fans of the *Batman* comic strip, which frequently showed the "Caped Crusader" delivering blows to long-haired radicals.

By using adult guest stars, the studio sacrificed not only the concept of heroic young wanderers but also the quality of the series. To be sure, guests Sonny and Cher Bono, Sandy Duncan, and Davy Jones fit into the formula because of their appeal to contemporary youth. The program also lured in viewers of *The Harlem Globetrotters* by bringing in that show's cast. However, older stars like Don Knotts, the Three Stooges, and Phyllis Diller were odd mismatches with the young sleuths. Still other caricatures like those of the famed comedy duo Laurel and Hardy were even stranger guest stars because both had been deceased since 1965.

While *The New Scooby-Doo Movies* figuratively illustrated a generation gap, two new television cartoon series literally featured middle-age adults dealing with the concerns of the counterculture. DePatie-Freleng's Saturday morning show *The Barkleys* and Hanna-Barbera's syndicated series *Wait Till Your Father Gets Home* fashioned themselves after the current top-rated television sitcom *All in the Family*. Both cartoons did not use animation to its fullest but focused on verbal humor instead. They avoided explicit one-liners about taboo subjects like U.S. policy in Indochina, African Americans, Jews, and homosexuals, unlike *All in the Family*. Instead, the animated parents and children of both programs clashed on the less controversial and more trivial issues of fashion, work ethics, and rock music. *Wait Till Your Father Gets Home* lasted two seasons in syndication—one longer than *The Barkleys* on network television. Still, both programs were pale imitations of Norman Lear's classic series.

A positive aspect of *Wait Till Your Father Gets Home* lay in its ability to satirize the generation gap from both sides—one of very few cartoons since *Marvin Digs* (1967) to do so. Hanna-Barbera presented people of the older generation as intolerant and paranoid. Neighbor Ralph, for example, expresses exaggerated fears of rampant communism in some episodes. On the other hand, the plot of one episode, "The Hippie," focuses on the neighborhood's efforts to remove a member of the counterculture, which it successfully does. In addition, the series depicts the younger generation from the point of powerlessness; both the shiftless, long-haired son Chet and Alice, the daughter supporting women's liberation live under the roof of their conservative parents. Despite the typical low-budget animation from the studio, the program offers wittier dialogue and less reliance upon slapstick comedy than *Scooby-Doo, Where Are You* or *Josie and the Pussycats*.

Like *Wait Till Your Father Gets Home*, the groundbreaking animated feature *Fritz the Cat* offers audiences a complex illustration of the counterculture. The plot focuses on an anthropomorphic cat enjoying recreational drug use and casual sex. Directed by Ralph Bakshi, the featured contains even more psychedelic imagery than his Paramount short subject *Marvin Digs* and explores the drug use and political activism only implied in the earlier film. As a director in his thirties, Bakshi was half the age of his contemporaries like Lantz and the directors at DePatie-Freleng; for example, Friz Freleng and Art Davis had animated cartoons approximately an entire decade before Bakshi was born. With his age came an approach to the counterculture that did not condescend to its members, unlike the pummeling of the "flower child" Roland in *Hurts and Flowers* (1969) or the king's disappointment of his hippie son in *Woody's Magic Touch* (1971). In addition, his film focused less on the superficial aspects of the counterculture and more on the ideological ones.[3]

Fritz the Cat is one of many films that capitalized on the popularity of X-rated movies with American audiences during the early 1970s but is also the first animated cartoon to have done so. Ever since the Motion Picture Association of America had created the ratings system in 1968, the number of viewers of sexually graphic features steadily grew. Independent filmmakers then began churning out more such movies. Hollywood took notice and made its own suggestive live-action films. Animation wings of Hollywood distributors wanted no part of this trend, largely remaining content with making G-rated cartoons, However, Bakshi — now his own boss and not tied to a major distributor — had the power to experiment with X-rated content.[4]

Fritz the Cat broke the mold in U.S. animation and not just because of sexual content. Bakshi satirized the politics of antiwar radicals — a departure from earlier broad caricatures of hippies as long-haired, unemployed dimwits seeking peace. In the movie Fritz involves himself with people devoted to revolution but only to attract women for sexual pleasure. Thus, he at least has a motive for his embrace of the antiwar movement — however shallow — whereas both the character Marvin from *Marvin Digs* and DePatie-Freleng's figure Roland give people flowers at random for no apparent reason. In addition, Fritz's manipulation of radicalism for sex demonstrates Bakshi's contempt for the white liberalism of the Vietnam War era.[5]

Fritz the Cat also differs from earlier films in that the hippie has a "happy ending" of sorts. Other cartoons end with flower children receiving punishment for their behavior. For example, Rattfink breaks a flowerpot over Roland's head in the conclusion of *Hurts and Flowers*, and Woody magically changes a hippie into a dragon at the end of *Woody's Magic Touch*. However, *Fritz the Cat* finishes with the title-character engaging in sexual intercourse with several different female cats. Thus, the animators enable him to engage in behavior that other studios avoided for their characters. In addition, unlike the old Hays Code, the "X" rating did not mandate the suffering of consequences by characters for sexual promiscuity.

Fritz the Cat was a counterculture exercise itself. The cast consisted of representations of hippies, black militants, and other social and political radicals of the time. In addition, the star himself was a counterculture icon, having appeared in underground comic books by Robert Crumb in the 1960s and early '70s. In a similar situation to the movie's small exposure due to its rating, Crumb's comics lacked the approval of the Comics Code and, therefore, did not enjoy as wide a circulation as code adherents Marvel Comics and DC Comics. Still, Crumb's work attracted a loyal cult following. The built-in fan base and the film's notoriety as animation's first X-rated work made *Fritz the Cat* a respectable hit. However, Crumb disapproved of Bakshi's efforts at adapting the character to animation and subsequently killed the cat in the comic book series. The rebuff hurt Bakshi, who chose to create his own characters for his next feature-length cartoon.[6]

Not every studio borrowing characters received little cooperation from their creators, as Bakshi had with Crumb. DePatie-Freleng continued to have a very profitable relationship with Dr. Seuss. The studio took a rare stab at social commentary via the television special *The Lorax*. The program, which concerns an industrialist's destruction of trees despite the cries of protest from a forest-dweller, has an ecological theme. The broadcast was popular enough to warrant repeat airings over the next few years, but the studio did not immediately convert to "message cartoons." On the other hand, Dr. Seuss did not write "message books" for the studio to convert to animation.

DePatie-Freleng took longer than its competitors in breaking its color barrier but did so in grand fashion in November. By that time Filmation's series *The Hardy Boys* had left the air, and Hanna-Barbera's program *The Harlem Globetrotters* was in its third and final season. DePatie-Freleng's television special *Clerow Wilson and the Miracle of PS 14* brought to animation several characters created and popularized by African American comedian Flip Wilson on his weekly variety program *The Flip Wilson Show* (1970–74). The special is very similar to *Fat Albert and the Cosby Kids*, for both shows are based on the stand-up routines of black humorists — Flip Wilson and Bill Cosby — about their childhoods. Wilson had one advantage over Cosby in that while Cosby only vocally imitated the people with whom he spent his youth before bringing them to animation, Wilson had performed his characters in costume on television for years. Such figures as the flirtatious, mini-skirted Geraldine were already familiar with viewers by 1972, although they were not geared specifically for children. Thus, with his special, Wilson attempted to reach an entirely different age demographic.

Flip Wilson was one of a few African Americans involved themselves directly in the production of animated adaptations of their work. This year the studios went beyond caricaturing black performers and sought characters created by black artists. Rankin-Bass produced a cartoon version of Morrie Turner's comic strip "Wee Pals." Titled *Kid Power*, the series promoted racial integration by boasting a cast consisting of white, black, Asian, Latino, and Native American children. Turner assessed the program, "I think the strength of the show was simply seeing all races cavorting (getting along) together each week." Indeed, such imagery had not been part of network television programming for children — making the show very radical for its time.[7]

Even the title of the series had radical connotations. Turner recalled that Rankin-Bass had first heard of his comic strip through a collection of "Wee Pals" reprints in a book called *Kid Power*. In compliance to the current rules of television animation, the show did not contain violence. However, the message of interracial tolerance was not enough for viewers uncomfortable with the title. To be sure, several activist groups had used the word "power" for their own agendas in the years since SNCC first introduced the phrase "Black Power" to the public in 1966. Thus, people had difficulty taking the word "power" out of a context of either radical political rhetoric or violent demonstration. Consequently, according to Turner, "ABC received resistance mail to the word 'power.'"[8]

Ironically, those who complained of the radical implications of Turner's title may not have known of his support of the U.S. troops during the Vietnam War. He visited soldiers in South Vietnam a few years before working on *Kid Power*. Few artists and entertainers made such trips. Many of the most outspoken advocates of the conflict suffered unofficial blacklisting from Hollywood; for example, the career of actress Martha Raye went into decline due to her public hawkish stance. However, Turner's strip did not lose subscribers as a result of his trip. What he remembered the most about that trip was "the black sergeant, in the hospital, obviously dying, who had to tell me about the circumstances that brought about his injuries, in spite of the distress it caused him in the retelling and the difficulty he had breathing in doing so."[9]

Sadly, violence at home during the 1960s also influenced *Kid Power*. The strip "Wee Pals" had modest success in the early and middle part of the decade. However, after the assassination of Rev. Dr. Martin Luther King, Jr. in 1968, Turner experienced a dramatic increase in the number of newspapers printing his strip in their "comics" sections. When asked why, he gave the simple reason of "GUILT." The sudden rejuvenation of "Wee Pals" was on par with other immediate innovations in African American art in the wake of King's death. That fall, NBC premiered the television series *Julia*— the first program with an African American female lead in over a decade and the first to not feature said lead in a domestic servant ("mammy") role.[10]

Kid Power was not the only pro-social series inspired by African American expression to debut in September 1972. Moreover, Filmation's *Fat Albert and the Cosby Kids* had more success than *Kid Power* in balancing education with entertainment. Whereas Turner's show aired on ABC-TV for two seasons, Bill Cosby's ran for twelve years on CBS-TV. To be sure, the latter series was helped by live-action scenes of Cosby, who provided commentary on the behavior of the animated figures. By then he had appeared on prime-time television for the past six years, from *I Spy* (1965–68) to *The Bill Cosby Show* (1969–71). In addition, as his cartoon premiered, he began hosting his own variety show *The New Bill Cosby Show*.[11]

Both *Kid Power* and *Fat Albert and the Cosby Kids* preach against racism but in very different styles. The former program tackles specific racial stereotypes. In one episode the cast sings, "Uncle Tom, He Is Gone." The latter series is more circumspect. It devoted only one episode that year to the subject of racism. The all-black cast met a group of white students at a campground, and at the end the Cosby Kids sang the song "One World," promoting interracial harmony.

The songs in both shows illustrate the heavy influence of both watchdog groups and public television upon audiences. The Public Broadcasting Service (PBS) network's *Sesame Street* (1969–present) proved to commercial networks that education and entertainment could effectively combine and reach young audiences. Meanwhile, criticisms started to mount against animation studios for making too many cartoons starring teenage rock musicians. As viewers tired of the Archies' "bubblegum" sound anyway, the producers of *Kid Power* and *Fat Albert and the Cosby Kids* capitalized on the new trend of educational music in cartoons.

Fat Albert and the Cosby Kids presents scenery that illustrated the cost of the Vietnam War to urban America. After President Johnson had begun spending more on the war than on combating poverty in the 1960s, cities nationwide fell into disarray. Likewise, *Fat Albert and the Cosby Kids* includes dilapidated buildings and garbage-filled junkyards in its backgrounds. In addition, the role of the junkyard as the space for the juvenile black characters to play represents the absence of community centers or public playgrounds — facilities frequently sacrificed by cities confronted with shrinking funds for public play areas. The children make toys out of junk, showing not only creativity but also the financial inability to purchase toys. Such imagery was on par with contemporary movies focusing on urban African American hardship such as *Shaft* (1971) and *Superfly* (1972).[12]

However, *Fat Albert and the Cosby Kids* only passively deals with African American urban issues, unlike the racial humor of contemporary television. Series such as *The Flip Wilson Show, All in the Family,* and *Sanford and Son* feature jokes about poverty, racism, and African Americans themselves. Meanwhile, the cartoon does not even mention the racial or ethnic identification of its characters. The lessons the children learn in their adventures — honesty, no hero worship, no sexism — also have little to do with their brown skin color. The only racially political aspect of the program is the "Afro" hairstyle worn by the figures — a hairstyle that only recently became widely accepted among African Americans.[13]

Other cartoons starring African American characters were even less ambitious than *Fat Albert and the Cosby Kids.* Studios mostly settled for tokenism in their series. In Hanna-Barbera's *Josie and the Pussycats in Outer Space,* Valerie remains the only character of color touring with her band but aboard a spaceship this time. The studio's *The New Scooby-Doo Movies* teams white teenage detectives and their Great Dane with celebrity guest stars; the Harlem Globetrotters appear with them twice. Only Hanna-Barbera's *Sealab 2020*— a science-fiction program about an underwater laboratory — offers an African American figure in a drama instead of a comedy. As with *Fat Albert and the Cosby Kids,* these shows also avoid discussions on race and ethnicity.[14]

Animation studios similarly exploited Asian American caricature without exploring the concerns of Asian Americans. The artists developed several Asian American figures as events on the Asian continent dominated U.S. news throughout 1972. President Nixon's historic visit to China early in the year launched a blitz of television programs and movies exploiting Asia over the next few years, from ABC-TV's series *Kung Fu* to martial arts films starring Bruce Lee. Meanwhile, after years as comical sidekicks, Asians now starred in animated films as lead characters. However, some ethnic stereotypes remained.

The cartoons presenting the grossest caricatures of Asians were DePatie-Freleng's "Blue Racer" theatrical shorts. The episodes star a lisping snake chasing the Japanese Beetle of the cartoon *Hop and Chop* (1970). As with the Tijuana Toads in the earlier film, the Beetle bests the serpent by wit and by karate. His skill with martial arts coincides with the increasingly popular martial arts fad of the 1970s. In addition, the Beetle's victories against the Racer reveal the changes in animated depictions of American-Asian conflict over the previous three decades. Many of the cartoons of World War II feature American characters not only defeating Japanese caricatures on battlefields but also killing them completely. Rarely do figures representing the Japanese armed forces survive to the end of an American cartoon. For example, Friz Freleng, the co-producer of "The Blue Racer," directed the Warner Brothers cartoon *Bugs Bunny Nips the Nips* (1944) — a cartoon ending with Bugs giving Japanese soldiers hidden live grenades, all of which exploded before the concluding "That's All, Folks" title. Therefore, Freleng's supervision of the Beetle's successful self-defense represents a significant shift in American sentiment concerning Asians, especially the Japanese.[15]

However, in more superficial ways, the Beetle is a throwback to the unflattering Japanese images of World War II. He wears horn-rimmed glasses and sports bucked teeth. He often peppers his sentences with "Ah so" and "So sorry." In addition, the studio continued the tradition of "Asian minstrelsy" by retaining white actor Tom Holland for the Beetle's voice. Although World War II had ended twenty-seven years earlier, editorial cartoonists regularly transferred the broad stereotypes of the old Japanese figures to contemporary drawings of Southeast Asians during the Vietnam War. Thus, anti-Asian imagery still appeared on a frequent basis.

The Blue Racer was one of very few colonialist characters from DePatie-Freleng. As in *Snake in the Gracias*, the Racer is a snake in a foreign country, looking for a meal. However, in his new series, he slithers across Japan, not Mexico, and tries to catch a Japanese insect instead of Latino frogs. Nevertheless, "The Blue Racer" calls for the audience to merely accept the colonialism at face value. No episode offers an explanation as to why a "Western" figure is zooming across Japan. To be sure, the serpent is not interested in the culture or social norms of the country; he merely wants one of its commodities: food. Still, the audience has no idea why he goes across the Pacific Ocean to find it instead of staying at home.

The existence of such crude racial caricature in American animation in 1972 also reflects the career of "Blue Racer" co-producer Friz Freleng.

He developed several racial caricatures at Warner Brothers, and some of them became stars. He animated the studio's first protagonist — a black-face figure named Bosko — in the 1930s. Moreover, the Beetle was not Freleng's first broad ethnic minority figure to conquer a "Western" foe. In the 1950s and '60s, he had directed films starring the sombrero-topped Mexican mouse Speedy Gonzales, who regularly outwitted Sylvester Cat and Daffy Duck. In addition, all of the previous DePatie-Freleng series, except for "Pink Panther," drew from ethnic stereotypes for humor. "The Blue Racer" followed the paths laid by "The Inspector" (humor at the expense of the French), "Roland and Rattfink" (Roland speaking in a British accent), "The Ant and the Aardvark" (Aardvark's voice resembling Jewish comedian Jackie Mason), and "Tijuana Toads" (borrowing Mexican gags from Speedy Gonzales).

The muted violence in "The Blue Racer" differentiates the episodes from other theatrical series by DePatie-Freleng. When Stan Paperny replaced Jim Foss as the studio's production executive in 1972, the cartoons under his leadership exhibited more sensitivity to the concerns of animation watchdog groups than the films of his predecessors. To be sure, the beetle uses karate chops on his adversary — including a painful scene of chopping through Blue Racer's teeth in *Punch and Judo* — and repeatedly slams the serpent's body to the ground. However, an increasing number of scenes in the studio's cartoons imply brutality instead of showing it. For example, in *Hiss and Hers*, when the Racer swallows the Beetle, the bug beats up the serpent while inside his belly. Meanwhile, the audience only sees the snake twitch and tie itself into a knot; viewers do not witness the blows from inside.

As for the Blue Racer, he represents via animation the new trend in Hollywood movies of the "anti-hero" figure. The snake has a similar characterization but as the result of an odd combination of Vietnam-era cartoon stars from Warner Brothers. He has the speed of Speedy Gonzales but, like Sylvester Cat, is a lisping antagonist searching for a creature to eat. And in keeping with the recent lack of creativity at DePatie-Freleng, the serpent starred in remakes of Sylvester's cartoons. Both the Racer's *Yokohama Mama* and the cat's *Fowl Weather* concern an animal's unsuccessful attempts to raid a henhouse for a meal.

Ending five decades in the animation business with ethnic stereotypes, Walter Lantz joined DePatie-Freleng in displaying old, derisive Asian characterizations. One of the last "Woody Woodpecker" cartoons ever made (and one of Lantz's final films), *Show Biz Beagle* tells the story of Woody Woodpecker buying a celebrity-impersonating dog and putting him in a solo stage show. The dog approximates the voices and faces of the personalities he imitates except for one — the famous live-action movie character Charlie Chan. For this fictional Chinese detective, Lantz's animators merely had the animal put on horn-rimmed glasses and phony bucked teeth, close his eyes into slants, and speak a fractured English sentence with various "Ah so" declarations thrown in for good measure. Here, minstrelsy took place through two different methods. First, the animators altered the dog's face to visually appropriate the Chinese ethnicity. Second, white actor Dal McKennon tried to sound Chinese via phony dialect and fractured English.

The Chan figure in *Show Biz Beagle* demonstrates the inability of longtime theatrical animators to modernize their humor. Some of them had worked in the industry since the 1930s and continued to draw from the entertainment of that decade. As a result, their cartoons exemplified a "generation gap" between the artists and the juvenile target audience. In addition to the detective, the dog also impersonated Laurel and Hardy, W. C. Fields, and Jimmy Durante. Only Durante, however, was still alive in 1972 but confined to a wheelchair due to illness by that point. Children watching animated cartoons were not even born when the caricatured actors were in their prime.

In the fall of 1972, Hanna-Barbera modernized Chan in order to adapt him to current trends in television animation. CBS aired *The Amazing Chan and the Chan Clan,* in which the sleuth solved mysteries with the help of his children. The series borrowed from animated programs *Scooby-Doo, Where Are You* and *The Archie Show.* The former show had already popularized the half-hour cartoon mystery genre. Meanwhile, the latter program pioneered the exploitation of original songs through cartoon characters. Chan and his family formed a rock group, not unlike the Archies. Hanna-Barbera even utilized the same singers as Filmation had for *The Archie Show.*

Despite these contemporary twists to the old character, *The Amazing Chan and the Chan Clan* still implemented ethnic stereotypes, although much more subtle ones than those of the Japanese Beetle. Continuing Hollywood's tradition of presenting people of color without intact families, Charlie Chan had no wife. Thus, his children lacked a mother. Also, the series resorted to "Asian minstrelsy" by casting white actors to provide voices for some Asian characters; one of these performers was a very young Jodie Foster. Even the theme song by music director Hoyt Curtin sounded like a Hollywood interpretation of Asian music. In addition to these generalizations, Hanna-Barbera avoided discussing Chinese culture in a substantial manner.

For all its ethnic caricature, *The Amazing Chan and the Chan Clan* managed to break new ground in Asian imaging in Hollywood cartoons. Asian actor Keye Luke played the role of Chan — an irony, considering that he appeared as Chan's "number-one son" in the movies. He was the only Asian American to provide voice characterization for a lead character in a cartoon until actor Robert Ito's vocal performance as martial arts mentor Mr. Miyagi in the animated series adaptation of the popular live-action movie *The Karate Kid* in 1989; then, another decade passed before action star Jackie Chan voiced his cartoon likeness nearly three decades later. The originality of *The Amazing Chan and the Chan Clan* also lay in its depictions of Chan's children. Juvenile Chinese American human figures had not previously appeared in Hollywood cartoons, and the most recent Asian American child characters in U.S. animation were the son and daughter of Hashimoto from the Terrytoons films produced between 1959 and 1963.

Rankin-Bass' animated series *Kid Power* used Chinese and other ethnic groups to attempt to put stereotypes to rest. Among the cast was a Chinese character named George — another new Asian juvenile in American animation since the "Hashimoto" cartoons by the Terrytoons studio had ceased in 1963. In addition, thanks to the show's promotion of ethnic diversity and interracial friendships, George bore the distinction as the first Asian character in American animation to be placed as a social equal to whites. He was neither a servant nor a strong martial arts expert but rather one person in a group of innocent children. When the series left the air two years later, he and the Chan kids were the only Asian American juvenile characters in animation at the time.

For another Saturday morning cartoon (*The Brady Kids*), Filmation shoehorned Chinese figures to an established property. The animated spinoff to the live-action sitcom *The Brady Bunch* (1969–74) starred only the juvenile characters of the original series plus a talking bird, a dog, and Chinese pandas named Ping and Pong. As with *The Amazing Chan and the Chan Clan*, *The Brady Kids* incorporated several elements of successful television cartooning. Like *The Archie Show*'s musical exploitation, each episode of *The Brady Kids* featured a song from the children, who had become a recording group for the Famous Music label. Filmation reused animation of the members of the Archies for musical scenes in *The Brady Kids*. The dog Moptop looked exactly like Hotdog, the pet dog on *The Archie Show* but with brown hair instead of white. Borrowing from the magician characters of Filmation's *Sabrina the Teenage Witch*, the talking bird in *The Brady Kids* cast magic spells. The Chinese Pandas, however, were unique figures in that they did not speak English in the cartoon.

As a result, the language barrier left the pandas with little to do on the show.[16]

Another problem with *The Brady Kids* lay in its animalizing of the Chinese. To be sure, thanks to the Chan-imitating dog and the Japanese Beetle, the pandas were not the only non-human Asian figures of 1972. However, only Ping and Pong had neither autonomy nor lines written in the English language. As the pets of the Brady Kids, they did not move around freely like the Beetle but were the property of others and under their authority. Because of their lack of clear speech, they did not have as strong a power to communicate as the year's other Asian characters had.

The Brady Kids encapsulates U.S. popular music in 1972, which was at a crossroads. Pop groups like the Jackson Five and the Osmonds waned in popularity, while introspective singer-songwriters performed sophisticated if not danceable songs. Filmation exploited various musical genres in order for the Bradys to replace the Archies as animated hitmakers. Songs like "Sunshine Day" were lightweight, but the ambitious "We Can Make the World a Whole Lot Brighter" is pro-ecology "message music." The serious tune's inclusion in *The Brady Kids* recalls the integration of "Nowhere Man" into the series *The Beatles* and the movie *Yellow Submarine*.

As *The Brady Kids* premiered in the fall, the networks stopped airing most violent theatrical cartoons. ABC-TV cancelled *The Road Runner Show* after six years on the air. In the previous year, the network had taken the series from CBS-TV and strictly censored the cartoons packaged in each half-hour. CBS-TV, meanwhile, finally put *The Tom and Jerry Show* out of its Sunday morning misery. The series had languished there since 1968, when the public backlash against animated violence started.

Thanks to parental activism, syndicated cartoons televised throughout the war's duration suddenly disappeared in 1972. Action for Children's Television (ACT) successfully pressured the Federal Communications Commission (FCC) to prohibit programs whose hosts pitched products to juvenile viewers. The FCC set New Year's Day 1973 as the date in which the mandate went into effect. As a result, local children's shows all across the country went off the air in December. Some independent television stations continued to air the animated films that had appeared on the shows but stopped using hosts to introduce them. Other stations, however, replaced both the cartoons and the hosts with public affairs programming, syndicated talk shows, or syndicated game shows. In these cases, such films as King Features Syndicate's "Popeye" cartoons and UPA's "Dick Tracy" episodes became "homeless" for the first time in over a decade.

The triumph of ACT was representative of the effects of political activism on domestic and foreign policy. Throughout the election year, both President Nixon and his opponent George McGovern talked about ending the Vietnam War instead of achieving a military victory. Thanks to the legislative victories of the civil rights movement, African Americans achieved remarkable political milestones in 1972, including the election of the first black congressman representing a southern state since the Reconstruction Era (1863–1877). Now, grass-roots protest obliterated one of the most profitable avenues of revenue for animation distributors.

A few of the older cartoon characters survived, thanks to the current nostalgia craze. For example, Betty Boop — a flapper figure in animation producer Max Fleischer's Paramount cartoons from 1930 to 1939 — was very popular in June 1972. Originally produced in black-and-white, a company reanimated the "Betty Boop" episodes in color in the early 1970s and successfully sold them into television syndication. Various businesses capitalized on her returned exposure by manufacturing products bearing her likeness. Ironically, a newspaper story about her resurgence had the same short length as the periodical's obituary for Fleischer three months later, and the producer was not even mentioned in the report about the new "Betty" craze.[17]

By 1972 animation studios had found ways to develop nonviolent story formulas for formerly violent characters. A wave of old stars, long gone from the theaters or from television, returned that fall on Saturday morning cartoons. The first of these was the superhero Batman, appearing in an episode of *The New Scooby-Doo Movies* on September 16. Without throwing a single punch, he and Robin team with the mystery-solving teenagers to catch villains Joker and Penguin.

Hanna-Barbera drew from the defunct live-action *Batman* program to fit the heroes into the "teenage adventure/comedy" genre. Robin retains his affinity for bad puns, often starting exclamations with the word "holy." In another *Scooby-Doo* episode that December, Batman's utility belt serves as a prop for comedy. When the character Shaggy mentions his hunger, the hero pulls a "bat-cookie" out of the belt. The scene originates from a recurring joke in the original series, in which Batman manages to remove exactly whatever he needs for a situation — no matter how specific — from his belt.

The New Scooby-Doo Movies also keeps Robin's appearance from the *Batman* program, which underscored the still-present politics of hair length. By 1972 the comic book version of the hero had evolved from a young teenager to a college student. DC Comics called him the "Teen

Wonder" instead of the "Boy Wonder." Most importantly, he wore a shorter mask and longer hair. In contrast, Hanna-Barbera's version is frozen in the mid–1960s — wearing his old mask, responding to the "Boy Wonder" nickname, and having short-length hair.

Both the campy *Batman* television show and slapstick *The New Scooby-Doo Movies* catered to a younger audience than the dramatic *Batman* comic book series. Thus, the absence of any similarity between the periodical and Hanna-Barbera's cartoon is not surprising. Also, the studio had only created hirsute heroes by making them rock musicians (the Impossibles), and Robin was no rocker.

Not every effort to adapt superheroes to nonviolence succeeded. Filmation brought both Superman and Wonder Woman to *The Brady Kids* for different episodes. However, neither character integrated well into the series. Especially in Superman's appearance, the program awkwardly tried to balance the comedy of the teenagers and pet animals with the dramatic subplot of the hero trying to catch criminals. Unlike Batman, Superman did not have a campy precedent from which Filmation could have extracted humor. Still, one upshot in casting the figure was that the studio used several opportunities to reuse animation from its own series *The New Adventures of Superman* from 1966 — a tactic that reduced production costs in animation. On the other hand, the six-year-old character designs clashed stylistically with the more contemporary Brady caricatures. Even Lois Lane, who in comic books now sported miniskirts and shoulder-length hair, retained her short "bob" hairdo and conservative knee-length dress from the mid-1960s.

Wonder Woman's appearance on the show illustrates the growing visibility of empowered women in the media in the waning years of the Vietnam War. Filmation made a political statement in how it presented the character. In the summer of 1972, *Ms.* Magazine reprimanded DC Comics for taking away Wonder Woman's superpowers and accessories (bulletproof bracelets and a magic lasso), replacing her patriotic uniform with civilian clothes, and making her into a martial arts expert mentored by elderly gentleman I Ching. Those recent changes transformed the heroine from independent and physically strong to dependent and weak. The periodical emphasized its complaint by placing Wonder Woman, in her former costume and towering over a city, on the cover of its first issue. Just as DC restored the heroine's original look by the end of the year, the "old" Wonder Woman greeted the young Bradys.[18]

Classic slapstick characters joined the superheroes in returning from exile. On October 9, King Features Syndicate Television brought Popeye back after a decade-long absence for an episode of *The ABC Saturday Superstar Movie*. To do so, King had to devise a different reason for Popeye to eat spinach other than to strike Brutus. In "Popeye Meets the Man Who Hated Laughter," a villain captures a spate of characters from the syndicate's comic strips. The figures actually save themselves from their adversary and only need the spinach-eating sailor to push the captor's submarine out from between two boulders.

Like Wonder Woman's costume, Popeye's uniform underwent a political change in 1972. After having appeared in "navy whites" in animated cartoons since 1941, "Popeye Meets the Man Who Hated Laughter" returns the sailor to his dark comic-strip costume. Because the simple design and minimal color of the navy whites would have made Popeye cheaper and easier to animate, the switch to the old uniform is very poignant. The change signaled that the animation industry knew that television networks and viewers no longer found military figures attractive, especially after so many years of U.S. combat in the Vietnam War.

In addition to taming the sailor, *The ABC Saturday Superstar Movie* toned down the actions of characters who had defined the animated physical humor of the previous thirty years. In "Daffy Duck and Porky Pig Meet the Groovie Goolies," the most famous stars of the defunct Warner Brothers Cartoons teamed with Filmation's caricatures of monsters. Both sets of figures have in common an identity as a repertory company of sorts. Warner Brothers Cartoons had developed diverse pairings of their characters over the years: Bugs Bunny and Daffy Duck, Porky Pig and Daffy, and, most recently, Speedy Gonzales and Daffy. In addition, in Filmation's television series *Groovie Goolies* (1971–72), Frankenstein, Dracula, a werewolf, and assorted witches and ghosts told one-liner jokes to one another in a fashion similar to *Rowan & Martin's Laugh-In*.

"Daffy Duck and Porky Pig Meet the Groovie Goolies" was one of the few opportunities in the 1972-73 season for television audiences to see animated animal characters. For example, for the first time in its existence, Hanna-Barbera offered no programs starring animal figures as the lead characters. Instead, its new programs starred human figures, especially teenagers. Meanwhile, even the older series were falling out of favor with contemporary audiences. When *Help! It's the Hair Bear Bunch* ended its one-year run in September 1972, it was the last "animal" show by the studio airing on network television.

While getting rid of some established properties, Hanna-Barbera worked to reinvent others. The studio retooled the long-defunct series *The Flintstones* (1960–66) for a new audience. The popularity of *Pebbles and*

Bamm-Bamm inspired the studio to milk the characterizations from that show and *The Flintstones* as much as possible. Debuting in September 1972, *The Flintstone Comedy Hour* (1972–74) not only aired reruns of *Pebbles and Bamm-Bamm* but also presented new five-minute episodes of *The Flintstones*, comedy vignettes by the cast of *Pebbles and Bamm-Bamm*, and two songs by the teenage figures — now dubbed the music group the Bedrock Rockers. In bringing back *The Flintstones*, the studio capitalized on the nostalgia craze. Hanna-Barbera borrowed from *Rowan & Martin's Laugh-In* by having characters pop out of windows to deliver short jokes. The rock band was an attempt to make Pebbles and Bamm-Bamm into the Stone Age "Archies."

The graphics of *The Flintstone Comedy Hour* come from previous rock cartoons. In one musical sequence a representation of the sun has a similar design to that in the "Singalong" segment "Good Day Sunshine" from *The Beatles*. Visual effects such as colors sliding across transparent designs of the characters originated with Rankin-Bass' *The Jackson 5ive*, whose popularity journalist David Rider reported in August 1972. He was thrilled that a British studio had animated a series that was successful in the United States and smugly bragged that "British animation [has] beaten the Americans at their own game." He noted that the series attracted more viewers than some Hanna-Barbera offerings, and he revealed, "In fact, Hanna-Barbera have been intrigued by some of the visual effects created for the programmes and are eager to know how they were achieved." *The Flintstone Comedy Hour*'s psychedelic musical vignettes confirm Rider's article.[19]

The failure of Hanna-Barbera's new "anachronistic suburbia" cartoon *The Roman Holidays* to find an audience underscores the waning appeal of the formula without new gimmickry like the psychedelic imagery and quick one-liners in *The Flintstone Comedy Show* to accompany the social satire. Airing only in the 1972-73 season, *The Roman Holidays* concerns a family living in Rome during the Roman Empire. The studio revised its "prehistoric appliance" jokes from *The Flintstones* to fit the new time period. However, the Roman Empire does not work well for a caricature of modern society. Ancient Rome has a significant amount of documented social history about its society, unlike the prehistoric era of *The Flintstones* or the futuristic setting of *The Jetsons*. The history, therefore, does not allow as much of a suspension of disbelief for a completely fabricated version of Rome as it does for a similarly caricatured Stone Age or future. In addition, the new series does not have a strong foundation for humor. *The Flintstones* borrowed from the very funny *Honeymooners*, and gags in *The*

Jetsons about automation and the future had been staples in animation for decades. In contrast, Hollywood had not extracted much comedy from the Roman Empire by September 1972.

Rankin-Bass' *The Osmonds* copies *The Jackson 5ive* to a greater extent than *The Flintstone Comedy Show* does. The group inspiring the series admittedly approximated the sound of the Jacksons. As with the Motown group, the Osmonds star in cartoons set around the world. Both series also share psychedelic graphics for song-sequences. However, the music of the real-life Osmonds was not as popular as that of the Jacksons. Correspondingly, *The Osmonds* lasted only one year, in contrast to the two seasons of *The Jackson 5ive.*

Rankin-Bass was not the only studio struggling to compete with Filmation and Hanna-Barbera. Terrytoons — the cartoon studio that had originally started television animation in the 1950s — did not survive the changes of the early '70s. Throughout all of 1972, new owner Viacom did not offer a single cartoon from the Terrytoons studio for 20th Century–Fox to distribute. In the meantime, studio employees failed to successfully pitch new ideas to networks for cartoon series. Before the year ended, Viacom finally saw no point in keeping its animation facility active. On December 29, the corporation sold the building that had housed the Terrytoons studio. Now out of the business of cartoon production, Viacom concentrated on syndicating the Terrytoons cartoons through television and on helping 20th Century–Fox to facilitate the distribution of films to foreign theaters.[20]

Meanwhile, the racism and social divisions of the Vietnam War remained an important part of American animated comedy, despite the overtures made by Hanna-Barbera and Filmation towards integrationist imagery. Only major developments bringing about the war's conclusion the next year would inspire U.S. animators to make drastic changes.

10

THE CARTOONS
OF 1973

The year 1973 started with great success for the United States in foreign and domestic affairs. On January 23, President Richard Nixon announced that North and South Vietnam and the United States had agreed to a cease-fire to end the war in the next four days. Extremely proud of the accomplishment, he frequently referred to the event as the achievement of "peace with honor" for the remainder of his presidency. The agreement had come after a month of escalation of hostilities. After a three-month hiatus, Nixon had resumed daily bombing of North Vietnam in late December 1972. The North shot down some of the B-52s and captured new U.S. prisoners of war, and public outcry over Nixon's escalation of U.S. military activity intensified. However, peace talks progressed, and Nixon halted the bombings after eleven days. In addition, while concluding U.S. involvement in the war, the federal government also ended the draft, thus transforming the U.S. Armed Forces into an all-volunteer military for the first time since before the United States had entered World War II.

Within a short time, the effectiveness of the agreement became apparent. The Vietnam War did not end when its cease-fire went into effect on January 28. North and South Vietnam still fought for two additional years. Casualties on both sides were as high in 1973 as in the previous year, and as late as December, U.S. servicemen operating in non-combat roles sporadically died in Southeast Asia. The United States funded South Vietnam's military, although in decreasing amounts, during that period. Meanwhile, U.S. B-52s continued to bomb neighboring Cambodia between February and August 1973. In addition, reports circulated regarding the continued presence of U.S. servicemen disguised as civilians in South Vietnam and the U.S. Government's deliberation of the legality of restarting combat in Indochina.

However, most Americans considered the war finished on March 29, 1973, when the last prisoners of war were freed and the last U.S. troops left South Vietnam. The media soon focused on domestic affairs such as the rising price of meat and the Watergate scandal. Southeast Asia left the front pages newspapers, resulting in less than ten percent of polled Americans considering the Vietnam War a pressing problem. Even as the war intensified throughout the remainder of the year, most commentators reported America's military role in the past tense after March. The deaths of U.S. pilots on bombing missions over Cambodia that spring and summer were too few to arouse the anger of a war-weary public. To secure the finality of the withdrawal of the United States from Vietnam, Congress prohibited funding for U.S. combat in Southeast Asia after August 15 — effectively ending the bombing of Cambodia — and limited presidential power to conduct war by passing the War Powers Act in November.[1]

The American cartoon followed popular culture in putting Vietnam War-era imagery to rest. After all, with the end of the draft, even a recent cartoon like DePatie-Freleng's *Trick or Retreat* (1971) was now obsolete because of its joke about an Indian burning his draft card. In the spring of 1973, television networks canceled some of the most popular shows of wartime, including *Mission: Impossible* and *Rowan & Martin's Laugh-In*. Jefferson Airplane and the Doors — two of the most successful psychedelic, antiwar rock music groups — disbanded. Meanwhile, the broad animated Asian, military and counterculture figures of the past twelve years no longer had relevance. Throughout the year the studios searched for ways to revise these figures for post-war animated films with varying degrees of success.

The cancellation of *The Bullwinkle Show* came as U.S.-Soviet tensions slightly eased. In this new era of détente, Soviet caricatures Boris Badenov and Natasha became passé. Even the federal government itself was not as committed to investigating domestic Communism as when the 1970s had started. In 1973 the Subversive Activities Control Board and the Department of Justice's Internal Security Division were abolished. Also, the House of Representatives proposed eliminating the infamous House Internal Security Committee — formerly the House Un-American Activities Committee (HISC) — on December 7, as part of its first revision of House committees since 1946. Barely one week earlier, the HISC had held its final hearing specifically on U.S. Communism after forty-five years of hearings.

Underdog— another staple of wartime Saturday morning television — also left network television. The era of satirizing violence was over. The series was one of the few to outlive the studio that had produced it; Leonardo-Total Television had not made a new cartoon since *The Beagles* in 1966. Formerly a comedy relief figure among superheroes, Underdog's popularity suffered over the years when audiences no longer found violence funny anymore, whether satirized or not. In addition, the voice of the title-character, Wally Cox, died in February.

The Japan-based Mushi Studios, which had once captured America's attention with *Astro Boy*, also had trouble adjusting to new viewer tastes. In the 1970s, instead of starting animation trends like the boy-superhero genre of the '60s, Mushi evolved from leader to follower. For the past year, the facility had animated classic novels and folktales for the series *Festival of Family Classics*. In addition the films the studio made originally for Japanese television no longer reached the United States; the only Mushi cartoons airing stateside by 1973 were films it made by arrangement with Rankin-Bass. Then, in November of that year, the company filed for bankruptcy and made no further cartoons for many years.

As durable cartoons and studios disappeared, the press spent much of the year waxing nostalgic for cartoons of long ago. Over a year after the passing of Max Fleischer, the New York *Times* finally paid homage to his contributions to animation; the periodical put its tribute within a review for a film compilation of old "Betty Boop" episodes. Meanwhile, *Time* magazine published a biographical sketch of Chuck Jones. The article featured more discussion of his career at Warner Brothers Cartoons than on his current television special *A Very Merry Cricket*. Interestingly, the periodical did not mention any of his films from his recent stint at Metro-Goldwyn-Mayer — not even his Academy Award-winning film *The Dot and the Line* (1965).[2]

The year 1973 is also notable in that it marked the first time in decades that no studio released any theatrical cartoons starring Latino stereotypical figures. Ever since the 1910s, various studios had produced films in which characters donned sombreros or appeared in bullfights. Warner Brothers Cartoons became increasingly reliant on the imagery in the 1950s and '60s after the debut of Speedy Gonzales won an Academy Award in 1956. DePatie-Freleng, however, was even more dependent. Every year since the studio's first cartoon in 1964, at least one DePatie-Freleng release per year starred Latino figures: Speedy (1964–67), Deaux Deaux (1965–68), and "Tijuana Toads" (1969–72). When the studio ceased production of "Tijuana Toads" in 1972, it did not develop a new Latino character to co-opt the phrases used since Speedy's heyday like "Holy *frijoles!*" Rather, it stopped anti–Latino humor altogether as a crutch and moved on to other types of humor.

Also in 1973 DePatie-Freleng followed the lead of television studios by capitalizing on the popularity of the guest appearances of nonviolent heroes in *The New Scooby-Doo Movies* and *The Brady Kids* from the previous year. The studio created its own nonviolent lead for the theatrical "Hoot Kloot" series. Sheriff Hoot Kloot of the Old West never fires a gun in any of his cartoons. Moreover, he wears a belt instead of a gun holster. To be sure, the series was in theaters instead of television, thus giving the studio greater leeway with content. On the other hand, NBC-TV, which aired DePatie-Freleng's older theatrical shorts as *The Pink Panther Show*, edited the violent scenes of older films for television broadcast. By producing inoffensive cartoons for theaters, DePatie-Freleng saved networks possibly interested in broadcasting "Hoot Kloot" from needing to do such work for the series' entries.

As the year progressed, the studio gradually rid itself of violent slapstick in the "Hoot Kloot" shorts. In June 1973, *Apache on the County Seat* featured a Native American character using his fist to pound the sheriff into the ground. Four months later United Artists released *Stirrups and Hiccups — Ten Miles to the Gallop*, the first completely self-censored theatrical cartoon from DePatie-Freleng. In this episode, every time the villain prepares to clobber Kloot, the film cuts away to Fester listening to punches, grunts and thuds from another room. Thus, the audience never sees any violence but merely hears suggestions of it. Episode director Gerry Chiniquy was experienced in camouflaging comical fisticuffs, for he had handled the scenes of the beetle hitting the Blue Racer from the inside in *Hiss and Hers* the previous year.

"Hoot Kloot" presents a twist on another character type — the war veteran. At first glance the sheriff's horse Fester displays the signs of the usual Hollywood cartoon interpretation of the veteran: wearing a hat from the Civil War, walking with a limp, and having old age. However, DePatie-Freleng cast the horse as an entertaining co-star instead of a throwaway character used for jokes about deafness and senility. He appears in every episode of the series. He often provides a voice of reason to Sheriff Kloot's lack of insight; in *Apache on the County Seat*, for example, the horse warns Kloot about Native Americans wanting to kill him, but the officer, oblivious to the Native Americans' scowls and flying arrows, thinks that they love him.

DePatie-Freleng incorporated elements from several popular, established characters of the Vietnam War era for "Hoot Kloot." Despite the demise of Terrytoons the previous year, the defunct studio influenced this new series via the concept of the bumbling southern lawman ("Deputy Dawg"). Voice actor Bob Holt made Kloot holler and rant in the same manner as Mel Blanc had for the Warner Brothers character Yosemite Sam, whose last cartoon had arrived to theaters nine years earlier. DePatie-Freleng even borrowed from its own "Inspector" series in developing the sheriff as an officer who either catches crooks by accident or has sidekicks apprehend criminals for him.

The episode *Ten Miles to the Gallop* is one of the last theatrical cartoons to evoke vaudeville. Ever since the Silent Era, animation studios had made several films featuring an act on a stage, vegetables thrown at bad performers, or both. As vaudeville lost ground to movies in the 1920s, such scenes gradually disappeared from cartoons. They were virtually nonexistent by the release of *Ten Miles to the Gallop* in 1973. In the cartoon Kloot sings on a stage. Crazywolf throws eggs at him during his unremarkable performance.

Although these elements had worked in other series, "Hoot Kloot" was not a success. The title-character, like DePatie-Freleng's Blue Racer, is the unsympathetic star of his own series. He often speaks condescendingly and abusively towards Fester, especially by constantly reminding him about the glue factory. In addition, the episodes inconsistently alternate between Western parody and cartoon fantasy. Most episodes consist of the sheriff's attempts to catch a criminal, and the talking horse provides comic relief. Other shorts, however, feature an anthropomorphic, cross-eyed wolf who lives to tease and harass Kloot. The failure of the series was more pronounced by the absence of competition, because Walter Lantz had closed the previous year and the Disney studio released no new shorts in 1973. In fact, between September and December of that year, "Hoot Kloot" cartoons were the only new commercial animated shorts released to movie houses. The nonviolent cowboy left the theaters after only seventeen episodes and was not missed.

"The Blue Racer" proved even worse at adapting to post–Vietnam animation trends. The episodes released from 1973 onward do not feature the Japanese Beetle, nor does the snake remain in Japan. As a result, the crude ethnic jokes at the expense of Asians are gone — an appropriate development as U.S. forces totally withdraw from South Vietnam. However, the snake evolved into a fearful creature pursued by others instead of doing the pursuing for food himself. The "new" Blue Racer, as a craven coward, is an atypical characterization from the veterans of Warner Brothers

Cartoons, who gained popularity by creating self-assured and cocky protagonists. Thus, the snake becomes a blank personality, and "guest stars" like caricatures of celebrities and clumsy antagonists overshadow the serpent within his own films.

The evolution of the Blue Racer is completely opposite of that of the Warner Brothers character Daffy Duck. In contrast to the snake's transformation from a clearly defined predator to a nondescript prey, the duck began as a hunting target who hooted and pranced but ended as a sinister villain to Speedy Gonzales. Ironically, DePatie-Freleng had handled the change in Daffy's characterization with enough success for the bird to appear for another few years. The studio could not work the same magic for the snake.

In contrast to the studio's references to contemporary culture in many of its earlier cartoons, the new "Blue Racer" episodes draw significantly from the past. In *Freeze a Jolly Good Fellow*, the serpent squares off against a bear looking and sounding like the long-deceased comedian W. C. Fields only four years after the final "Merlin the Magic Mouse" film from Warner Bros.-Seven Arts Cartoons. Also, the snake's most frequent new adversary is a hungry crane who sounds like comedian Red Skelton, who had first performed on radio in the 1930s and had starred in his own television series from 1951 to 1971. In addition, the bird had previously appeared in the studio's own "Tijuana Toads" cartoons to chase the title-characters for food.

The "Blue Racer" films of 1973 are most notable in that they bring the theatrical cartoon chase — as it had existed ever since the silent era of animation — to an end. For decades cats had chased mice, dogs ran after cats, and the coyote pursued the Road Runner. As time progressed, the cartoon chase became more elaborate, with animals setting traps and using weapons to catch their prey. However, the public backlash against violence during the Vietnam War resulted in the animation industry's watering down of such scenes. As the "chase cartoon" genre died, figures began to talk more and hurt themselves less. On August 10, the studio released two episodes in which the snake is involved in a chase for food. In *Aches and Snakes*, he chases a bee, and in *Snake Preview* a crane chases Blue Racer. After these lackluster releases, neither DePatie-Freleng nor any other studio ever produced another theatrical "chase cartoon."

Despite DePatie-Freleng's efforts to bring trends in television animation such as nonviolence to theatrical shorts, theatrical and television animation continued to diverge that year. DePatie-Freleng — the only commercial theatrical studio in operation that year — still produced films that poked fun at indigenous people. The theatrical cartoons were not accountable to network rules but rather to the movie ratings system, which did not prohibit ethnic generalizations. On the other hand, Filmation used animation and the medium of television to inform audiences about the inaccuracy of Native American stereotypes.

For DePatie-Freleng, making contemporary images of Native Americans meant modernizing ethnic generalizations. In the cartoon *Apache on the County Seat*, a sheriff pursues an Indian — a typical plot for a Western-genre film. However, upon finding the culprit, the lawman arrests him for over-parking and reads him some revised Miranda rights: "You have the right to make one smoke-signal." In addition, the Indian's name is the Jolly Red Giant — a reference to both the mascot of Green Giant foods and the color associated with the skin of Native Americans.

Apache on the County Seat degrades Native Americans while making them sympathetic. It is one last gasp at racial humor from DePatie-Freleng, apparently struggling to develop new gags after having abandoned the Latino figures in "Tijuana Toads" and the derogatory Asian character the Japanese Beetle. The film provides a negative image of imperialism. The sheriff invades tribal land and starts confiscating the tribe's property for clues. In return, the Indians become enraged and shoot arrows at him. To be sure, the scene with the arrows smacks of basic ethnic generalization. Still, for the first time, a white character is discouraged from imposing his will upon Native Americans. Even the sheriff's talking horse warns him that his snooping will anger the tribe.

Filmation's series *Fat Albert and the Cosby Kids* tried to put many of the stereotypes from *Apache on the County Seat* to rest a few months later. When the series returned in the fall of 1973, it addressed social issues previously ignored by commercial cartoon producers. One of these issues was racism towards Native Americans. An Indian moving to Fat Albert's neighborhood spends the entire episode disproving the myths about indigenous people that the Cosby Kids believe. Such nonsense that the characters tell him include, "Indians can't shoot straight." Only an awful pun at the end spoils the episode; the new friend announces that he is moving to "*Indian*-apolis."

The second season of *Fat Albert and the Cosby Kids* also tackles the problems of the inner city. One episode discusses the sale of illegal drugs — a problem that grew rampant in urban environments throughout the Vietnam War era. The program, however, avoids giving audiences a glimpse of the damage inflicted by drugs to African American communities, nor did the studio educate about how drugs infiltrate such areas. Rather, the show reduces the issue to the conflict between a boy whose brother is arrested in a drug bust and Fat Albert, who informs the police about the drug dealer. Still, the avoidance by Filmation and Bill Cosby of dialogue about race ensured the popularity of the series with white viewers as well as viewers of color.[3]

As with *Fat Albert and the Cosby Kids*, Ralph Bakshi's new movie *Heavy Traffic* presents the ghetto in animated form. Bakshi's version is much grittier and more daring than Cosby's. *Heavy Traffic* blends live-action and animation — a frequent gimmick in Walt Disney's movies of the 1940s like *Song of the South* (1946), which may have prompted *New York Times* writer Martin Kasindorf to call Bakshi an "X-Rated Disney." Photographs of actual urban tenements serve as the backdrop to animated winos and prostitutes. In addition to poverty and drugs, however, *Heavy Traffic* explored race in ways that broke new ground in U.S. animation. The young protagonist Michael has an Italian father and a Jewish mother. Also, he pursues a black female bartender. In contrast, television animation was only recently beginning to cast black and white figures together without deepening their relationships.[4]

Most of the animation of African American figures in 1973 reflects the country's progress towards racial integration more than urban strife. In that year the cities of Los Angeles, Atlanta, and Detroit elected their first black mayors. Also, two state-level spy organizations dedicated to preserving racial segregation — the Mississippi State Sovereignty Commission and the Alabama State Sovereignty Commission — lost their funding from their respective states and folded. Meanwhile, Hanna-Barbera's *The New Scooby-Doo Movies* teamed the all-white detectives with Josie and the Pussycats on one occasion and with the Harlem Globetrotters for the third time in two years. Filmation offered two new series with integrated casts: *Star Trek* and *Mission: Magic*. Even the all-white "Peanuts" gang welcomed black child Franklin in the holiday special *A Charlie Brown Thanksgiving*. None of these programs specifically addressed race, yet the presence of so many diversely cast cartoon series on television showed where the networks and studios stood on the issue of ethnic representation in the media. They were now ready for superficial gestures of sensitivity if nothing else.[5]

Years after the first tolerant African American cartoon characters had come to television, Asian images finally followed suit in 1973. To be sure, some of the characters of the previous year still appeared in theaters and on television. Reruns of *The Amazing Chan and the Chan Clan* and *Kid Power* comprised a portion of children's weekend television for the 1973-74 season. In addition, Filmation produced five new episodes of *The Brady*

Kids, complete with Ping and Pong. Meanwhile, the only animated Asian image appearing in sixteen new episodes that year was the introspective character of Sulu in Filmation's adaptation of *Star Trek*; the episodes made their debut on NBC Saturday mornings from September to December. Sulu's arrival in animated form introduced a new kind of Asian image to the medium.

Sulu was one of American animation's first non-comedic Asian characters in a protagonist role. As a member of the U.S.S Starship Enterprise, he works for the United States. He does not attempt to sabotage the ship, as had Japanese figures to an American plane in Paramount's propagandistic World War II–era cartoon *Japoteurs* (1942). He does not wear horn-rimmed glasses or bucked teeth, nor does he behave in an exaggerated servile manner. In addition, the vocal performance of Asian American actor George Takei, who played Sulu in the original show, gave ethnic credibility to Filmation's depiction of Sulu.

Unfortunately, the animated adaptation of *Star Trek* accentuated the limitations of Sulu's character from the live-action series. In the cartoon, for example, Sulu rarely appears elsewhere besides in a seated position in front of his control panel aboard the enterprise. The frequency of this scene reflected Sulu's minor role in the original program; rarely did Filmation make the character central to the plots of episodes. In addition, because of budgetary constraints, the studio constantly reused the same animation of Sulu at the spaceship controls. Thus, while he has more personality than the Japanese Beetle, he has less to do than the insect.

Star Trek and other cartoons display cultural effects of the Vietnam War by presenting no violent acts by the characters. Whenever lasers beam from spaceships, they are aimed at other vessels instead of the aliens themselves. Similarly, for the first time since activist parent groups pressured networks to pull cartoon super-heroes from weekend television in 1970, the characters starred in a new animated Saturday morning series in the fall of 1973. National Periodical Publications (a.k.a. DC Comics) licensed its superhero characters to Hanna-Barbera for the *Super Friends* program. However, from its debut in September, the stars of the long-running series — Superman, Batman, Robin, Wonder Woman, and Aquaman — did not throw punches at anyone. Rather, they display their heroism by stopping natural disasters and destroying gadgets created by scientists for evil purposes.

Super Friends also features the military in this new restrained manner. The superheroes often receive word of potential disasters through a military official speaking to them by a sort of videophone called the

"TroubAlert." The officer's appeals to the heroes to protect the world from danger paralleled the backing away of the U.S. armed forces from long-term commitments in the wake of the Vietnam cease-fire. After 1973 the media and critics of U.S. foreign policy tended to describe any new military occupation by the United States, such as the nation's support of Israel in its war with Egypt that year, as "another Vietnam." In addition, the serviceman's reliance on the nonviolent Super Friends to resolve conflicts without using physical aggression implies the ineffectiveness of military force — another common theme of the postwar media. Even the name *Super Friends* suggested pacifism and the building of relationships.

Hanna-Barbera even managed to produce a "spy cartoon" without resorting to firepower and fists. Its program *Butch Cassidy and the Sundance Kids*— no relation to the western movie *Butch Cassidy and the Sundance Kid* (1969) — combines the global interventionism of films from the past twelve years with the post–Vietnam War nonviolent sensibilities. The show features teenage rock musicians solving international crimes. Some of the content originates from other films focused on espionage. As with Terrytoons' character James Hound, Cassidy and his team report to a boss, who gives them foreign assignments. The spies receive their orders from a computer named Mr. Socrates instead of an actual person. What separates the musicians from their animated predecessors in the "spy cartoon" genre is that the agents catch their villains without causing them physical pain.

Although primarily a show about foreign intrigue, *Butch Cassidy and the Sundance Kids* replaces action scenes with derivative content from programs aimed at children and teenagers. The studio modeled the character "Butch Cassidy" after David Cassidy, the "teen idol" star of ABC-TV's situation comedy *The Partridge Family* (1970–74). Butch sports David's "shag" hairdo, slightly resembles David facially, and sings in a similar "pop music" style and vocal pitch. The series also borrows from the studio's own Saturday morning cartoon *Scooby-Doo, Where Are You* by presenting a cast of teenagers and a comical pet dog. The premise of the new show is identical to Hanna-Barbera's *The Impossibles*, except that the musicians are undercover agents instead of disguised superheroes. ABC-TV broadcast new episodes between September and December and did not air reruns past the following August.

With *Butch Cassidy and the Sundance Kids* and *Super Friends*, Hanna-Barbera challenged the taboo against long-haired heroes. The former series was not much of a stretch because of its similarity to *The Impossibles*. However, the latter broke from the trend in television animation of portraying long-haired protagonists as rock musicians. In a major change from the previous year, Hanna-Barbera modernized the character Robin similarly to how DC Comics had done to him for his appearances in periodicals. He is much older and has lengthier hair in *Super Friends* than in *The New Scooby-Doo Movies*. Moreover, he does not play any musical instruments, nor does he sing. Instead, he serves as a full member of the Justice League of America.

The images of women defending justice — Wonder Woman in *Super Friends* and Merilee and Stephanie of *Butch Cassidy and the Sundance Kids*— represent the peak of female empowerment in animation. They are a far cry from the dependent Olive Oyl from the *Popeye* cartoons of the early Vietnam War. They face both male and female adversaries with their colleagues. Thus, as male superheroes become less aggressive in television animation, heroines ironically grow more aggressive.

Wonder Woman was more of a feminist icon on television than in her own comic book series. On the one hand, the character in both media was a superhero and displayed technological savvy in piloting her airplane. Her debut in *Super Friends* broke an interesting color barrier in that the only other female pilots in cartoons in 1973 were African American — Uhuru of *Star Trek* and Valerie of *Josie and the Pussycats in Outer Space*. On the other hand, in the comics the members of the Justice League of America monitor Wonder Woman's stories as they decide whether to reinstate her membership; when she lost her powers in 1968, she resigned from the league. However, on *Super Friends*, she is already a member of the organization. In addition, she embarks on solo adventures within each episode without the presence of her male colleagues supervising her performance.

Not every new animated woman for 1973 displayed empowerment as Wonder Woman did. The female image regressed substantially when Hanna-Barbera's series *Jeannie* promoted the concept of man as woman's master. The program is a loose adaptation of the live-action situation comedy *I Dream of Jeannie* (1965–70). Whereas a female genie serves an astronaut in the original series, two teenage boys are her masters in the cartoon. The stereotype of the supernatural woman had disappeared from network television in July 1972, when *Bewitched* ended its eight-year run. However, *Jeannie* did not single-handedly revive the image. At the same time NBC-TV tried to give the characterization a more realistic twist in the live-action series *The Girl with Something Extra* (1973–74), in which Sally Field played a woman possessing the gift of Extra-Sensory Perception (ESP). Ironically, Screen Gems, which produced the series, had also made both *Bewitched* and *I Dream of Jeannie*.

Walt Disney Productions also took a retrogressive approach to female characterization in its feature-length cartoon *Robin Hood*. The character Maid Marian is nondescript and has little to do in the movie. Her minimal characterization is similar to those of other female protagonists in Disney movies, especially ones in which the figures are overshadowed by anthropomorphic animals and wait for men to rescue them. On the other hand, the "Robin Hood" character himself also suffers a lack of development in this movie. The true stars are the characters voiced by distinctive personalities; the studio called upon Phil Harris once again to use his distinctive voice for "Little John," who is consequently indistinguishable from *The Jungle Book*'s "Baloo" and *The Aristocats*' "O'Malley."

Disney further drew from the past by producing the film in a "classic" style. The studio replaced the psychedelic filmmaking style of Ward Kimball in favor of the detailed backgrounds, musical numbers, and full animation — all standard practices before 1969. Some of the animation itself was "classic." Disney reused animation of a scene from *Snow White and the Seven Dwarfs* (1937) for *Robin Hood*. The disappearance of Kimball's approach, meanwhile, was on par with the evolution of U.S. animation in 1973. With the successful return of heroes and spies to cartoons, studios did not need superficial counterculture imagery. For example, the only new television cartoons to employ psychedelic visual gimmickry that year were *Butch Cassidy and the Sundance Kids* and *Mission: Magic*.

Disney's past movies also influenced Hanna-Barbera's final theatrical feature of the Vietnam War era. Instead of making a movie starring its own popular characters like Yogi Bear or Fred Flintstone, the studio borrowed Disney's winning formula of adapting children's literature to animation. Based on E. B. White's book, Hanna-Barbera's movie *Charlotte's Web* contains such standard Disney elements as songs, talking animal figures, and a death scene. Hanna-Barbera even copied Disney by giving characters and scenery more details and fuller animation than usual, which constituted a far cry from Barbera's infamous declaration in 1961, "All that motion is passé." The feature — the first animated film distributed by Paramount since the close of its own cartoon studio in 1967 — generated respectable business, which proved that nearly a year after *Fritz the Cat* (1972), audiences still desired family-friendly cartoon movies.

Audiences liked Hanna-Barbera's television series *Wait Till Your Father Gets Home* enough for its syndication distributor to renew the program for the 1973-74 season. However, the studio began to lose interest in the program's original focus on the generation gap. The cast of characters remained intact for the new episodes, but Hanna-Barbera used celebrity guest-stars to lure viewers. Many of them — Jonathan Winters, Don Knotts, and Phyllis Diller, for example — had appeared in the studio's series *The New Scooby-Doo Movies* during the previous year. The reliance on famous characters and voices signaled that the conflict between the conservative parents and their liberal offspring had worn thin with viewers after the Vietnam War's cease-fire.

The shift in focus for *Wait Till Your Father Gets Home* also represented the disappearance of the generation gap as a pressing homefront issue. Intergenerational tension still existed, but both sides of the gap lost ground and spent more time regrouping as political forces than quarreling with each other. In the wake of the Vietnam War cease-fire, antiwar groups fizzled, unable to sustain momentum and membership without the war around which to rally. Conservative newspaper columnist William A. Rusher proclaimed in the fall, "The youth revolution is over." On the other hand, the year was not good for Nixon's supporters, because the Watergate scandal damaged his popularity with the nation and weakened his governing power to the point of losing the ability to wage war in Indochina without congressional approval after August 15. He was losing the support of the Silent Majority that he had pitted against young demonstrators in the first place.[6]

Animators illustrated counterculture concerns by promoting environmentalism instead of caricaturing hippies. The issue became a means for studios to educate viewers while entertaining them — a balance increasingly sought by television networks stinging from the loss of violent animated programming. Hanna-Barbera's *Yogi's Gang* features several old studio characters collectively thwarting pollution from various villains. Filmation's *Lassie's Rescue Rangers* loosely adapts the famous live-action series *Lassie* (1954–74) by placing a dog, usually the close companion of a boy, into a family of rangers. The initial episodes of both series were originally one-hour films for ABC-TV's anthology program *The ABC Saturday Superstar Movie* during the previous year. The network, however, decided to commission the respective studios to produce series spinoffs from both movies for the 1973-74 season.

Hanna-Barbera used humor in *Yogi's Gang* to replace slapstick, which had shaped the earlier cartoons of these characters. Gunshots and blows to the head appear quite frequently in the "Yogi Bear" and "Huckleberry Hound" episodes of the 1950s and '60s. However, networks prohibited such content in 1973. Thus, the studio put the vocal talents of Daws Butler, Don Messick, and other Hanna-Barbera stalwarts to much greater use than before.

Yogi's Gang borrows from contemporary animation trends instead of relying on the personalities of the characters. The popularity of *The Archie Show* and *Scooby-Doo, Where Are You* led studios to produce shows with large casts instead of focusing on one or two main figures. As a result, the characters are more distinguishable by their voices than by their personalities. Moreover, *Yogi's Gang* was one of the first series to capitalize on the success of the blend of education and entertainment in *Fat Albert and the Cosby Kids*. Yogi Bear and his co-stars taught viewers not to litter and so on. The bear had come a long way from his days as a picnic basket-stealer.

In fact, none of the lead characters stole anything or committed any other crimes. To be sure, the stars of *Yogi's Gang* had funny characterizations that would have worked well for their new roles as moral centers of the series. However, Hanna-Barbera did not develop any humor from the figures redefining themselves as behavioral instructors. As a result Yogi Bear, whose penchant for mischief contributed to the comedy of his personality in earlier cartoons, now is more solemn and less mischievous when telling characters to save the earth. To the studio the absence of Yogi's survivalist mentality (stealing baskets of food for sustenance) required this change. In effect, he transformed from a rebel bear to the "establishment."

Lassie's Rescue Rangers taught more than it entertained. It was a dramatic cartoon series. A family of rangers — the Turners — travels across the country, rescuing people from floods, forest fires, and other environmental disasters. As with other series, this program also is flooded with dialogue. The characters spend a significant amount of time talking about the geography of an area or scientifically explaining the origins of the disaster they are addressing. On the other hand, not unlike *The Archie Show* and *The Brady Kids*, *Lassie's Rescue Rangers* features animal figures serving as "comedy relief." However, the humor is strained and distracts from the action.

Surprisingly, *Lassie's Rescue Rangers* presents ethnic sensitivity without preaching to the audience. A Native American character named Jackie Fox joins the Turner family on their trips. As a fellow "Rescue Ranger," he is one of the first Native American protagonists to save the lives of other characters. He does not call attention to his ethnicity, nor does it figure into the plots of any episodes. Unlike other contemporary Native American characters, he is not a broad stereotype, and he does not educate others about his heritage. Rather, Filmation merely called on viewers to simply accept his presence among white rangers.

The presence of diverse animal and human figures in *Lassie's Rescue Rangers* proved that by the fall of 1973, teenage characters alone no longer ensured the success of an animated television program. In fact, no new cartoon program starring adolescent principals lasted beyond the 1973–74 season on Saturday mornings; they were either cancelled or moved to Sundays. That year was the last for the groundbreaking "teen adventure" series of the late 1960s. The final new episode of *The New Scooby-Doo Movies*, which aired on October 27, 1973, was also the final cartoon for three years starring the dog and his adolescent owners. Meanwhile, *Everything's Archie*, which aired for only four months, was a "cheater cartoon" series, consisting of portions from previous cartoons featuring the Archies. These developments symbolized the declining popularity of the "powerful youth" genre in television. That same fall, ABC-TV cancelled the live-action series *The Mod Squad* after five years.

Meanwhile, another adaptation of a '60s situation comedy — Filmation's *My Favorite Martians* — brought discussions of conformity to Saturday morning animation. As in the live-action television comedy *My Favorite Martian*, this animated sequel series depicts aliens in human form. The Martian figures only differ from Earthlings by having antennae emerge from their heads and sporting pointed ears. They only attract attention when using supernatural powers in public. Thus, these white immigrants from Mars share something in common with the nineteenth-century immigrants from Europe by matching WASP U.S. citizens in skin color but suppressing cultural activities in order to fit into society.

The teenage character Andy is not only a caveat to the current popularity of adolescent figures but also symbolically illustrates contemporary problems concerning the integration of public schools. He is the only alien attending an otherwise white–Earthling high school. Students tease him for looking and behaving differently from them. By this time, many African American students nationwide struggled to adjust to schools they were integrating. The controversial policy of busing blacks to predominately white schools exacerbated racial tensions in several U.S. communities.

Yet another adaptation of a live-action series of the '60s, the *Saturday Superstar Movie* episode "Lost in Space" combines white flight with colonialism. The original *Lost in Space* aired between 1965 and 1968. The lead characters in both versions are members of a white family and two white crewmen traveling through outer space. The cartoon, produced by Hanna-Barbera, resembles the studio's own *The Jetsons* in its premise of "white flight" to outer space. It is, therefore, out of step with current trends in animation such as the racially integrated crew of Filmation's *Star Trek*.

As the year 1973 drew to a close, American animation, like the nation itself, completed its transformation from wartime to peacetime. To be sure, North and South Vietnam continued their violent conflict, and Cambodia's civil war worsened. However, while in Paris in December to confer with North Vietnamese Politburo member Le Duc Tho on the Vietnam War, Secretary of State Henry Kissinger assured reporters that the United States was not involved in "that mess" and that renewed military intervention in Indochina was unlikely. The previous twelve years of gruesome news coverage of the Vietnam War had largely soured American tastes for long-term foreign military commitments and for violence on television. Consequently, solving problems through communication instead of fists, bullets, and bombs was now the norm for animated characters. The ethnic integration on the battlefront finally carried over to the casts of television cartoons. In addition, with the United States no longer at war in Indochina, American cartoons considerably softened Asian caricature and gave Asian actors vocal agency over their own ethnic representations. Mostly because of the Vietnam War, ethnic sensitivity and the absence of physical aggression defined commercial American animation for the next several years.[7]

Hanna-Barbera adapted best to the post–Vietnam War years. The studio continued its successful business formula of creating popular original characters and making savvy licensing choices. New indigenous creations included *Jabberjaw* and several sequel series to *The Flintstones*; in the 1990s the studio supervised the live-action feature adaptation of the latter. In addition, Hanna-Barbera's animated version of comic strip artist Peyo's "The Smurfs" was one of the most watched television cartoons of the 1980s. Now operating at Cartoon Network Studios, the facility shows no signs of slowing down as of this writing.

Meanwhile, Filmation Associates struggled to survive. It never made a popular original series. However, it redefined television animation by contracting with Mattel Toys to animate the already-popular "Masters of the Universe" line of toys and arranged for Group W Productions to syndicate the series to local stations. It was the first television cartoon in years to present violent fights; without the restrictions from television networks, the syndicated program had greater leeway in content. Also, Filmation worked around the FCC's prohibition against advertisements in children's programming by essentially bringing the toy to "life" and avoiding direct sales pitches within the show. But when the "Masters" craze cooled, the studio still had no original characters upon which to fall back. After years of having to share the profits of the studio's most loved series with its licensing parties, Filmation folded at the end of the 1980s.

Rankin-Bass lasted nearly as long as Filmation after 1973 but by different means. Like Filmation, Rankin-Bass contracted with a television syndicate (Telepictures) to distribute its series to local markets. However, the program was an original creation by the studio; *Thundercats*, which first aired in 1985, belonged to Rankin-Bass instead of a toy company. To be sure, the studio licensed toy manufacturers to capitalize on the popularity of the show's super-powered anthropomorphic cats. Rankin-Bass created and produced similar shows in the wake of *Thundercats*, but none matched its success. After the 1980s the studio made no further cartoons.

As for DePatie-Freleng, the studio turned away from its own creations towards exclusive licensing after the war ended. The studio stopped producing theatrical cartoons after 1976, and its original characters declined in popularity, except for the Pink Panther. In the 1980s DePatie and Freleng parted company, and the former created a new studio dedicated to animating properties owned by Marvel Comics. By serving as the head of an animation wing of a thriving company, DePatie did not have to worry about generating income or developing new characters. The new facility produced successful adaptations of "G.I. Joe" and "Transformers"—both of which were not only comic book titles but also popular toy lines from Hasbro. Marvel Entertainment also periodically brought Spider-Man and the Incredible Hulk back to animation. It also licensed from other parties, including Jim Henson for another well-received program of the 1980s—*Muppet Babies*.

Last but not least, the Disney Studio became more of a follower than a leader. After other studios had made pioneering moves in animation, Disney capitalized on them. Years after Filmation's *He-Man*, Disney entered television animation with *Ducktales* and syndicated the program itself. In addition, some of the later cartoons did not even come from the studio but from subcontracted facilities like Pixar (for *Toy Story*). After some middling success with animated features in the 1980s, the studio rebounded with *The Lion King*, *Aladdin*, and *Pocahontas* the following decade. Disney had found a way to modernize its traditional "musical adventure" formula by injecting irreverent humor and diversifying characterizations.

Many of the animators themselves were among the least receptive to the changes in their industry during the Vietnam War. Some lamented new technical trends. In the 1970s Fred "Tex" Avery, an innovative director for Warner Brothers, MGM, and Lantz from the 1930s to the '50s, responded to the shift to dialogue humor by complaining that contemporary characters talked too much. He added that he would not return to the industry in its current state. Meanwhile, other animation veterans resorted to stereotypes while defending their work. After noting that his characters never bled and likening the physical humor of his work to slapstick, Walter Lantz referred to the largely female members of cartoon activist groups as ignorant, self-appointed censors who spent insufficient time at home with their children.[8]

As time has passed, the cartoons of the 1961–73 period have received an increasing number of tributes. Some people poke fun at kitschy fashions or dated characterizations, while others treat the films with reverence. In recent years Hollywood has produced live-action features loosely based on cartoon properties *Josie and the Pussycats* (2001) and *Fat Albert* (2004). Cool Cat appeared occasionally on *The Sylvester and Tweety Mysteries*— a television cartoon series produced by the reopened Warner Brothers Animation Studio and airing on Cartoon Network from 1995 to 2002. In addition, a few websites dedicated to DePatie-Freleng cartoons have emerged on the Internet. These developments show that the popularity of many of the wartime cartoons has withstood the test of time.

Still, another legacy is that the least overtly political cartoons gained the most favor from audiences. Animation in the United States has not been as political since the Vietnam War. To be sure, U.S. Presidents were caricatured for cameos in *The Simpsons* and *Animaniacs* during the 1990s. Nonetheless, cartoons rarely explore issues of race, class, war and peace. Television networks prefer to air cartoons containing as few timely references as possible in order to minimize potentially outdated content. Animators last explored social division about war in Ralph Bakshi's *Fritz the Cat* in 1972. The most recent cartoon intelligently discussing nuclear war was much earlier in 1964 in the Hubleys' *The Hat*. For studios to revive sociopolitical content in animation, audiences will have to demonstrate that a market for such films exists.

Appendix A

SELECTED ANIMATED THEATRICAL SHORTS OF THE VIETNAM WAR ERA, BY STUDIO

DePatie-Freleng

David H. DePatie and Friz Freleng formed the studio in 1963. Warner Brothers distributed the studio's films from 1964 to 1967, and United Artists distributed DePatie-Freleng cartoons from 1964 to 1977. The following cartoons are United Artists releases unless otherwise noted.

The Pink Phink (1964): The Pink Panther engages in a color war with a house painter. The cat wants pink paint, but the painter wants blue. This film won the studio's only Academy Award.

Pinkfinger (1965): In one of the first animated spy spoofs, the Pink Panther has a difficult first — and only — day as a secret agent.

Assault and Peppered (1965): In this cartoon Daffy Duck and Speedy Gonzales fight each other from military forts over the issue of land ownership. Distributed by Warner Brothers.

Pink Panzer (1965): Tension between a human figure and the Pink Panther escalate to warfare, which pleases the devil himself.

Pink Punch (1966): The Pink Panther battles with an asterisk over the color pink. For the first time, the cat loses a color battle.

Sugar and Spies (1966): This "Looney Tune" cartoon is an unusually topical episode for Wile E. Coyote and the Road Runner. The coyote uses spy gadgets to try to catch the bird. Distributed by Warner Brothers.

Pink Posies (1967): In the Pink Panther's final color war, he secretly replaces a gardener's yellow flowers with pink ones.

Psychedelic Pink (1968): The Pink Panther has an abstract adventure inside a hippie's bookstore.

Les Miserobots (1968): The Inspector becomes a vigilante, trying to destroy a robot officer in order to regain his job with the police force.

Hawks and Doves (1968): The debut of the "Roland and Rattfink" series, this cartoon satirizes war via World War I references. It also pokes fun at peace treaties and reconstruction aid. As in most episodes of the series, there is no clear winner or loser, although "good" and "evil" are clearly delineated.

Pinkcome Tax (1968): Pink Panther is unsuccessful in his efforts to commit civil disobedience as Robin Hood. The Sheriff of Nottingham foils him at every turn.

Hurts and Flowers (1969): This "Roland and Rattfink" cartoon depicts Roland as a hippie and Rattfink as a lover of hate. Rattfink is frustrated by Roland's constant friendliness to him, no matter how the hater tries to get the hippie to hate him.

Trick or Retreat (1971): Roland and Rattfink reuse old Warner Brothers cartoon gags in a film that pokes fun at several aspects of the Vietnam War — from draft card-burning to peace conferences.

Apache on the County Seat (1973): One of the last cartoons to stereotype Indians, this "Hoot Kloot" film modernizes the cowboy v. Indian formula with references to over-parking, search warrants, and Miranda rights.

Stirrups and Hiccups (1973): This cartoon shows how nonviolence in television animation influenced theatrical animation by the end of the Vietnam War. Every scene involving Hoot Kloot receiving blows to the body is censored. The audience instead sees supporting characters listening to the punches from outside the scene of the fight.

Walt Disney Productions

This cartoon studio evolved into a major force in Hollywood entertainment during the Vietnam War. As Disney branched out into television, amusement parks, and feature films, shorts' releases became more sporadic. Disney distributed all of the following films through his own company, Buena Vista.

Aquamania (1961): Goofy is a suburbanite father taking his son on a boat outing that goes horribly awry. The film won an Academy Award nomination.

A Symposium on Popular Songs (1962): The second Oscar nomination in a row for Disney, this film tells the story about how one intelligent duck influenced music in the twentieth century. It is one of few cartoons of the early 1960s to not treat rock and roll music with contempt.

Freewayphobia (1965): This cartoon is one of two episodes about highway safety. It is more educational than funny, and it stars Goofy.

Goofy's Freeway Trouble (1965): This sequel to *Freewayphobia* also instructs on driving safety. It is Goofy's final theatrical short.

Winnie the Pooh and the Honey Tree (1966): This cartoon is the only Disney release for 1966, and it stars a completely unoriginal creation.

Winnie the Pooh and the Blustery Day (1968): This second "Winnie the Pooh" episode won the studio's first Academy Award in fifteen years. It employs some psychedelic graphics — very timely for the late 1960s.

It's Tough to Be a Bird (1969): This film — the first Disney cartoon produced and directed by Ward Kimball — humorously discusses the evolution of flight. It features a mixture of media besides animation in a Laugh-In-type fashion. It won an Academy Award; the studio had not won back-to-back Oscars since the 1930s.

Dad, Can I Borrow the Car (1970): This cartoon is similar to Kimball's debut except that it focuses on automobiles.

Hubley Studio

A married couple — John and Faith Hubley — ran this independent studio. John had worked for commercial studios before starting his own business with Faith. Paramount Pictures distributed some of their films, which they made from 1959 until John's death in 1977.

The Hole (1962): This film consisting of political dialogue between two characters — one black and one white — won an Academy Award one day after one of the most violent demonstrations of the civil rights movement.

The Hat (1964): This cartoon satirizes war. Two military figures separated by a boundary line argue over one character's hat that accidentally falls to the other side of the line.

Walter Lantz Productions

This studio was the last of the pre–Vietnam War cartoon facilities to produce theatrical shorts. Universal Pictures distributed them from 1929 to 1947 and again from 1950 to 1972.

Robin Hoody Woody (1963): Woody Woodpecker commits civil disobedience in a spoof of the legend of Robin Hood.

Secret Agent Woody Woodpecker (1967): This unusually topical cartoon from the studio stars Woody as a spy. Included is a gag referring to the new technology of the "instant replay."

A Lad in Bagdad (1968): Woody Woodpecker is protected by a blond genie against an indigenous villain.

Project Reject (1969): Chilly Willy destroys a military base that has wreaked havoc on his home.

Woody's Magic Touch (c. 1971): A hippie becomes a comic foil for Woody in a medieval setting.

The Rude Intruder (1972): This film is one of the few from Lantz to take a political stance. Here, a pro-ecology Chilly Willy sabotages the efforts of an oil driller to strike "black gold" in the North Pole.

The Genie with the Light Touch (1972): Woody plays "Aladdin" to a phony genie — a mouse wearing a fez. This film is one of the last animated "Aladdin" spoofs, the last film featuring Buzz Buzzard, and the penultimate "Woody Woodpecker" cartoon.

Metro-Goldwyn-Mayer

This company distributed films from independent cartoon studios as well as its own studio for nearly four decades. The following cartoons come from MGM's final cartoon department (1963–71), which Chuck Jones headed.

Snowbody Loves Me (1965): This cartoon, like many "Tom and Jerry" episodes by Chuck Jones, has no cat-and-mouse chase. Instead, Jerry tries to warm Tom's heart towards him by dancing for him. In doing so, the mouse hopes to stay out of the snow and inside the cat's warm house.

Much Ado About Mousing (1965): This cartoon borrows from another "Tom and Jerry" film in which Jerry saves the life of a dog who, in turn, vows to protect him from Tom.

The Dot and the Line (1965): One of only two non–"Tom and Jerry" cartoons produced during the 1960s, this film is a love story between a rigid line and a carefree dot. The antagonist squiggle is musically represented by rock-and-roll. The film won the studio's last Academy Award for animation.

Shutter Bugged Cat (1969): This cartoon consists mostly of old "Tom and Jerry" episodes, one of which features the cat and the mouse battling during World War II. The new animation is inventively superimposed over the classic footage at times.

Paramount Cartoon Studio

Once an independent cartoon facility run by cartoon pioneer Max Fleischer from the 1910s to 1942, Paramount Pictures assumed total control of it in and kept it open until December 1967.

The Robot Ringer (1962): This film is a rare social commentary from the studio. In this satire of social conformity, an android looking just like white-collar workers rises in rank at the office.

Drum Up a Tenant (1963): In this "Modern Madcap" episode, a beatnik's drumming frustrates his neighbor in an apartment building.

Robot Rival (1964): This film addresses automation and colonialism. A robot threatens to displace a taxi driver in outer space, which consists of planetary bodies colonized by human figures.

Laddy and His Lamp (1964): A white boy plays "Aladdin" to a brown genie in an American suburb.

Homer on the Range (1964): A white cowboy and his indigenous sidekick keep the peace in the Old West.

Poor Little Witch Girl (1965): This debut of the "Honey Halfwitch" character established the formula for the series. A little sorceress inadvertently causes trouble for her much older cousin Maggie.

My Daddy the Astronaut (1967): The cartoon is revolutionary for the studio. A sole harmonica provides the score for this film stylized in a childlike manner. The cartoon has a good line about an imaginary US lunar landing: "We own the moon."

Marvin Digs (1967): In this "generation gap" comedy, a hippie paints the family apartment in order to please his father. However, the psychedelic graphics horrify dear ol' Dad instead.

Mouse Trek (1967): The final cartoon from this studio consists of a small cat and a large mouse destroying the planet while trying to destroy one another.

Rembrandt Films

This cartoon studio located in Czechoslovakia was highly sought by animation producers for theaters and television throughout the 1960s.

Munro (1960): In this independent film, a boy is mistakenly drafted into the army. It was the last theatrical cartoon to win an Academy Award before the United States began military involvement in South Vietnam under President John F. Kennedy. Distributed by Paramount Pictures.

The Tom and Jerry Cartoon Kit (1963): Tom Cat and Jerry Mouse are in their most stylized chase. Props pop out of nowhere, and backgrounds are minimal. Distributed by Metro-Goldwyn-Mayer.

Terrytoons

This studio produced cartoons from 1930 to 1968. Twentieth Century--Fox distributed them from 1938 to 1968 and then distributed made-for-television cartoons to theaters for the next three years. CBS-TV owned Terrytoons from 1955 to 1971, at which point Viacom became the owner. Viacom sold the studio facility on December 29, 1972.

Spooky-Yaki (1963): This film is not only the "Hashimoto" finale but also the last sympathetic Asian animated image for nearly a decade.

Brother from Outer Space (1964): Astronut arrives from outer space to start a friendship with nervous white-collar worker Oscar Mild. It is a rare plot for a story involving aliens, for most films depict outer-space visitors as villains. This cartoon, therefore, has an unusually positive symbolic representation of racial integration.

Gadmouse the Apprentice Good Fairy (1965): In a bizarre remake of *Cinderella*, a fairy mouse enables Sad Cat to attend a ball, which dismays the cat's two "dear mean brothers."

The Phantom Skyscraper (1966): This cartoon stars spy dog James Hound, who tries to keep Professor Mad from launching a rocket disguised as an apartment building. The film features a topical reference to "the housing shortage."

Warner Brothers

The studio existed from 1930 to 1963. After DePatie-Freleng made films with the studio's stars, the distributor — now Warner Bros-Seven Arts — created a new cartoon division in 1967. The studio shut down for good in 1969.

Rebel without Claws (1961): As the Civil War centennial began, the studio produced this cartoon about Union cat Sylvester chasing Confederate Tweety. Made during the civil rights movement era's early years, the film goes against the grain of Civil War-set cartoons by avoiding any depictions of African Americans.

The Jet Cage (1962): Tweety is in another military role. This time he is a pilot dropping Sylvester as if the cat were a bomb.

Chili Weather (1963): Speedy Gonzales engages in civil disobedience, stealing cheese from a factory to feed his fellow Mexican mice.

Banty Raids (1963): This "Merrie Melody" starring Foghorn Leghorn features a very one-dimensional beatnik who plays rock and roll.

Dumb Patrol (1964): In World War I, Bugs Bunny and Yosemite Sam (as Sam Von Shamm) engage in dogfights.

Cool Cat (1967): The title-character blends the Pink Panther with the counterculture. He is a tiger trying to escape British hunter Colonel Rimfire in the jungle. The colonel is one of the last colonialist characters created during the Vietnam War. Cool Cat, meanwhile, is a self-consciously "hip" figure.

Merlin the Magic Mouse (1967): W. C. Fields — a long-deceased Hollywood actor revered in the 1960s as a counterculture icon — receives a conventional cartoon treatment here. The title-figure impersonates Fields.

Norman Normal (1968): N. Paul Stookey of Peter, Paul and Mary conceived of this "Cartoon Special," which criticized conventional attitudes of middle and upper class citizens.

Skyscraper Caper (1968): In the penultimate cartoon for both Daffy Duck and Speedy Gonzales, the mouse tries to save the duck from accidentally killing himself by sleepwalking into danger. The two figures are friends — a rarity for this particular pair and unprecedented regarding an interracial pair of protagonists in any animated cartoon.

Flying Circus (1968): In another World War I-set cartoon, two pilots — one German and the other American — have a dogfight and accidentally land in each other's air bases.

Bunny and Claude (1968): This cartoon stars the last female recurring character in theatrical animation. It also has imagery of violent vigilantism. Two hungry rabbits steal carrots and shoot machine guns at the sheriff pursuing them.

Bugged by a Bee (1969): In this episode, Cool Cat strains to be hip by uttering, "Baseball is my bag. It's not just a happening. It's my thing." As a college student, the tiger tries to play on a football team against Hippie College but keeps getting distracted by a bee. The mysterious floating beret is now gone.

Injun Trouble (1969): Cool Cat appears in a very *Laugh-In*-like cartoon. Several one-liners involving Native American stereotypes comprise the film.

Appendix B

SELECTED ANIMATED TELEVISION PROGRAMS OF THE VIETNAM WAR ERA, BY STUDIO

Walt Disney Productions

Mouse Factory (1971–73): This series is a mixed bag of film genres, including animation, produced by Ward Kimball.

Filmation Associates
(All series produced by Norm Prescott and Lou Scheimer and directed by Hal Sutherland)

The New Adventures of Superman (1966–70): The program popularized the trend of superheroes in television cartoons because of its huge ratings success. The actors of the radio series of the 1940s reprised their roles for this show.

The Adventures of Batman (1968–70): Only two years after *The New Adventures of Superman*, this series was the last from the studio to star violent superheroes.

The Archie Show (1968–69): This series is the first of many by the studio to star Bob Montana's comic-strip characters and the studio's first foray into pop music exploitation.

The Hardy Boys (1969–71): This show is noteworthy as the first animated series to have an African American figure among its principals.

Archie's Funhouse (1970–71): The series utilizes the format of *Rowan &*

Martin's Laugh-In—assorted one-liners interrupted by non-sequiters and musical numbers.

Sabrina and the Groovie Goolies (1970–71): The series also drew from *Rowan & Martin's Laugh-In* but had monsters tell jokes. It also borrows from *Bewitched*.

The Brady Kids (1972–74): This animated spinoff of *The Brady Bunch* starred the juvenile actors of the series, promoted the music of their albums, and reused animation from *The Archie Show*.

Fat Albert and the Cosby Kids (1972–84): This landmark series from Bill Cosby was the first to blend comedy, music, and education. Its success led to imitative series from other studios as well as Filmation itself.

Lassie's Rescue Rangers (1973–75): This program used the famous collie of radio, movies, and television to promote ecology. It also featured a sympathetic Native American character.

Star Trek (1973–76): This series used the actors from the live-action program and was one of the few cartoons to feature an integrated cast, including a sympathetic Asian American figure.

Format Films

The Alvin Show (1961–65): The show pioneered the "musical comedy" television cartoon later popularized by *The Beatles*. It consisted of short adventures and song-sequences.

Grantray-Lawrence Animation

Marvel Superheroes (1966): This program used extremely limited animation to bring several characters from Marvel Comics to the cartoon medium. Paramount Cartoon Studio animated episodes of the show's component "The Mighty Thor."

Hanna-Barbera Productions
(All series produced and directed by William Hanna and Joseph Barbera unless otherwise noted)

The Flintstones (1960–66): This program is one of the longest running prime-time animated television series. It satirizes US society in the early 1960s via a comical prehistoric setting.

The Yogi Bear Show (1961–63): The title-character is confined to Jellystone Park under human supervision but makes the most of his restrictions by stealing food. He is one of the studio's most popular animal characters.

Top Cat (1961–65): The title-character leads a gang of cats in get-rich-quick schemes as they try to leave the poverty of their alley.

Wally Gator (1962): The title-character escapes from the zoo where he lives and from the zookeeper's authority but returns there every time.

The Jetsons (1962–63): This "social satire" series is similar to *The Flintstones*, except that the setting is outer space in the future.

The Adventures of Jonny Quest (1964–65, 1967–72): This adventure series offered colonialism and imagery reminiscent of Milton Caniff's comic strip "Terry and the Pirates."

The Magilla Gorilla Show (1964–66): The title-character is sold from a pet store where a storekeeper cares for him, but the gorilla somehow returns to the store by the end of each episode.

The Atom Ant–Secret Squirrel Show (1965–68): The studio cleverly capitalized on the current popularity of both superheroes and secret agents with this series.

Frankenstein, Jr. and the Impossibles (1966–68): The Impossibles are superheroes disguised as rock and roll musicians. They are the first animated "good guys" of the 1960s to have long hair.

Space Ghost and Dino Boy (1966–68): This series is one of the most popular original "superhero cartoons" of the Vietnam War era. Space Ghost's voice came from future *Rowan & Martin's Laugh-In* star Gary Owens.

The Space Kidettes (1966–67): The title-characters are extremely young heroes, foiling the schemes of Captain Skyhook.

The Fantastic Four (1967–70): This team of heroes is based on the comic-book series from Marvel Comics.

Scooby-Doo, Where Are You (1969–72): This program gives some depth to a beatnik character, albeit in a still unflattering manner. Ironically, music and slang have little to do with his personality; instead, cowardice and hunger define him. In the second season, the show featured a musical number during lengthy chase sequences.

The Harlem Globetrotters (1970–73): The well-known team of basketball showmen is caricatured in this animated television series — the first to feature all-black principals. Don Kirshner served as music supervisor in the second season of the show.

Josie and the Pussycats (1970–74): These adventures of a racially integrated rock group star the first black female cartoon character since the hefty housemaid of Hanna and Barbera's "Tom and Jerry" cartoons for Metro-Goldwyn-Mayer. It was retitled *Josie and the Pussycats in Outer Space* in 1972.

Help! It's the Hair Bear Bunch (1971–72): The *Yogi Bear* formula is given one last try here, in which bears improve their lot within the Wonderland Zoo by resorting to assorted schemes.

Pebbles and Bamm Bamm (CBS 1971–72): The title-characters are teenagers whose adventures are similar to those of *The Archie Show*. The main difference is that *Pebbles and Bamm Bamm* is set in prehistoric times.

The New Scooby-Doo Movies (CBS 1972–74): The studio made some noteworthy episodes of this series — essentially *Scooby-Doo, Where Are You* with guest stars and an extra half-hour. Batman and Robin captured crooks without fighting them. Also, the all-black Harlem Globetrotters teamed with the all-white teenage sleuths.

The Flintstone Comedy Hour (CBS 1972–74): The studio gives *The Flint-stones* a *Laugh-In* treatment while revamping the teenage cast of *Pebbles and Bamm Bamm* as a rock band like the Archies.

Butch Cassidy and the Sundance Kids (NBC 1973–74): Borrowing from the studio's own *The Impossibles*, this new series features secret agents disguised as rock stars.

Super Friends (ABC 1973–75): DC Comics superheroes give up fisticuffs for nonviolent means to saving the world.

King Features Syndicate Television
(All series credit Al Brodax as executive producer)

Popeye the Sailor (1960–61): The company arranged for several cartoon studios to produce short episodes starring Popeye and his comic-strip co-stars. Producers were Larry Harmon, Jack Kinney, Seymour Kneitel, Gerald Ray, and William Snyder. Directors were Gene Deitch, Paul Fennell, Jack Kinney, Seymour Kneitel, and Gerald Ray.

King Features Trilogy (1962): King again subcontracted animation of its own comic-strip characters. Producers were Seymour Kneitel and William Snyder. Directors were Gene Deitch and Seymour Kneitel.

The Beatles (ABC 1965–69): John Lennon, George Harrison, Ringo Starr, and Paul McCartney are caricatured in short adventures produced in European studios. Actors voice the caricatures, but actual Beatles musical recordings are in each episode.

Leonardo-Total Television Productions

Tennessee Tuxedo and His Tales (1963–66): This series featured "The World of Commander McBragg"—one of the most colonialist and militaristic sets of cartoons of the Vietnam War.

The Underdog Show (1964–70): This spoof of Superman was the longest running series from the studio.

The Beagles (CBS 1966–68): It capitalized on the Beatles in name only. Otherwise the program's characters hardly resemble the "Fab Four." Rather, they are a duo of musical dogs.

Paramount Cartoon Studio

The New Casper Cartoon Show (1963–69): This series starred a juvenile heroic apparition. He was one of the most profitable theatrical stars created by the studio, but Paramount had sold him to Harvey Comics and ironically had to arrange with that company to make television cartoons starring Casper. Seymour Kneitel produced and directed.

Rankin-Bass Productions
(Both series produced by Arthur Rankin, Jr. and Jules Bass)

The Jackson Five (ABC 1971–73): The famous musical group of brothers is caricatured in half-hour installments. Similar to the format of *The Beatles*, actors voice the Jacksons, but Motown recordings of the band are in each episode. Robert Balser of *Yellow Submarine* directed.

The Osmonds (ABC 1972–74): The studio capitalized on its success with *The Jackson Five*, trying to make lightning strike twice by caricaturing a white group of musical brothers and showcasing the group's music. Tony Guy directed.

Terrytoons
(Owned and operated by CBS 1956–71 and Viacom 1971–72)

The Mighty Heroes (CBS 1966–67): This series cashed in on the "superhero craze" of the mid–1960s. Bill Weiss produced and Ralph Bakshi directed.

Jay Ward Productions
(Both series produced by Jay Ward)

The Bullwinkle Show (NBC 1961–64, ABC 1964–73): This series concerned the exploits of Bullwinkle Moose and Rocket J. Squirrel. Originally a prime-time series, it had a successful rerun life on network television throughout the Vietnam War.

George of the Jungle (1967–70): This program was one of the last efforts of television animation to bring satire to Saturday mornings.

Warner Brothers Cartoons

The Bugs Bunny Show (1960–62): The series had a short prime-time run but reran in several formats from 1962 to 2000. It blended new animation with old studio cartoons within the context of vaudeville. Directors were Friz Freleng, Chuck Jones, and Robert McKimson.

Appendix C

SELECTED ANIMATED THEATRICAL FEATURE FILMS OF THE VIETNAM WAR ERA, BY STUDIO

Walt Disney Productions
(All features produced by Walt Disney unless otherwise noted, directed by Wolfgang Reitherman and distributed by United Artists)

The Sword in the Stone (1963): King Arthur as a boy fulfills his destiny in this medieval-set musical.

The Jungle Book (1967): Rudyard Kipling's novel is very loosely adapted to animation through jazzy songs and comical animals.

The Aristocats (1970): Hippies and swing musicians cavort to psychedelic strobe lights and jazz in early twentieth-century France. Produced by Wolfgang Reitherman.

Hanna-Barbera Productions
(All features produced and directed by William Hanna and Joseph Barbera unless otherwise noted)

Hey, There, It's Yogi Bear (1964): Yogi Bear "goes straight," confessing his pilfering of picnic baskets in order to rescue girlfriend Cindy Bear. Distributed by Columbia Pictures.

The Man Called Flintstone (1966): The Flintstones are the misplaced cast in this spy adventure-comedy-musical. Distributed by Columbia Pictures.

Charlotte's Web (1973): E. B. White's famous novel about life, death, and self-confidence is given a musical, animated treatment. Directed by Charles A. Nichols and Iwao Takamoto. Distributed by Paramount Pictures.

King Features Syndicate

Yellow Submarine (1968): The Beatles battle against the Blue Meanies via love in mystical, psychedelic Pepperland. Produced by Al Brodax. Directed by George Dunning. Distributed by United Artists.

Steve Krantz Productions
(Both features produced by Steve Krantz and directed by Ralph Bakshi)

Fritz the Cat (1972): Robert Crumb's underground comic book character comes to life in a satire of liberal politics of the 1960s. Cinemation was the distributor.

Heavy Traffic (1973): This movie about a boy surviving in an inner city propelled director Ralph Bakshi to fame. American International Pictures distributed it.

Mendelsohn-Melendez Productions

A Boy Named Charlie Brown (1969): Charlie Brown, Linus, and Snoopy travel together for Charlie Brown's appearance in a championship spelling bee. Bill Melendez — the film's director — co-produced it with Lee Mendelsohn. National General Pictures distributed.

United Productions of America

Gay Purr-ee (1962): Two cats, male and female, romp all over France in this romantic musical adventure. Warner Brothers director Chuck Jones and his wife Dorothy wrote it. Henry Saperstein produced, and Abe Levitow — a future director for Jones at MGM — directed the movie. Warner Brothers Pictures distributed it.

CHAPTER NOTES

Chapter 1

1. Shull and Wilt, 127–128, 130.
2. "Well, It Isn't a Dog," 80.
3. Spigel, 49.
4. Scott, 110, 111.
5. Scott, 110.
6. Maltin, 51.
7. "Return of the Animals," 94.
8. Spigel, 47.
9. Hubley, letter to author, January 1999.
10. Hubley, letter to author, January 1999.

Chapter 2

1. Callenbach, 14.
2. Rider, "Just Good Friends," 31.
3. Benayoun, 25.
4. Maltin, 275; Beck and Friedwald, 343.
5. Schickel, 202.
6. Maltin, 259.
7. Branch, 508.
8. Branch, 230.
9. Schickel, 204.
10. Branch, 456–460.
11. Sennett, 134, 136.
12. Sennett, 136.

Chapter 3

1. Bart, 20.
2. "Put a Panther in Your Tank," 90.
3. Stark, 156.
4. Luckett, 113–114.
5. Branch, 290–291.
6. Stark, 133; Axelrod, 24–25.
7. Axelrod, 53, 55.
8. Stark, 152.

9. DeMain, 144.
10. DeMain, 144.
11. Posner, 136, 141–142; Branch, 229.

Chapter 4

1. "Top Off the Show with a Short," 14.
2. Lee, 75.
3. Hertsgaard, 154.
4. Bodroghkozy, 203.

Chapter 5

1. Sennett, 144.
2. "Pink Panther and the Inspector."
3. Lee, 17–18, 75.
4. Lee, 133, 136.
5. Scott, 270.
6. Scott, 262.
7. Spencer, 234–235.
8. Erickson, 14–15.
9. Stark, 188.
10. Crane, letter to author, 16 March 2005.
11. Gailzaid, interview with author, February 2005; Crane, letter to author, 16 March 2005.
12. Crane, letter to author, 16 March 2005.
13. Crane, letter to author, 16 March 2005; Gailzaid, interview with author, February 2005.
14. Crane, letter to author, 16 March 2005.
15. Crane, letter to author, 16 March 2005; Gailzaid, interview with author, February 2005.
16. Shortly after expressing her pacifism through writing the *Marvin Digs* theme, Gailzaid discovered that Scientology offered

a similar outlet, saying that it "gave me the answers on how to put my beliefs into action in the real world." She added, "I've learned how to break down cultural and political barriers and create better communication between people. My reason to be, so to speak, is to do all I can to 'Make Love, Not War' on a grandiose scale, and I mean spiritually, not in any degraded sense."

17. Gailzaid, interview with author, February 2005.

18. Erickson, 80; Branch, 189; Carson, 10–12.

19. Crane, letter to author, 17 March 2005.

20. "Live Action Is Theme of Paramount's Short Subjects," 14.

21. Crane, letter to author, 16 March 2005.

22. Crane, letter to author, 16 March 2005.

Chapter 6

1. Cawleti, 51–56.

2. Cawleti, 42–43; Beck and Friedwald, 367.

3. Samuels, 92.

4. "Bunny and Claude."

5. Cawleti, 49.

6. Cawleti, 48–49.

7. Schickel, 204.

8. Hieronimus, 118–121.

9. "*Yellow Submarine*," 78; "New Magic Art in Animation," 42.

10. Hieronimus, 85.

11. Hieronimus, 68.

12. Hertsgaard, 51.

13. Stark, 188; Hieronimus, 305, 374–375.

14. Hertsgaard, 247, 255.

15. Schickel, 205, 339.

16. Schickel, 302–303.

Chapter 7

1. Rider, "Animation: Disney World," 95.

2. Schickel, 203–204.

3. Maltin, 76.

4. Erickson, 149–150, 256.

5. Bodroghkozy, 204–205.

6. Jahn, 38:2.

Chapter 8

1. Spears, interview with author, August 1998; Spears, interview with author, 5 March 2005.

2. Spears, interview with author, 5 March 2005.

3. Ibid.

4. Spears, interview with author, August 1998.

5. Ibid.

6. Erickson, 80.

7. Small, 81–82.

8. Shawcross, 135, 144.

9. Posner, 237, 240; Woolery, 151.

10. Erickson, 14–15.

Chapter 9

1. Adamson, 212–214.

2. Isaacs, 18–19; Browne, 3: 1; Semple, 1: 8; Adamson, 214.

3. Maltin, 322.

4. Sklar, 297–299.

5. Kasindorf, 41.

6. Kasindorf, 41; Bakshi, 271–272.

7. Turner, letter to author, 13 December 2005.

8. Turner, letter to author, 13 December 2005.

9. Turner, letter to author, 13 December 2005.

10. Turner, letter to author, 13 December 2005.

11. Calta, "Bill Cosby to Star in Children's Show Saturdays on C.B.S.," 91: 4.

12. Hendershot, 205.

13. Hendershot, 206.

14. Calta, "N.B.C. Revises Its Schedule for Children Saturday in '72–73," 87: 3.

15. Beck and Friedwald, 149.

16. "A.B.C. Fall Lineup for Children Adds 4 Saturday Shows," 87: 4.

17. "Betty Boop Latest to Join Nostalgia Craze," 21: IV.

18. Daniels, 131–132.

19. Rider, August 1972, 82.

20. Bureau of Assessment, City of New Rochelle.

Chapter 10

1. Isaacs, 143.

2. Milstein, 17: IV; Cocks, 76–77.

3. Hendershot, 200–201, 206.

4. Kasindorf, 41.

5. Katagiri, 225–226.

6. Rusher, 2: 2.

7. Lewis, 3.

8. Avery, 199; Lantz, 199.

BIBLIOGRAPHY

Books, Articles, and Interviews

"A.B.C. Fall Lineup for Children Adds 4 Saturday Shows." *New York Times* (27 April 1972), 87: 4.

"'Action Plus' Theme of WB-7A Short Subjects." *Film Bulletin* (2 December 1968), 12.

Adamson, Joe. *The Walter Lantz Story: With Woody Woodpecker and Friends.* New York: Putnam, 1985.

Adler, Renata. "Yellow Submarine." Review. *New York Times* (4 November 1968), 56: 1.

Avery, Tex. Quoted in Joe Adamson. *Tex Avery: King of Cartoons.* New York: Da Capo, 1975.

Axelrod, Mitchell. *Beatletoons: The Real Story Behind the Cartoon Beatles.* Pickens, SC: Wynn, 1999.

Baily, Charles A. "Shorts Have Definite Place on Theatre Screens — Baily." *Film Bulletin* (27 November 1967), 16.

Bakshi, Ralph. Quoted in Patrick McGilligan. "A Talk with Ralph Bakshi." In *The American Animated Cartoon.* Danny Peary and Gerald Peary, eds. New York: Dutton, 1980.

Barrier, Michael. *Hollywood Cartoons: American Animation in Its Golden Age.* New York: Oxford University Press, 1999.

Bart, Peter. "Studios to Revive Animated Shorts." *New York Times* (15 January 1965), 20: 4.

Beck, Jerry, and Will Friedwald. *Looney Tunes and Merrie Melodies: A Complete Illustrated Guide to the Warner Bros. Cartoons.* New York: Henry Holt, 1989.

Beckerman, Howard. Interview with author. 28 July 1996.

Benayoun, Robert. "Animation: The Phoenix and the Road-Runner." *Film Quarterly* (Spring 1964), 25.

Bernstein, Irving. *Guns or Butter: The Presidency of Lyndon Johnson.* New York: Oxford University Press, 1996.

"Betty Boop Latest to Join Nostalgia Craze," *New York Times* (16 June 1972), sec. IV, 21.

Bodroghkozy, Aniko. "The Smothers Brothers Comedy Hour and the Youth Rebellion." In *The Revolution Wasn't Televised: Sixties Television and Social Conflict*. Lynn Spigel and Michael Curtin, eds. New York: Routledge, 1997.

Branch, Taylor. *Pillar of Fire: America in the King Years, 1963–65*. New York: Simon & Schuster, 1998.

Brion, Patrick. *Tom and Jerry: The Definitive Guide to Their Animated Adventures*. New York: Harmony, 1990.

Browne, Malcolm W. "No G.I. Killed in Week in Indochina, U.S. Says." *New York Times* (22 September 1972), 3: 1.

"Bunny and Claude." Advertisement. *Film Bulletin* (2 December 1968).

Callenbach, Ernest. "Animation." *Film Quarterly* (Spring 1964), 14.

Calta, Louis. "Bill Cosby to Star in Children's Show Saturdays on C.B.S." *New York Times* (26 April 1972), 91: 4.

_____. "N.B.C. Revises Its TV Schedule for Children Saturday in '72–73." *New York Times* (25 April 1972), 87: 3.

Carson, Clayborne. *In Struggle: SNCC and the Black Awakening of the 1960s*. Cambridge: Harvard University Press, 1981.

Cawleti, John G. "The Artistic Power of *Bonnie and Clyde*." In *Focus on Bonnie and Clyde*. Ronald Gottesman and Harry M. Geduld, eds. Englewood Cliffs, N.J.: Prentice-Hall, 1973.

Cocks, Jay. "The World Jones Made." *Time* (17 December 1973), 76–77.

Cohen, Karl F. *Forbidden Animation: Censored Cartoons and Blacklisted Animators in America*. Jefferson, NC: McFarland, 1997.

Crane, Doug. Letter to author. 16 March 2005.

_____. Letter to author. 17 March 2005.

Culhane, Shamus. *Talking Animals and Other People*. New York: St. Martin's, 1986.

Daniels, Les. *Wonder Woman: The Complete History*. San Francisco: Chronicle, 2000.

DeMain, Bill. "Come Together." In *The Beatles: Ten Years that Shook the World*. Paul Trynka, ed. London: Mojo, 2004.

Erickson, Hal. *From Beautiful Downtown Burbank: A Critical History of* Rowan and Martin's Laugh-In, *1968–1973*. Jefferson, NC: McFarland, 2000.

Gailzaid, Vickie Lee. Interview with author. February 2005.

Hendershot, Heather. *Saturday Morning Censors: Television Regulation Before the V-Chip*. Durham, NC: Duke University Press, 1998.

Hertsgaard, Mark. *A Day in the Life: The Music and Artistry of the Beatles*. New York: Delacorte, 1995.

Hieronimus, Dr. Robert R. *Inside the Yellow Submarine: The Making of the Beatles Animated Classic*. Iola, WI: Krause, 2002.

Hubley, Faith. Letter to author. January 1999.

Isaacs, Arnold R. *Without Honor: Defeat in Vietnam and Cambodia*. Baltimore: Johns Hopkins University Press, 1983.

Jahn, Mike. "The Archies Are Fictional, but Their Success Is Not." *New York Times* (5 November 1969), 38:2

Kasindorf, Martin. "A Kind of X-Rated Disney: Cartoon Vision and Brownsville Reality." *New York Times* (14 October 1973), sec. IV, 41.

Katagiri, Yasuhiro. *The Mississippi State Sovereignty Commission: Civil Rights and States' Rights*. Jackson: University Press of Mississippi, 2001.

Kimball, Jeffrey P. *Nixon's Vietnam War*. Lawrence: University Press of Kansas, 1998.

Lantz, Walter. Quoted in Danny Peary. "Reminiscing with Walter Lantz." In *The American Animated Cartoon*. Danny Peary and Gerald Peary, eds. New York: Dutton, 1980.

Lee, Stan. *Origins of Marvel Comics.* New York: Simon and Schuster, 1974.

Lenburg, Jeff. *The Great Cartoon Directors.* Jefferson, NC: McFarland, 1981.

Lewis, Flora. "Kissinger and Tho in Paris Discuss Vietnam Fighting." *New York Times* (21 December 1973), 3.

"Live Action Is Theme of Paramount's Short Subjects." *Film Bulletin* (27 November 1967), 14.

Luckett, Moya. "Girl Watchers: Patty Duke and Teen TV." In *The Revolution Wasn't Televised: Sixties Television and Social Conflict.* Lynn Spigel and Michael Curtin, eds. New York: Routledge, 1997.

Maltin, Leonard. *Of Mice and Magic: A History of American Animated Cartoons.* Rev. ed. New York: Plume, 1987.

Mayerson, Mark. "The Lion Began with a Frog." *Velvet Light Trap,* Spring 1978.

Milstein, Fredric. "'Betty Boop Scandals' Screen at the Regent." *New York Times* (2 November 1973), sec. IV, 17.

"New Magic Art in Animation." *Time* (27 December 1968), 42–47.

"Pink Panther and the Inspector." Advertisement. *Film Bulletin* (27 November 1967).

Posner, Gerald. *Motown: Music, Money, Sex and Power.* New York: Random House, 2002.

"Put a Panther in Your Tank." *Time* (1 October 1965).

Reeves, Richard. *President Kennedy: Profile of Power.* New York: Simon & Schuster, 1993.

"Return of the Animals." *Newsweek* (22 May 1961), 94.

Rider, David. "Animation." *Films and Filming* (August 1972), 82.

_____. "Animation: Disney World." *Films and Filming* (June 1970), 95.

_____. "Just Good Friends." *Animation* (July 1963), 31.

Rusher, William A. "The Youth Revolution: It Never Really Happened." St. Paul *Pioneer-Dispatch* (20 October 1973), 2: 2.

Samuels, Charles Thomas. "*Bonnie and Clyde.*" In *Focus on Bonnie and Clyde.* Ronald Gottesman and Harry M. Geduld, eds. Englewood Cliffs, N.J.: Prentice-Hall, 1973.

Schickel, Richard. *The Disney Version.* New York: Simon and Schuster, 1968.

Schulz, Charles M. *Peanuts: A Golden Celebration.* New York: HarperCollins, 1999.

Scott, Keith. *The Moose that Roared.* New York: St. Martin's, 2000.

Semple, Robert B., Jr. "Nixon Rules Out Duty in Vietnam for New Draftees." *New York Times* (29 June 1972), 1: 8.

Sennett, Ted. *The Art of Hanna-Barbera: Fifty Years of Creativity.* New York: Viking Studio Books, 1989.

Shawcross, William. *Sideshow: Kissinger, Nixon, and the Destruction of Cambodia.* Rev. ed. New York: Cooper Square, 1987.

"Short Talk — and to the Point." *Film Bulletin* (2 December 1968), 12.

Shull, Michael S., and David E. Wilt. *Doing Their Bit: Wartime American Animated Short Films, 1939–1945.* 2nd ed. Jefferson, NC: McFarland, 2004.

Sitkoff, Harvard. *The Struggle for Black Equality, 1954–1992.* Rev. ed. New York: HarperCollins, 1993.

Sklar, Robert. *Movie-Made America: A Cultural History of American Movies.* New York: Vintage, 1994.

Small, Melvin. *The Presidency of Richard Nixon.* Lawrence: University Press of Kansas, 1995.

Spears, Ken. Interview with author. August 1998.

_____. Interview with author. 5 March 2005.

Spencer, Neil. "Eastern Rising." In *The Beatles: Ten Years that Shook the World.* Paul Trynka, ed. London: Mojo, 2004.

Spigel, Lynn. "White Flight." In *The Revolution Wasn't Televised: Sixties Television and Social Conflict.* Lynn Spigel and Michael Curtin, eds. New York: Routledge, 1997.

Stark, Steven D. *Meet the Beatles: A Cultural History of the Band that Shook Youth, Gender, and the World.* New York: HarperCollins, 2005.

Stookey, Noel Paul. Letter to author. 8 February 2005.

"Top Off the Show with a Short." *Film Bulletin* (27 November 1967), 14.

Trynka, Paul, ed. *The Beatles: Ten Years that Shook the World.* London: Mojo, 2004.

Turner, Morrie. Letter to author. 13 December 2005.

"Warner Bros–Seven Arts Cartoons." Advertisement. *Film Bulletin* (27 November 1967).

"Well, It Isn't a Dog." *Time* (21 December 1962), 77.

Wells, Tom. *The War Within: America's Battle over Vietnam.* Berkeley: University of California Press, 1994.

Woolery, George W. *Children's Television: The First Thirty-Five Years.* Part One. Metuchen, NJ: Scarecrow, 1983.

"Yellow Submarine." Time (22 November 1968), 78.

Vietnam War-Era Cartoons Available on DVD-Video

"Apprentice Good Fairy." Video Treasures.

"Archie: Volume One." Thorn EMI Video.

"Archie: Volume Two." Thorn EMI Video.

"Archie's TV Funnies Featuring Broom Hilda." New Age Video.

"Boy Named Charlie Brown." Paramount Home Video.

"Charlie Brown Christmas." Paramount Home Video.

"Fat Albert and the Cosby Kids: The Ultimate Collection." Urban Works (DVD).

"Flintstones: The Complete First Season." Turner Home Entertainment (DVD).

"Flintstones: The Complete Second Season." Turner Home Entertainment (DVD).

"Flintstones: The Complete Third Season." Turner Home Entertainment (DVD).

"Flintstones: The Complete Fourth Season." Turner Home Entertainment (DVD).

"Go for Croak." MGM/UA Home Video.

"Hashimoto-San." Video Treasures.

"Jetsons: The Complete First Season." Turner Home Entertainment (DVD).

"Jonny Quest: The Complete First Season." Turner Home Entertainment (DVD).

"Lassie's Rescue Rangers." Family Home Entertainment.

"Mr. Winlucky." Video Treasures.

"My Favorite Martians." United American Video.

"Pink Panther Classic Cartoon Collection." MGM (DVD).

"Popeye's 75th Anniversary." Koch Video (DVD).

"Rocky and Bullwinkle and Friends: The Complete First Season." Sony Wonder (DVD).

"Rocky and Bullwinkle and Friends: The Complete Second Season." Sony Wonder (DVD).

"Rocky and Bullwinkle and Friends: The Complete Third Season." Sony Wonder (DVD).

"Star Trek: The Animated Series." Vols. 1–10. Paramount Home Video.

"Super Powers: Aquaman." Warner Home Video.
"Super Powers: Batman." Warner Home Video.
"Super Powers: Superboy." Warner Home Video.
"Super Powers: Superman." Warner Home Video.
"Sweet and Sourdough." MGM/UA Home Video.
"Top Cat: The Complete Series." Turner Home Entertainment (DVD).
"Underdog Boxed Set." Sony Wonder (DVD).
"Yogi Bear: The Complete Series." Turner Home Entertainment (DVD).

INDEX

215